Manufacturing in Colonial Zimbabwe, 1890–1979

RELATED JAMES CURREY TITLES ON CENTRAL & SOUTHERN AFRICA

Roots of Rural Poverty in South Central Africa
ROBIN PALMER & NEIL PARSONS

Diamonds, Dispossession and Democracy in Botswana
KENNETH GOOD

Crossing the Zambezi: The Politics of Landscape on a Central African Frontier
JO-ANN MCGREGOR

Circular Migration in Zimbabwe and Contemporary Sub-Saharan Africa
DEBORAH POTTS

Remaking Mutirikwi: Landscape, Water and Belonging in Southern Zimbabwe
JOOST FONTEIN

The War Within: New Perspectives on the Civil War in Mozambique, 1976–1992
ERIC MORIER-GENOUD ET AL. (eds)

Faith, Power and Family: Christianity and Social Change in French Cameroon
CHARLOTTE WALKER-SAID

Manhood, Morality & the Transformation of Angolan Society: MPLA Veterans & Post-war Dynamics
JOHN SPALL

Protestant Missionaries & Humanitarianism in the DRC: The Politics of Aid in Cold War Africa
JEREMY RICH

Across the Copperbelt: Urban & Social Change in Central Africa's Borderland Communities
MILES LARMER ET AL. (eds)

Inside Mining Capitalism: The Micropolitics of Work on the Congolese and Zambian Copperbelts
BENJAMIN RUBBERS (ed.)

Namib: The Archaeology of an African Desert
JOHN KINAHAN

The Politics of the Dead in Zimbabwe 2000–2020: Bones, Rumours & Spirits
JOOST FONTEIN

Competing Catholicisms: The Jesuits, the Vatican & the Making of Postcolonial French Africa
JEAN LUC ENYEGUE, SJ

Transport Corridors in Africa
HUGH LAMARQUE & PAUL NUGENT (eds)

Manufacturing in Colonial Zimbabwe, 1890–1979

Interest Group Politics, Protectionism, and the State

Victor Muchineripi Gwande

JAMES CURREY

First published 2022

ISBN 978 1 84701 333 0

James Currey is an imprint of Boydell & Brewer Ltd
PO Box 9, Woodbridge, Suffolk IP12 3DF, UK
and of Boydell & Brewer Inc.
668 Mt Hope Avenue, Rochester, NY 14620–2731, USA
website: www.boydellandbrewer.com

A CIP catalogue record for this book is available from the British Library

To my parents, siblings, and family

Contents

Illustrations

Map

Figures

Tables

Full credit details are provided in the captions to the images in the text. The author and publisher are grateful to all the institutions and individuals for permission to reproduce the materials in which they hold copyright. Every effort has been made to trace the copyright holders; apologies are offered for any omission, and the publisher will be pleased to add any necessary acknowledgement in subsequent editions.

Preface

This book examines the relationships between organised secondary industry, the state, and other economic interest groups (farmers, miners, and commerce) during the industrialisation of Southern Rhodesia (colonial Zimbabwe) between 1890 and 1979. Using diverse and fresh archival material that includes minutes and reports of industrialists' congresses, industrial journals, business newspapers, legislative debates, and government and commissions of enquiries' reports, it demonstrates that this relationship was conflictual, uneven, and irregular, and often shifted depending on time and context. The book argues that the great expansion and diversification of industry which took place were attributable, among other factors, to the efforts of private entrepreneurs.

Industrialists galvanised and formed representative organisations, starting with the Salisbury and Bulawayo Manufacturers' Association (*c.*1920), which then evolved into the Salisbury and Bulawayo Chambers of Industry (*c.*1930s), the Association of Chambers of Industries of Rhodesia (1941–1949), the Federation of Rhodesia Industries (1949–1957), the Association of Rhodesia and Nyasaland Industries (1957–1964), and the Association of Rhodesian Industries (1964–1979). These organisations engaged the state in pursuit of industrial development. Often, industrialist associations' requests, demands, and suggestions were opposed, if not dismissed, by the government and other economic interest groups, and yet, remarkably, secondary industries expanded. By privileging the voice of industrialists which hitherto has been neglected in the historiography, the book moves beyond the existing scholarship's emphasis on the actions of the state in the industrialisation of colonial Zimbabwe through planning, regulation, and establishment of major industries of national importance. While this existing analysis is correct, it is incomplete.

Between 1890 and 1965, farmers, miners, and commerce, with the state's support, believed in the supremacy of the primary exporting industries of agriculture and mining in propelling the economy of Southern Rhodesia. As we will see, the state adopted the policy of 'imperial preference'. It opened the colony for imports of manufactured goods from other parts of the British Empire in return for market opportunities for the primary products. This policy deliberately favoured the mining and agricultural sectors. It also sacrificed industrial interests in negotiating trade agreements, thus depriving the secondary industry of tariff protection. Further, the state routinely accepted advice which labelled the manufacturing sector as of secondary importance to mining and agriculture. The result was government policy based on the idea that industrial development was a field of private enterprise whose growth ought to be voluntary. Industries were left to their own devices and to develop as opportunity occurred.

The exception to this policy was during the crisis periods of the Second World War and the Unilateral Declaration of Independence (UDI). Faced with the shortages of imported manufactured goods in the domestic market induced by the interruptions in international trade because of the war, the Southern Rhodesian government realised the imperative of developing local industries. The nascent industrialists seized the opportunity and prevailed upon the state to adopt an active policy to foster industrial growth. At the instigation and lobbying of industrialists, the government agreed, but no sooner had the war ended than the state retreated from its temporary support of local industries, reiterating its avowed policy of leaving industry to its own devices. This policy continued in the post-war years and throughout the period of the Federation of Rhodesia and Nyasaland (1953–1963). The other exception was during UDI. Determined to survive under sanctions, the government and organised industry cooperated and collaborated (societal corporatism) to keep the wheels of industry in particular, and the economy in general, going. In an effort to preserve foreign exchange in the face of sanctions, the government introduced import control measures; this had the consequential effect of encouraging the establishment of import substitution industries, which were able to take advantage of the protection it afforded.

Acknowledgements

This book is a product of many years of research and writing. That would not have been possible without the support, generosity, advice, and insights of friends, colleagues, family, and mentors. I owe a debt of gratitude to Ian Phimister, Admire Mseba, and Tinashe Nyamunda for their mentorship throughout my time at the International Studies Group (ISG) at the University of the Free State. I am grateful to Ilse le Roux and Tari Gwena for all their administrative support and ensuring that my welfare was catered for. Your dedication was amazing.

A number of institutions assisted me during my research. Many thanks to archivists and librarians at the National Archives of Zimbabwe (NAZ), the National Archives of South Africa, The National Archives at Kew, University of the Free State Library, and Herald House for all their help in navigating through repositories and reading rooms. I am thankful to the American Council of Learned Societies' African Humanities Fellowship Program, funded by the Carnegie Corporation of New York, for their financial support during the preparation of this manuscript.

The writing process was also made less arduous by the welcoming, stimulating, intellectual, and collegial environment I had at the ISG. Members of the ISG were very helpful with their constructive criticism and suggestions as I shared my work with them through seminars or personal discussions. Thank you Duncan Money and Dave Patrick for reading through draft chapters of this manuscript. My stay at the ISG also earned me many friendships that I will cherish forever. Special mentions go to Kundai Manamere, George Bishi, Sibanengi Ncube, Unaludo Sechele, Abraham Mlombo, Lotti Nkomo, Hyden Munene, and Anusa Daimon; my life-long friends Kelvin Zahaya, Bosteer Takawira, Teverayi Muguti, and Anesu Goba; and my role model and inspiration, Dr Sylvester Dombo – thank you for your support, always.

I reserve my utmost gratitude for my family. To my wife Tsitsi Paidamoyo and our two boys, Taremekedzwa and Wenyasha, thank you for your support and all the sacrifices. Words fail me. My brother Chamu and *maiguru* Priscilla, my 'twin' Oscar, and my siblings, I am grateful for your faith in me. To my parents, your sacrifices were not in vain.

Abbreviations

AAG	Affirmative Action Group
ACIR	Association of Chambers of Industries of Rhodesia
AfCFTA	African Continental Free Trade Area
AGM	Annual General Meeting
ARNI	Association of Rhodesia and Nyasaland Industries
ARnI	Association of Rhodesian Industries
BCI	Bulawayo Chamber of Industries
BSAC	British South Africa Company
CAF	Central African Federation
CATMA	Central African Textile Manufacturers' Association
CZI	Confederation of Zimbabwe Industries
DCC	Development Coordinating Commission
EAC	East African Community
EPT	Excessive Profit Tax
EPTA	Excessive Profit Tax Act
ESAP	Economic Structural Adjustment Programme
FBI	Federation of British Industries
FRI	Federation of Rhodesian Industries
FROLIZI	Front for the Liberation of Zimbabwe
GATT	General Agreement on Trade and Tariffs
GDP	Gross domestic product
GNU	Government of National Unity
IBWO	Indigenous Business Women's Organisation
ICA	Industrial Conciliation Act
ICS	Import Control System
IDAC	Industrial Development Advisory Committee

IDC	Industrial Development Commission or Corporation
ISCOR	Iron and Steel Corporation
ISI	Import Substitution Industrialisation
LAA	Land Apportionment Act
MDC	Movement for Democratic Change
MECC	Ministerial Economic Coordination Committee
MP	Member of Parliament
NASA	National Archives of South Africa
NAZ	National Archives of Zimbabwe
NCI	No-Currency-Involved
NLHA	Native Land Husbandry Act
NPC	National Priorities Committee
OPEC	Organization of the Petroleum Exporting Countries
P&F	*Property and Finance*
PSCC	Private Sector Coordinating Committee
RF	Rhodesian Front
RHISCOM	Rhodesia Iron and Steel Commission
RNFU	Rhodesia National Farmers Union
RTA	Rhodesia Tobacco Association
SADC	Southern African Development Community
SCI	Salisbury Chamber of Industries
TAC	Tariff Advisory Committee
TILCOR	Tribal Trust Land Development Corporation
UANC	United African National Council
UDI	Unilateral Declaration of Independence
UIPG	United Indigenous Pressure Group
UK	United Kingdom
USA	United States of America
USAID	US Agency for International Development
ZANU-PF	Zimbabwe African National Union–Patriotic Front
ZAPU	Zimbabwe African People's Union
ZEDP	Zimbabwe Enterprise Development Programme

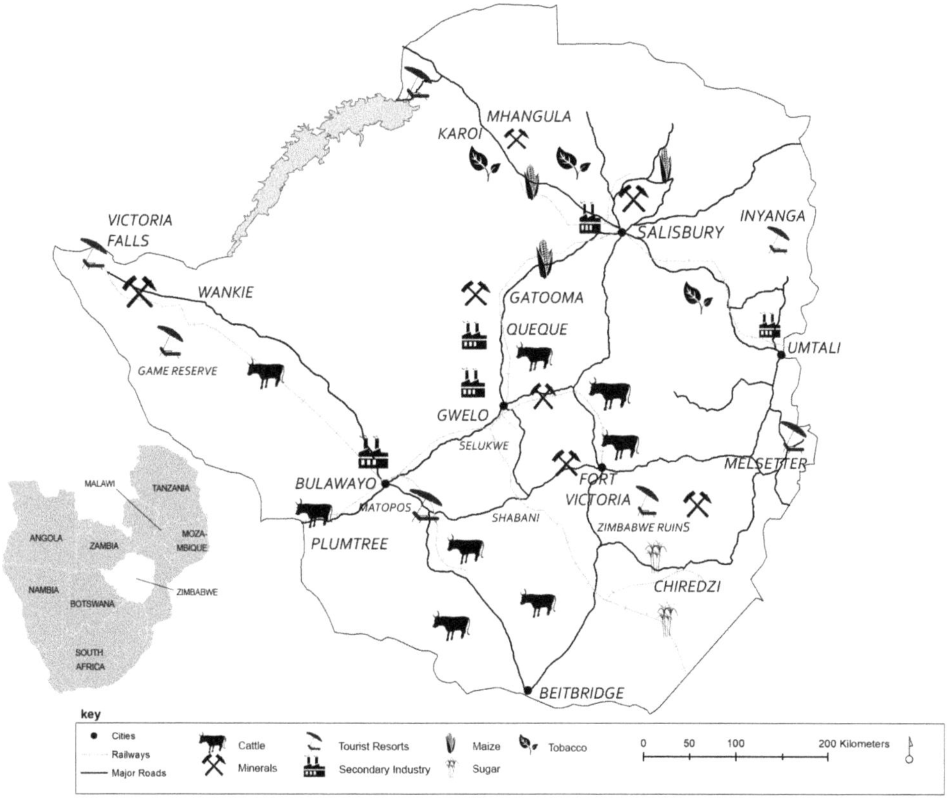

Economic Map of Rhodesia (Source: Adapted from *Economic Survey of Rhodesia*, 1966–1972; redrawn by Russell Kapumha, 2022).

Introduction

On 1 July 2016, the government of Zimbabwe gazetted Statutory Instrument 64 of 2016 (SI 64/2016), aimed at boosting domestic industrial production through the protection of local industries from unfair competition from foreign firms.[1] However, Zimbabwe's neighbours, in particular Zambia and South Africa, formally complained to the Southern African Development Community (SADC). They claimed that SI 64/2016 adversely affected their economies and violated the SADC Protocol on Trade, which promotes free trade among member countries.[2] The two countries further argued that Zimbabwe's introduction of the statutory instrument was unilateral and unprocedural because, for instance, 'the Government of Zimbabwe was supposed to approach the SADC Committee of Ministers Responsible for Trade to justify its promulgation before implementation'.[3] The rationale was that Zimbabwe, as a member of the World Trade Organization, the Common Market for Eastern and Southern Africa, Economic Partnership Agreements, and the SADC, was bound by the various trade agreements of these organisations and, therefore, had an obligation to adhere to their terms and conditions.

Around the same time, in 2016, the East African Community (EAC), comprising Rwanda, Kenya, Tanzania, Uganda, and Burundi, adopted a phased ban on the importation of used clothing over three years.[4] Just like Zimbabwe, the EAC intended to protect its domestic textile industry because the second-hand clothing imports, estimated at roughly USD 151 million in 2015, stifled the

1 B. Sibanda, *Zimbabwe's Statutory Instrument (SI) 64 Of 2016 On Control of Goods on the Open General Import License: The Gains and Pains* (Harare: Parliament of Zimbabwe, 2017).

2 *Ibid.*, 2.

3 *Ibid.*

4 E. A. Wolff, 'The global politics of African industrial policy: the case of the used clothing ban in Kenya, Uganda and Rwanda', *Review of International Political Economy*, 28, 5 (2020), 1308–1331.

local sector.[5] The proposed ban alarmed the Secondary Materials and Recycled Textiles Association (SMART), an association of United States (US)-based used clothing exporters. They sought the intervention of the US Trade Representative (USTR). The USTR responded by evoking 'an out-of-cycle review of AGOA privileges', which would result in the revocation of 'preferential market access' for the EAC's textile exports to the USA.[6] Against the backdrop of this threat, within two years all EAC states except Rwanda had reversed their decision.

The two cases of Zimbabwe and the EAC brought to the fore the globalism, imperialism, inequality, and state–capital relations associated with African industrial policy as it strives to achieve meaningful industrialisation. Examining industrial policy is even timely, as the topic has also become resurgent after a lapse of almost three decades.[7] At a continental level, the African Union, under the auspices of the Agenda 2063, launched the African Continental Free Trade Area (AfCFTA) in March 2018, 'a single market for goods and services in Africa that aims to unlock manufacturing potential and facilitate industrialisation, driving sustainable growth and jobs among other objectives'.[8] The initiative has given currency to the politics of industrialisation in Africa at global, continental, regional, and national levels. These current debates on industrialisation in Africa have their antecedents in history. I use the case study of Zimbabwe's historical industrial development to show that Africa's industrialisation has always been a contested path.

However, this endeavour is by no means novel. Roger Riddell *et al.* and Colin Stoneman attempted a similar venture in 1990.[9] During the 1980s, Western donors and international institutions, especially the World Bank and the International Monetary Fund, produced reports analysing the crisis of

5 Wolff, 'The global politics of African industrial policy', 1310.

6 *Ibid.*, 1311.

7 For current debates in the utility of industrial policy, see H. Chang and A. Andreoni, 'Industrial policy in the 21st century', *Development and Change*, 51, 2 (2020), 324–51. See also, *African Development Bank, Industrialise Africa: Strategies, Policies, Institutions and Financing* (African Development Bank Group, 2017), http://bit.ly/2AfU14P, Accessed 10 November 2020, 1:07pm.

8 https://au.int/en/agenda2063/flagship-projects, Accessed 7 September 2020, 5:01pm. See also https://www.tralac.org/documents/resources/faqs/2377-african-continental-free-trade-area-faqs-june-2018-update/file.html, Accessed 7 September 2020, 5:05pm.

9 R. C. Riddell, 'Zimbabwe', in R. C. Riddell (ed.), *Manufacturing Africa: Performance and Prospects of Seven Countries in Sub-Saharan Africa* (London: James Currey, 1990), 337–411; R. C. Riddell, 'A forgotten dimension? The manufacturing sector in African development', *Development Policy Review*, 8 (1990), 5–27; and C. Stoneman, 'Industrialisation in Zimbabwe: past, present and future', *Afrika Focus*, 6, 3–4 (1990), 245–82.

development in sub-Saharan Africa and recommended policy reforms.[10] The hallmark of these economic reforms became known as the Structural Adjustment Programmes (SAPs). The policy prescriptions of the SAPs emphasised market-oriented adjustment measures such as trade liberalisation policies, currency devaluation, and privatisation in African economies. In essence, the World Bank argued that the state's role should be rolled back. It is to these recommendations that Riddell and Stoneman reacted.

Surprisingly missing in the contemporaneous debate was the role of the manufacturing industry in Africa's development. The World Bank reports stated that the sector 'should be developed in response to market opportunities.'[11] Yet, during this period, industrialisation occupied the minds of African leaders and organisations. For example, in the 1980s, African leaders undertook key initiatives like The Lagos Plan of Action for the Economic Development of Africa, 1980–2000; A Programme for the Industrial Development Decade for Africa; and the Economic Commission for Africa's 1989 report – *African Alternative Framework to Structural Adjustment Programmes for Socio-Economic Recovery and Transformation* – all geared towards industrial development on the continent.[12] What was clear was the critical role the manufacturing sector would have to play in Africa's development. The World Bank either missed or ignored this.

Riddell and associates, therefore, sought to examine the state of the manufacturing sector in Africa vis-à-vis World Bank reports. They criticised the World Bank policy prescriptions, arguing that they were 'based on incorrect data' and would actually 'exacerbate the vulnerabilities of African industry rather than promote efficiency and competitiveness', resulting in

10 See World Bank, *Accelerated Development in Sub-Saharan Africa: An Agenda for Action* (Washington, DC: World Bank, 1981); *Financing Adjustment with Growth in Sub-Saharan Africa 1986–90* (Washington, DC: World Bank, 1986); *Zimbabwe: An Industrial Sector Memorandum* (Washington, DC: International Bank for Reconstruction and Development, 1987); and *Zimbabwe: A Strategy for Sustained Growth* (Washington, DC: International Bank for Reconstruction and Development, 1987); *Sub-Saharan Africa: From Crisis to Sustainable Growth* (Washington, DC: World Bank, 1989); and World Bank and UNDP, *Africa's Adjustment and Growth in the 1980s* (Washington, DC: World Bank, 1989).

11 Riddell, 'A forgotten dimension?', 7.

12 Organization for African Unity (OAU), *Lagos Plan of Action for the Economic Development of Africa, 1980–2000* (Geneva: International Institute for Labour Studies, 1982). United Nations Economic Commission for Africa (UNECA), OAU, and United Nations Industrial Development Organization (UNIDO), *A Programme for the Industrial Development Decade for Africa* (New York: United Nations, 1982) and UNECA, *African Alternative Framework to Structural Adjustment Programmes for Socio-economic Recovery and Transformation* (Addis Ababa: UNECA, 1989).

'further disinvestment, deindustrialisation, and more urban unemployment'.[13] Riddell further pointed out the inadequacy of the SAPs as a panacea to Africa's economic recovery and industrial development. As their case studies demonstrated, there was no 'one particular road to industrialisation or mould into which either these or other [sub-Saharan] countries could or should be made to fit'.[14] Instead, Riddell suggested that 'a policy of *benign intervention* rather than *benign neglect*, together with an upgrading of the role of aid to the sector, is likely to enhance the growth and deepening of the manufacturing sector and in so doing to assist in, rather than hinder, attempts to solve the "African crisis."'[15]

With regard to Zimbabwe specifically, the World Bank argued that the state was interventionist and its protectionism had produced an industrial structure that was highly inefficient and inhibited further growth. Riddell responded that 'carefully chosen interventionist policies, not sole reliance on market forces, were necessary to encourage local industries ... more systematic import substitution should be the goal, as well as policies to raise the efficiency of current enterprises'.[16] Stoneman also disagreed with the World Bank's assessment of the manufacturing sector in Zimbabwe. Whereas the World Bank recommended the liberalisation of the economy and the rolling back of the state, Stoneman argued that the state had been central in the earlier industrialisation and that there was still a need for an intelligent state role.[17] Even as both Riddell and Stoneman rebutted the World Bank's assessment of the Zimbabwean manufacturing industry, their examination of the manufacturing history missed a crucial aspect of how the country had industrialised.

According to Riddell, Zimbabwe's manufacturing sector growth derived from import substitution activities underpinned by

> government support for industrial promotion and expansion, a sustained period without balance-of-payments problems, a long period of overall growth and continued diversification in the rest of the economy, a fairly developed and efficiently operating supporting physical, transport and financial infrastructure, a developed capital market, high levels of local management and engineering skills, knowledge of production processes and ability to adapt machinery to local conditions, international confidence in the economy leading to inflows of foreign investment and technology (in the crucial pre-UDI period), trade agreements which ensured relatively captive neighbouring and larger markets for goods, tariffs and quantitative

13 A. Gordon, 'Review of Riddell (ed.), *Manufacturing Africa*', *Journal of Modern African Studies*, 29 (1991), 334.

14 Riddell (ed.), *Manufacturing Africa*, 47.

15 Riddell, 'A forgotten dimension?', 7.

16 *Ibid.*

17 Stoneman, 'Industrialisation in Zimbabwe', 252–58.

> restrictions which provided protection to newly established firms and, in the case of some firms, the payment of subsidies.[18]

He thus concluded that what made Zimbabwe's success possible was the 'convergence of so many supportive elements for long periods of time, together with the ability of both the government and manufacturers to adapt as circumstances, internal and externally induced, changed'.[19]

For Stoneman, Zimbabwe became the most industrialised country in sub-Saharan Africa outside South Africa because of 'the relative success of the mining and agricultural sectors and the early attainment of a measure of domestic control of the economy', which in turn allowed for 'a state-led process of industrialisation favouring settler interests, in part at the expense of the economically dominant British South Africa Company'.[20] Stoneman further noted that

> Circumstances played a major role in creating a climate conducive to the development of industry: although the state was somewhat interventionist, 'natural protection', World War II and UDI also played a major role. Indeed, the professed ideology throughout was of a free market, open-economy nature which was at odds with the interventionist, semi-autarchic policies actually being pursued. Government, however, did not play a very large direct role in industry, although its catalytic effect in steel and cotton were probably crucial.[21]

What is clear from both Stoneman and Riddell's analyses is that a combination of factors gave Zimbabwe a head start. Among those factors was the crucial role played by the state. While all these factors are acknowledged, their significance could have mattered only if there was a committed national capital prepared to risk its investments and set up shop in a country with a small market, far removed from the newest technology and, more importantly, in antagonism to the contemporaneous imperial policy that stifled industrial development in the colonies. To be sure, Stoneman and Riddell are correct in pointing out that circumstances like the domestic control of the economy, the Great Depression, the Second World War, and the Unilateral Declaration of Independence (UDI) were crucial in stimulating industrial development in colonial Zimbabwe. However, although these are important, they only tell part of the story of the development of secondary industries. For instance, the Second World War may account for the opportunistic development of the manufacturing sector but hardly informs us of its persistence after the war. Similarly, political moments like the Federation of Rhodesia and Nyasaland

18 Riddell, 'A forgotten dimension?', 12–13.

19 *Ibid.*

20 Stoneman, 'Industrialisation in Zimbabwe', 245–46.

21 *Ibid.*, 247.

and the UDI may have offered conditions for further industrial growth, but that growth depended on various internal dynamics and variables. These included the relationship between industrialists and the state.

This book thus explores policy proposals and political pressure exerted on the state by industrialists through their organised Chambers of Industry over the trajectory of industrialisation in colonial Zimbabwe (1890–1979). The development, expansion, and diversification of industry which took place in the colony was, among other factors, attributable to the efforts of industrialists, who galvanised and formed representative organisations to advance their interests, pitting them against the state and other blocs of capital – farmers, miners, and commerce. The book's focus on organised industry differs remarkably from the previous studies of Stoneman, Riddell, and others which invariably emphasised on the role of the state and other factors of production in the development of the manufacturing industry. While the state was a significant player, analyses that privilege its role in the industrialisation of Zimbabwe are incomplete. The colonial state did not *mero motu* support industrialisation in Zimbabwe as suggested by Riddell and Stoneman.

Instead, as I will show in this book, private enterprise in general, and industrialists in particular, played an often underestimated role in the country's industrialisation. The book demonstrates that the significant point of contention between the state, industry, and other economic interest groups was protection. Pursuing this contestation reopens a long-standing debate on the best way for developing countries to achieve economic development: free-market enterprise, state-protected development, or import substitution industrialisation (ISI)? More broadly, the book also casts light on the implications of Southern Rhodesia's industrial development on its neighbours and trading partners, especially South Africa, Zambia, and Malawi. By so doing, it speaks to regional trade in SADC, which preoccupies African leaders, as manifested in the member states' adoption of the AfCFTA. By focusing on the contested history of industrial policy in colonial Zimbabwe, the book also contributes to growing literature on settler colonial studies, with broader implications on our understanding on settler colonialism and its legacies.

Colonial Zimbabwe's remarkable and exceptional success story can be best appreciated if contrasted with Africa's experiences of industrialisation. According to Ana Paula F. Mendes, Mário A. Bertella, and Rudolph F. A. P. Teixeira, 'the road to the first stage of the industrialisation process in Sub-Saharan Africa was long, and paved with a great deal of conflict of interests between national and international economic agents ... international agents and particularly local colonial Governments never encouraged the introduction of a vigorous industrial policy in African colonies.'[22] Larry J. Butler shares

22 A. P. F. Mendes, M. A. Bertella, and R. F. A. P. Teixeira, 'Industrialization in sub-Saharan Africa and import substitution policy', *Brazilian Journal of Political Economy*, 34, 1 (2014), 120–38, at pp. 121–22.

the same view, stating that 'among the most entrenched criticisms of the record of European colonial rule in Africa is that it discouraged, or actively obstructed, the emergence of diversified colonial and post-colonial economies ... the colonial state failed to create the climate in which industrialisation might have been possible.'[23] The neglect was informed by the desire to ensure that the colonies remained suppliers of desired commodities to the metropolitan economies and to protect the market share of metropolitan exporters and manufacturers.

Another economist view advances three explanations in accounting for the unequal spread of industrialisation in colonial Africa. To begin with, it is argued that 'barriers to the spread of industrialisation were cultural. Some societies simply did not possess those attitudes to work, savings, risk-taking or cooperation, which are necessary for the efficient operation of markets and modern industries.'[24] From the 1950s, the argument shifted to economic factors such as 'narrow markets, poor infrastructure, weak financial institutions, falling terms of trade, and rapid population growth', and the final explanation of the three lays the fault at the door of 'disequalising tendencies emanating from world capitalism.'[25] Economists have also made a crucial observation regarding how the nature of colonialism impacted Africa's capacity to industrialise. Specifically, they suggest that colonies with settler colonialism fared better than those without. As M. Shahid Alam posits,

> The presence in any colony of large numbers of settlers from the metropolitan country can also create conditions favorable to local industrialisation. The settlers bring valuable industrial and entrepreneurial skills; they constitute a potential market for domestic manufactures; but most importantly, they will be able to exploit their close social ties with colonial governments to extract policies supportive of industrialisation. It is not surprising, therefore, that those African countries which made some progress in industrial development had large settler populations.[26]

Though not incorrect, Shahid's argument is problematic. To argue as he does that the number of settlers was a crucial variable is essentialist. One need only think of colonial Algeria and Angola, both of which had far larger settler populations than Southern Rhodesia, but nothing remotely approaching its industrial development after the Second World War. Rather, it was the constitutional autonomy and the capacity to shape the economy accordingly that

23 L. J. Butler, 'Industrialisation in late colonial Africa: a British perspective', *Itinerario*, 23, 3–4 (1999), 123–35, at p. 123.

24 M. S. Alam, 'Colonialism and imperialism: empirical results', https://mpra.ub.uni-muenchen.de/37866/ Munich Personal RePEc Archive Paper No. 37866, Posted 7 Apr 2012, 12:32pm UTC, 2.

25 *Ibid.*

26 *Ibid.*, 8.

was fundamental. Southern Rhodesia had the crucial advantage of having been a self-governing colony since 1923. Under the Responsible Government, and unlike other typical colonies, it had domestic control of the economy and was free to manipulate tariffs.[27] Shigeru Akita observes that there was a similar tendency in British India during the Great Depression. Quoting from a *Commercial Report on India*, Akita writes: 'There is little doubt that a self-governing India will take full advantage of her fiscal autonomy in order to promote her industries. [Lancashire's] efforts to regain a footing in the Indian market may be frustrated by the fiscal policy of an autonomous India.'[28] Just as in British India during this period, this autonomy allowed Southern Rhodesia to determine its economic policies independently of the metropole, except in matters of African affairs, currency, and foreign policy.[29] But even with this relative freedom from the metropole, the colonial state did not, on its own, initiate policies favourable to the development of secondary industries. As Stoneman and Riddell have shown, certain events such as the Great Depression (1929–1933) and the Second World War (1939–1945) led industrialisation to take root.

These developments exposed the vulnerability of relying on the export-oriented primary industries of agriculture and mining, thus forcing the Southern Rhodesian state to concede the need to develop local secondary industries.[30] Even as the state realised this imperative, the lobbying power of the domestic industrial bourgeoisie was still needed to ensure an active industrial policy

27 For a detailed analysis on how Southern Rhodesia manipulated tariffs, especially with respect to Northern Rhodesia and the Congo, see A. M. Kanduza, *The Political Economy of Underdevelopment in Northern Rhodesia, 1918–1960: A Case Study of Customs Tariff and Railway Freight Policies* (Lanham: University Press of America, 1986).

28 S. Akita, 'British economic interests and international order of Asia in the 1930s', in S. Akita and N. J. White (eds), *The International Order of Asia in the 1930s and 1950s* (Farnham: Ashgate Publishing Company, 2010),), 17–48, at p. 38.

29 M. M. Burdette, 'Industrial development in Zambia, Zimbabwe and Malawi: the primacy of politics', in Z. A. Konczack *et al.* (eds), *Studies in the Economic History of Southern Africa: The Frontline States, Volume 1* (London: Frank Cass and Co. Ltd, 1990), 75–126, at p. 75; C. Palley, *The Constitutional History and Law of Southern Rhodesia 1888–1965 with Special Reference to Imperial Control* (Oxford: Clarendon Press, 1966); see also Phimister, 'Accommodating imperialism: the compromise of the settler state in Southern Rhodesia, 1923–1929', *Journal of African History*, 25, 3 (1984), 279–94.

30 Secondary industry is an economic sector that processes raw materials into finished and semi-finished products. It mainly consists of two branches: the manufacturing and construction sectors. These can also be divided into light industry or heavy industry. This study relates organised secondary industry to the manufacturing sector and does not differentiate between heavy industry and light industry. The manufacturing sector constitutes the automotive, electrical, chemical, energy, metallurgical, food, glass, textile and clothing, and consumer goods industries.

was put in place. The Great Depression resulted in the decline of commodity prices in international markets. Countries and mainly colonies like Southern Rhodesia, which relied on exporting primary products, suffered from contracting markets and, ultimately, a loss of revenue. To lessen the impact of the Great Depression, for instance, farmers in Southern Rhodesia encouraged the development of local factories that could process their farm products.[31]

The development of local factories during this period was not unique to Southern Rhodesia. In East Asia, particularly British India, 'the rapid development of cotton industries occurred under the Great Depression and its aftermath from the early 1930s'.[32] As discussions about colonial industries began, they were underpinned by tariff protections for those industries. Those deliberating believed that the nascent colonial industries would require protective tariffs, yet there was also a genuine 'fear that tariffs would encourage uneconomic or unviable industries, which would pass on to their consumers the costs of their lack of competitiveness'.[33] This argument continued to dominate conversations on industrial development in colonies. Sound as it may have been, the real motive behind discouraging local industries was the 'long-standing metropolitan hostility towards colonial industrialisation, anxious to defend existing British commercial interests, especially those ailing sectors, such as the textile industry, which had come to see African markets as providing some compensation for the irretrievable loss of markets in Asia'.[34]

While Southern Rhodesia was still reeling from the adverse effects of the Depression, the Second World War broke out in 1939. The war disrupted international trade patterns. Manufacturing industries in Western countries were geared towards the war and so too were shipping priorities. Thus goods formerly imported became practically unavailable, leading to shortages of manufactured goods on the local market. To meet the domestic demand, Southern Rhodesia turned to local factories. Nascent industrialists seized the impetus provided by the Second World War to expand. Noteworthy here is that the state and the industrialists had different expectations for the industrial development path the country would pursue. They disagreed on whether industrialisation should be a state-led and protected development or one based on free enterprise. For the state, secondary industrial development could best be achieved through free enterprise, while industrialists preferred state protection as and when it suited them. Other factors of production tied to industrial development, such as labour, markets, capital, and transport, also became central to the debate, attracting the attention of other economic interest groups like miners, farmers, and commerce. Industrialists coalesced around their interests and formed

31 O. Hulec, 'Some aspects of the 1930s depression in Rhodesia', *Journal of Modern African Studies*, 7, 1 (1969), 95–105.
32 Akita, 'British economic interests', 43.
33 Alam, 'Colonialism and imperialism: empirical results', 8.
34 Butler, 'Industrialisation in late colonial Africa', 123, 127.

representative organisations to push through their interests. It is these industrial representative organisations (organised secondary industry) established to represent and advance the interests of industrialists that form the crux of this book's discussion.

The book examines the relationship between organised secondary industry, the state, and other economic interest groups over the industrialisation of Rhodesia from 1890 to after 1979.[35] It investigates the extent to which the nature and structure of the secondary industry in colonial Zimbabwe was shaped by the relationship between the state and organised industry. It also examines the contribution of organised secondary industry to the development of policies on industrial relations, immigration, housing, and urbanisation in the post-Second World War period. In a way, it seeks to establish the extent to which organised industry rather than political considerations alone influenced the formulation of these policies. Furthermore, the study analyses the position of organised secondary industry in relation to the establishment of the Federation of Rhodesia and Nyasaland (henceforth, the Federation) in 1953; the UDI in 1965; the intensification of the liberation struggle and the negotiations for Zimbabwean independence in 1979. It further examines the effects of these historical and political developments on the relationship between the state and organised industry.

The general development of the secondary industry is traced over time, paying particular attention to policy debates, overall contribution to the gross domestic product (GDP), and the generality of the economy. In contrast to the emphasis that many scholars have placed on the role of the state as the driver of industrialisation, the book puts private enterprise represented by organised secondary industry at the centre of industrial development in Southern Rhodesia.[36] It takes 1890 as its starting point, for the origins of the capitalist manufacturing industry are traceable to the establishment of the colony. By 1979, on the eve of Zimbabwe's independence, Rhodesia had become the second most industrialised country in sub-Saharan Africa, after South Africa. It boasted a diversified economy, second only to that of its neighbour. That position, I argue, was a result of a conflictual, uneven, irregular, and often shifting but sometimes collaborative relationship between industrialists on one side and the state and other blocs of capital – farmers, miners, and commerce – on the other. A brief overview of the trends and trajectories post-1979 reveals elements of continuity from the colonial structures. But more importantly, the interventionist character of the state intensifies in the manufacturing sector, crowding out industrial lobby groups, if not muzzling them.

35 Because the study focuses on the colonial period, Zimbabwe is referred to by its colonial names: Southern Rhodesia up to 1964 and Rhodesia from 1965 to 1979.

36 See E. S. Pangeti, 'The state and manufacturing industry: a study of the state as regulator and entrepreneur in Zimbabwe' (PhD, University of Zimbabwe, 1996); and Stoneman, 'Industrialisation in Zimbabwe'.

Farmers, miners, and commerce, with the state's support, believed in the supremacy of the primary exporting industries of agriculture and mining in propelling the economy of Southern Rhodesia. Secondary industries, assumed then to be dependent upon the primary industries for their growth, could develop only if the latter expanded. The state's bias towards these sectorial interests manifested itself in the adoption of 'imperial preference', by which it opened the colony to imports of manufactured goods from other parts of the British Empire in return for market opportunities for the primary raw products (for further discussion, see Chapter 1). Further, the state routinely accepted advice which labelled the manufacturing sector as of secondary importance to mining and agriculture. Politically, the state hoped to turn Southern Rhodesia into a settled British territory, and a viable farming sector was crucial for that purpose. The result was an inert government policy based on the idea that industrial development was a field of private enterprise whose growth ought to be voluntary. Industries were left to their own devices and to develop as opportunity occurred. And, indeed, without government support, and aided only by the partial protection provided via the customs tariff, selectively granted only after careful consideration of various factors, industrialists risked their money and laid a sound base for the industrialisation and economic diversification that characterised colonial Zimbabwe. The exceptions to this was during the crisis periods of the Second World War and the UDI, when the state realised the imperative of local industrial growth, thereby opportunistically and temporarily adopting an active policy to foster it. Each pursuing their own selfish interests, the government and industrialists cooperated and collaborated to promote domestic industrial expansion.

In examining the industrial development of colonial Zimbabwe, this book uses certain terms and concepts that require some qualification: for example, economic interest groups, the state, ISI, and societal corporatism. The state refers to an organised political community and its apparatus, institutions, or structures used in the decision-making process – the exercise of authority and administration which manifests itself in a government. Because the emphasis is on the practice of administration or the decision-making process, the state and government are used interchangeably. This state is seen to be functioning at two levels – that is, the central state and the local state.[37] The central state refers to the successive Southern Rhodesian governments between 1890 and 1979, except during the federal period (1953–1963), when there was the federal government and the Southern Rhodesian territorial government. This state is of a specific kind – that is, it is self-governing. Municipalities or urban councils are considered the local state.

37 These demarcations are adapted from their application in J. Alexander, *The Unsettled Land: State Making & the Politics of Land in Zimbabwe, 1893–2003* (Oxford: James Currey, 2006).

As David J. Murray and Jeffrey Herbst observed in their studies, the state does not function in a vacuum.[38] Its ability to make and allocate decisions is determined by the '"match-up" between interest groups and state institutional structures'.[39] Thus, 'the state should be seen as a structure through which the developmental aims of a particular group are "conceived of and presented as being the motor force of a universal expansion, of a development of all the 'national' energies"'.[40] Building on this conceptualisation, this book adopts Tor Skålnes's notion of societal corporatism – that is, the changing role of interest groups vis-à-vis their relationship with the state (largely their collaboration) – to understand state–interest group relations, but focusing on industrial development.[41] The various interactions between the state and interest groups in this book reflect and represent this societal corporatism.

The economic interest groups that 'matched up' the state have been drawn from the four main sectors of the Rhodesian economy – namely, mining, agriculture, commerce, and secondary industry.[42] These interest groups represented private enterprise – that is, businesses established, owned, and operated by private individuals for profit. They established colony-wide representative associations in each of their sectors that engaged the state with an ultimate goal of advancing and protecting their sectorial and sometimes collective interests. The Chamber of Mines and the Rhodesian Mining Federation represented the mining industry, while agriculture had the Rhodesian National Farmers Union (RNFU) and the Rhodesia Tobacco Association (RTA). These organisations retained the same names throughout the period under study. The Chamber of Commerce catered for the colony's retail and merchant interests. The Salisbury Chamber of Commerce, established in 1894, became the Associated Chambers of Commerce in 1919 and in 1947 evolved to become the Rhodesian Federated Chamber of Commerce. With the establishment of the Federation in 1953, it had to reflect its geographical representation and thus changed to the Association of Chambers of Commerce of Rhodesia and Nyasaland (ACCORN).

38 D. J. Murray, *The Governmental System in Southern Rhodesia* (Oxford: Clarendon Press, 1970); and J. Herbst, *State Politics in Zimbabwe* (Berkeley: University of California Press, 1990).

39 Herbst, *State Politics in Zimbabwe*, 253. By 'match-up', he means 'an interest group directly confronting the particular part of the state that is making the allocation decision in such a way as to cause political conflict': 253.

40 L. Sachikonye, B. Raftopoulos and G. Kanyenze, *Building from the Rubble: The Labour Movement in Zimbabwe since 2000* (Harare: Weaver Press, 2018), 48.

41 T. Skålnes, *The Politics of Economic Reform in Zimbabwe: Continuity and Change in Development* (London: Macmillan Press, 1995).

42 Murray, *Governmental System in Southern Rhodesia*, and C. Leys, *European Politics in Southern Rhodesia* (Oxford: Clarendon Press, 1959), discuss these economic interest groups in detail.

After the Federation dissolved in 1963, ACCORN changed to the Association of Chambers of Commerce of Rhodesia (ACCOR) in 1964.

Whereas the formation of agricultural, commercial, and mining interest groups happened much earlier, in secondary industry this only occurred in the 1920s. However, even by then, these did not have colony-wide representation. Commercial and industrial interest groups emerged in Salisbury and Bulawayo, the two major urban centres where the emerging industries were located. Both the Salisbury Manufacturers' Association and the Bulawayo Manufacturers' Association were formed in 1922. Later, in 1930 and 1935, these manufacturers' associations were transformed into Chambers of Industry. These Chambers later formed a loose Association of Chambers of Industry of Rhodesia in 1941.

The Chambers' functions had limited coverage compared to the other interest groups in mining, agriculture, and commerce, which had a national scope. The Chambers of Industry were partially limited by a lack of clear differentiation between commerce and industry, as some industrialists were also affiliated to the Chambers of Commerce. It also reflected the state and the position of the sector in the Rhodesian economy. It was only in 1949, when industrialists formed the Federation of Rhodesian Industries (FRI), that secondary industry had a clearly defined national representation. The FRI subsequently evolved into the Association of Rhodesia and Nyasaland Industries (ARNI) in 1957 to reflect the geopolitics of the Central African Federation (CAF) and changed again to the Association of Rhodesian Industries (ARnI) in 1964, after the break-up of the Federation of Rhodesia and Nyasaland. Post-1979, ARnI evolved into the Confederation of Zimbabwe Industries. All these groups interacted with the state and among themselves as they pursued their interests.

The book also engages with broad debates on industrialisation in the Third World which stress the importance of ISI as a driver of industrial development. ISI was first implemented by some Latin American countries (Brazil, Argentina, and Chile) in the 1950s as a development policy aimed at reducing their dependence on the industrialised zones of North America and Western Europe.[43] Dependency theorists recommended that the so-called developing countries adopted the ISI.[44] They argued that for Third World countries (periphery) to develop, they must delink from the metropole (centre). Delinking, they

43 A. O. Hirschman, 'The political economy of import-substituting industrialization in Latin America', *Quarterly Journal of Economics*, 82, 1 (1968), 1–32; and W. Baer, 'Import substitution and industrialization in Latin America: experiences and interpretations', *Latin American Research Review*, 7, 1 (1972), 95–122.

44 See R. Prebisch, *The Economic Development of Latin America and Its Principal Problems* (New York: United Nations, 1950); P. A. Baran, *The Political Economy of Growth* (New York: Monthly Review Press, 1957); and A. G. Frank, *Latin America: Underdevelopment or Revolution: Essays on the Development of Underdevelopment and the Immediate Enemy* (New York: Monthly Review Press, 1969).

suggested, could be achieved through ISI. Early independent African countries adopted the same approach to their economic development.[45] To what extent colonial Zimbabwe's industrialisation can be explained by this phenomenon is partly answered in this book.

The Long History of the Manufacturing Industry in Zimbabwe

Secondary industrial development in Zimbabwe has received scholarly attention from different perspectives, with academics drawing on a number of sources and employing various methodologies. The major focus has been on its general development, as influenced by a number of factors.[46] These include the role of the state, the effect of exogenous and episodic developments such as the Second World War, the 1948 Customs (Union) Agreement with South Africa, the establishment of the CAF, and the UDI in 1965.[47] The factors are sometimes narrowed down to the specific sectorial fortunes of, for instance, the cotton and textile industries.[48] The earliest discussion on secondary industries appeared in the editorials and letters to the editor of various newspapers. Industrialists' reports, pamphlets, and journalistic accounts also emerged.[49] This literature focused on the prospects of secondary industries in Southern Rhodesia and encouraged their development. It argued against the

45 Burdette, 'Industrial development in Zambia, Zimbabwe and Malawi'; and see also Riddell (ed.), *Manufacturing Africa*.

46 A. S. Mlambo, E. S. Pangeti, and I. Phimister, *Zimbabwe: A History of Manufacturing, 1890–1995* (Harare: University of Zimbabwe Publications, 2000); and L. Tow, 'The manufacturing economy of Southern Rhodesia: problems and prospects' (PhD, Columbia University, 1960).

47 C. H. Thompson and H. W. Woodruff, *Economic Development in Rhodesia and Nyasaland* (London: Dennis Dobson Ltd, 1953); I. Phimister, *An Economic and Social History of Zimbabwe: Capital Accumulation and Class Struggle* (London: Longman, 1988); Pangeti, 'The state and manufacturing industry'; I. Phimister, 'Secondary industrialisation in Southern Africa: The 1948 Customs Agreement between Southern Rhodesia and South Africa', *Journal of Southern African Studies*, 17, 3 (1991), 430–42; C. Stoneman, 'Foreign capital and the reconstruction of Zimbabwe', *Review of African Political Economy*, 5, 11 (1978), 62–83; 'Foreign capital and the prospects for Zimbabwe', *World Development*, 4, 1 (1976), 25–58; J. A. Handford, *Portrait of an Economy: Rhodesia under Sanctions* (Salisbury: Mercury Press, 1976); and J. A. C. Girdlestone, 'Manufacturing and construction', in G. M. E. Leistner (ed.), *Rhodesia: Economic Structure and Change* (Pretoria: African Institute of South Africa, 1976), 120–35.

48 A. S. Mlambo and I. Phimister, 'Partly protected: origins and growth of colonial Zimbabwe's textile industry, 1890–1965', *Historia*, 52, 2 (2006), 145–75.

49 *Industrial Rhodesia: A Record of Industrial Development in Southern Rhodesia* (Salisbury: Rhodesian Publications, 1945); and *Industries of the Federation: A Study in Progress* (Salisbury: Industrial Press, 1954).

realisation that agriculture and mining dominated the economy and received much support from the state. Some of this early work also discussed the development and scope of the nascent manufacturing sector.[50] In their account of the emerging secondary industries, C. H. Thompson and H. W. Woodruff confined their attention to the cotton textile and iron and steel sectors.[51] Both sectors were under government control, so the data concerning them was readily available. What emerged from this work was that the state was pivotal in their growth and expansion. Thompson and Woodruff also noted that while state assistance was crucial, other factors, such as capital, skilled labour, and African advancement had equal importance in maintaining the momentum of manufacturing growth. Leonard Tow discussed in depth the significance of these factors.[52] He systematically examined how the Rhodesian economic environment conditioned the growth and expansion of the manufacturing sector. While this literature gave insights into the development of the sector, it was limited to its own time.

The development and scope of secondary industries later received considerable attention from scholarship which traced the history of manufacturing from the beginning of colonisation to the post-colonial period.[53] Various perspectives emerged. Ian Phimister's *An Economic and Social History of Zimbabwe* offered a starting point in understanding the origins and development of the manufacturing industry in Southern Rhodesia. Phimister argued that manufacturing in Southern Rhodesia began in the 1890s and picked up in the crisis periods of the Great Depression and the Second World War. He challenged earlier scholars who emphasised the outbreak of the Second World War as the starting point of the manufacturing sector in Southern Rhodesia. His work discussed the role of the state, from its initial reluctance to assist industrialists in their infancy to its shift in emphasis in the 1940s, when it began to help the sector by negotiating trade agreements with South Africa. Phimister stresses this point in a subsequent publication.[54]

50 Thompson and Woodruff, *Economic Development in Rhodesia and Nyasaland.*

51 *Ibid.*, 164.

52 Tow, 'The manufacturing economy of Southern Rhodesia.' Also in 1969, the Rhodesian Economic Society held a symposium on 'Industry in Rhodesia,' at which papers on various aspects of industry such as government industrial policy, factors influencing or inhibiting the growth of secondary industries, and the impact of industry on other economic sectors of mining, agriculture, and trade were presented. The symposium resulted in the publication of a special issue of the *Rhodesian Journal of Economics*, 3, 2 (1969), covering all the papers.

53 See, for example, Phimister, *An Economic and Social History of Zimbabwe*; Pangeti, 'The state and manufacturing industry'; and Mlambo, Pangeti, and Phimister, *Zimbabwe: A History of Manufacturing.*

54 Phimister, 'Secondary industrialisation in Southern Africa.'

E. S. Pangeti used company history, while Alois S. Mlambo and Phimister employed sectorial analysis of the textile industry to demonstrate the state's role in the manufacturing sector.[55] However, these studies were limited by the unavailability of data at the time of writing. For example, in writing *Zimbabwe: A History of Manufacturing*, Mlambo, Pangeti, and Phimister relied heavily on public and government official records which did not reveal critical information about the subject. This was because at the time of publication, some archival material, for example data on the UDI period, was mostly not available due to different archival access regimes. Sources for this period are now accessible. Their availability makes it possible to revisit developments of the time, and ask new and different questions about the relations between organised industry and the state and their implications on the trajectory of industrialisation in the colony.

Other scholars like Leonard Zinyama and Daniel Tevera focused on the distribution and location of the manufacturing sector in Southern Rhodesia.[56] They demonstrated that uneven distribution of the manufacturing sector around the country was one of the characteristics and challenges that accompanied industrialisation. Thus, decentralisation needed to be promoted to address this reality.[57]

The Second World War, the Federation, UDI, and Secondary Industry

Giovanni Arrighi discussed the development of secondary industries within a Marxist framework.[58] Arrighi's account of the industrialisation process illustrated how the emerging manufacturing sector created a new class of industrialists who played an important role in reshaping the colony's political economy. He also noted the impact of external factors and key events like the Second World War and the Federation in stimulating the growth of manufacturing. Discussing the effects of the Second World War on Southern Africa, Norman Mlambo examined the development of war-oriented industries in

55 Pangeti's thesis is a case in point: it examines the state's entrepreneurial role in manufacturing using the case studies of Zimbabwe Iron and Steel Company and the Industrial Development Corporation (IDC) to buttress its argument. See also Mlambo and Phimister, 'Partly protected'.

56 D. S. Tevera, 'Location of manufacturing industry in Zimbabwe: a geographical investigation' (PhD, University of Cincinatti, 1984); and L. Zinyama, 'Prospects and problems of industrial decentralization in Zimbabwe', in G. Williams and A. Wood (eds), *Geographical Perspectives on Development in Southern Africa* (Australia: Commonwealth Geographical Bureau, 1986), 122–36.

57 *Ibid.*

58 G. Arrighi, 'The political economy of Rhodesia', *New Left Review*, 39 (1966), 35–65.

Southern Rhodesia and South Africa.[59] He argued that while the war stimulated the development of industries, it placed limitations on the industrial war effort because the two countries lacked technology and skilled manpower.[60] Mlambo challenged the traditional historiography, which tended to limit and reduce Southern Rhodesia's war effort to the supply of labour, training airbases, manpower, and raw materials.

In the post-war period, Southern Rhodesia, at the behest of Britain, pursued the establishment of a federation with Northern Rhodesia and Nyasaland. The Federation of Rhodesia and Nyasaland was pronounced in 1953. In a contribution to the debate about the economics of the Federation, Arthur Hazlewood made an important point about industrialisation, suggesting that although the Federation had not brought substantial economic benefits to the three territories by the time of its dissolution, secondary industries had expanded.[61] He attributed this to the high inflow of capital and the operationalisation of the 1955 Federal Tariff Agreement.[62] For him, the Federation provided two important factors for secondary industry expansion: a protected domestic market and capital. Indeed, the creation of the Federation promoted the further growth of the manufacturing sector.

Following the break-up of the Federation in 1963, in 1965 Southern Rhodesia unilaterally declared independence from Britain after it rejected the idea of Black African majority rule in preference of an independent White minority rule. The proclamation of the UDI gave further impetus to the development of secondary industries in spite of sanctions. Scholars like John A. Handford and James A. C. Girdlestone analysed the impact of UDI and the attendant sanctions on the Rhodesian economy.[63] In a full-blown celebration of settler entrepreneurship during sanctions, Handford emphasised the positive influence of sanction-induced protection on the manufacturing industry. Equally, Girdlestone accounts for industrial expansion under sanctions. Both scholars used statistical data to depict the structure of and changes in the manufacturing sector. They also revealed the importance of a 'protected' market in stimulating local industries. Sanctions gave 'natural protection' to local industries, as they faced no competition from outside firms. In addition, UDI provided an environment conducive to pursuing ISI. Both Handford and

59 N. Mlambo, 'Arms production and war supply in Southern Africa, 1939–1945: Limitations of the industrial war effort of South Africa and Zimbabwe during the Second World War' (PhD, University of Cape Town, 2000).

60 *Ibid.*

61 A. Hazlewood, 'The economics of federation and dissolution in Central Africa', in A. Hazlewood (ed.), *African Integration and Disintegration: Case Studies in Economic and Political Union* (Oxford University Press: London, 1967), 185–250.

62 *Ibid.*

63 Handford, *Portrait of an Economy*; and Girdlestone, 'Manufacturing and construction'.

Girdlestone concur that the UDI was the period where industrial development became a remarkable success.

Another review of the Rhodesian economy during sanctions was made by David M. Rowe.[64] Rowe explained how sanctions induced institutional changes that strengthened rather than weakened the targeted country or government. Cornered into isolation, the beleaguered Rhodesian regime devised new ways of controlling various local institutions, interest groups (business community), and the market. It used this powerful position to win political support and loyalty from business in order to withstand the expected adverse impact of sanctions. In explaining the state's capture of the business community, Rowe foregrounded his analysis alongside Murray's account of the intergroup politics and the position of the state in Rhodesian politics and governance up to 1953. Before 1965 but especially before the 1950s, commercial and industrial interest groups, despite their antagonism, enjoyed much recognition and a close relationship with the state. The United Party government reflected the interests of these groups.[65] However, for Rowe, all this changed from 1962 onwards, when the Rhodesian Front government came to power. It usurped all the influence of commercial and industrial interest groups.[66] Rowe concluded that business was muzzled and became acquiescent, and suggested that the state dictated economic policy, especially industrial policy.

The reaction and position of these interest groups towards the state's new influence was investigated by Phimister and the present author.[67] Phimister and Gwande examined the political and structural relationship between settler colonialism and secondary industry, as well as the composition, capitalisation, ownership, or product range of the manufacturing sector in the immediate period before and after the UDI. They demonstrated the complicit role of big business in the economic project that sustained UDI and the expansion of secondary industry in the first half of the 1960s. This book in part expands on this. By tracing the operations and voices of organised secondary industry, it shows the continued influence of economic interest groups in statecraft, contrary to Rowe's conclusion. Industrialists continued to set the agenda for industrial development. Other scholars, such as Gann and Gelfand, Patrick Bond, and D. G. Clarke, highlighted that secondary industrial development impacted on other aspects such as urbanisation, housing, labour and capital,

64 D. M. Rowe, *Manipulating the Market: Understanding Economic Sanctions, Institutional Change and the Political Unity of White Rhodesia* (Chicago: Chicago University Press, 2001).

65 *Ibid.*, 40.

66 *Ibid.*, 106.

67 I. Phimister and V. M. Gwande, 'Secondary industry and settler colonialism: Southern Rhodesia before and after UDI,' *African Economic History*, 45, 2 (2017), 85–112.

and money markets.[68] Such aspects drew the attention of industrialists, but the scholarship has shied away from discussing these from the perspective of industry. This book amplifies the relationship between the Rhodesian state and organised secondary industry over the *longue durée.*

In the years after independence, a debate emerged over the best path to follow to keep the momentum of industrialisation.[69] Participants in this debate assessed the state and prospects of industrialisation under a Black government. Daniel B. Ndlela and David Wield recommended a number of policy changes in light of the challenges inherited from the colonial state. In their policy suggestions, however, they are silent on how interactions between the state and industrialists could be explored. This assessment occurred in the context of emerging questions about the role of the state in development. One school of thought, fronted by the World Bank, argued that the state's role should be rolled back.[70] It was against this background that Stoneman and Riddell published their accounts of Zimbabwe's industrialisation.[71]

The literature suggests that the industrialisation process in colonial Zimbabwe was spearheaded by the state and owes its expansion to exogenous conditions, episodic developments, and other factors of production. Yet, the same scholarship acknowledges the reluctance of the state to encourage industrial development and, in some instances, examines the fights between the two. Another observation is that the state may have somewhat assisted secondary industry, but the sector was largely privately owned, suggesting that individual industrialists worked hard to achieve the sectorial growth. Much as exogenous shocks might have given impetus to industrialisation, they hardly explain its persistence in times of relative normalcy. Some of the scholarship focused on specific issues. Its confinement to a particular sector, period, or aspect limits our knowledge of the industrialisation of the country. New perspectives on

68 See, for example, L. H. Gann and M. Gelfand, *Huggins of Rhodesia: The Man and His Country* (London: George Allen and Unwin, 1964); E. Gargett, *The Administration of Transition: African Urban Settlement in Rhodesia* (Gwelo: Mambo Press, 1977); D. G. Clarke, 'The political economy of discrimination and underdevelopment in Rhodesia with special reference to African workers, 1940–1973' (PhD, University of St Andrews, 1975); and P. Bond, *Uneven Zimbabwe: A Study of Finance, Development and Underdevelopment* (Trenton, NJ: Africa World Press, 1998).

69 D. B. Ndlela, 'Problems of industrialisation: structural and policy issues', in I. Mandaza (ed.), *Zimbabwe: The Political Economy of Transition, 1980–1986* (Dakar, Senegal: CODESRIA, 1986), 141–64; and D. Wield, 'Manufacturing', in C. Stoneman (ed.), *Zimbabwe's Inheritance* (New York: St Martin's Press, 1981), 151–70.

70 See World Bank Report No. 6349-ZIM, *Zimbabwe: An Industrial Sector Memorandum*, and World Bank Report, *Zimbabwe: A Strategy for Sustained Growth.*

71 Riddell (ed.), *Manufacturing Africa*; Riddell, 'A forgotten dimension?'; and Stoneman, 'Industrialisation in Zimbabwe'.

secondary industrialisation can be understood in terms of state and organised industry's actions and interactions. Noteworthy also is the dearth of literature on the manufacturing sector in the current historiography of Zimbabwe. For instance, the expansive histories of Zimbabwe published recently are striking in their comparative silence on industrialisation.[72] These histories are therefore inadequate and incomplete. Against this background, this book reinserts the role of industrialists into the narrative.

State and Interest Groups in Rhodesia

Examining organised industry and state relations requires an understanding of the dynamics of interest group politics. Colin Leys was among the first cohort of scholars to discuss interest groups and their interaction with the state.[73] Leys demonstrated how business civil society influenced politics structurally and systematically in Southern Rhodesia. He concluded that all the interest groups were organised around a common objective of maintaining White racial superiority over Black Africans. Whereas the European business community unanimously supported one political party, labour rallied behind the Rhodesian Labour Party that represented its interests. The economic interest groups Leys identified were 'not mutually antagonistic', and their 'rallying point was fear of African economic and political competition'.[74]

Leys's account of political dynamics and change was thus centred on a homogenised local European society that was monolithic and free of conflicts. As L. H. Gann demonstrates, this was not the case. In contrast, in his account of Europeans' early social, political, and economic history, Gann shows that there were heterogeneous interest groups.[75] The interest groups competed and conflicted among themselves and in the process affected the future trajectory of the colony. One example was the 1922 referendum to decide whether company rule in Southern Rhodesia would be replaced by a Responsible Government to create a self-governing colony or by joining the Union of South Africa as a fifth province. In his account of the referendum, Gann establishes that various interest groups, formally organised or not, were associated with one side or the other. Such competition had a huge impact on the outcome of the referendum.

72 See, for example, B. Raftopoulos and A. S. Mlambo (eds), *Becoming Zimbabwe: A History from the Pre-colonial Period to 2008* (Harare: Weaver Press, 2009); and A. S. Mlambo, *A History of Zimbabwe* (Cambridge: Cambridge University Press, 2014).

73 Leys, *European Politics in Southern Rhodesia*.

74 *Ibid.*, 174.

75 L. H. Gann, *A History of Southern Rhodesia: Early Days to 1934* (London: Chatto and Windus, 1965).

Leys was further challenged by Murray, who argued that a study of any country's political and administrative structure should not be limited to its formal institutions or structures of government.[76] Instead, 'the point of attention is the system of power relationships through which basic decisions are taken for the society'.[77] Murray disaggregated the governmental and administrative structure of Southern Rhodesia, showing how the various economic interest groups identified by Leys became part of that governmental structure. This enabled them to exert some influence over political decisions. He further observed that the various interest groups were full of conflict and in-fighting as they competed for the attention of the state. The state took advantage of these conflicts and moved in as an arbiter, thus manipulating interest groups to its own advantage. Gann and Murray revealed the degree to which interest groups and their varying and competing agendas can influence the trajectory of a country. While intergroup conflict is demonstrated in these works, there is little discussion on the impact of such conflicts on economic policy in general and industrialisation in particular.

Attempts to show the effects of interest group politics on policy making were undertaken by Jeffrey Herbst, Skålnes, John A. McKenzie, and Angus Selby.[78] Herbst analysed the state's decision-making process and concluded that its ability is determined by the power of interest groups to check the autonomy of the state in exercising its functions. Skålnes's work looks at the role of various interest groups in influencing economic reform in post-colonial Zimbabwe, especially in light of the adoption of the Economic Structural Adjustment Programme (ESAP). The 1993 study is particularly revealing of the influence of organised industry in supporting economic liberalisation. For him, this was a huge paradox, as the manufacturing industry would be negatively affected by the liberalisation of the economy. Yet industrialists embraced and even campaigned for structural adjustment. Skålnes's analysis was, however, limited to the ESAP period. Furthermore, organised industry in his discussion was treated as a homogeneous group. Yet this comprised of subsectorial representative organs. Also contributing to the discussions on interest group politics and state relations, McKenzie and Selby focused on commercial farmers' interests in both the governmental system and the promulgation of agricultural policy. While these studies demonstrated the politics of commercial farmers

76 Murray, *Governmental System in Southern Rhodesia.*

77 *Ibid.*, xvi.

78 Herbst, *State Politics in Zimbabwe*; Skålnes, *The Politics of Economic Reform in Zimbabwe*; 'The state, interest groups and structural adjustment in Zimbabwe', *Journal of Development Studies*, 29, 3 (1993), 401–28; J. A. McKenzie, 'Commercial farmers in the governmental system of Zimbabwe, 1963–1980' (PhD, University of Zimbabwe, 1989); and A. Selby, 'Commercial farmers and the state: interest group politics and land reform in Zimbabwe' (PhD, University of Oxford, 2006).

and their interactions with the state, they did not identify linkages between this group's interests and its equivalents in other sectors.

The latest literature analysing state–interest group relations has emerged. Tapiwa Madimu's work explores the 'entangled relationship between miners, farmers and the state'.[79] He engages with the protean nature of colonial state policies, investigating how they influenced the interaction of settler farmers and miners between 1895 and 1961, and how the sectors reacted. Madimu examines the changes which characterised the succeeding colonial governments, highlighting reasons that influenced the adoption of specific policies regulating agriculture and mining. The country's first administrative system, led by the British South Africa Company (BSAC), laid the foundation of a policy framework which dictated miner–farmer relations for six decades from 1890. Such relationships were always shifting and mainly characterised by friction. Madimu concluded that 'the government's mediating role constantly shifted and significantly influenced the nature of policies which regulated farmer-miner relations up to 1961'.[80] This book extends this analysis to cover the state–industry relations that developed as Southern Rhodesia industrialised.

Musiwaro Ndakaripa also investigated the relationship between the state and civil society organisations on matters regarding the indigenisation policy in post-colonial Zimbabwe.[81] He used various concepts to analyse state–civil society relations. Of interest here are the ideas of statism and public choice. Statism is described as 'the dominance of the state over social, economic and political groups'.[82] Ndakaripa's study revealed that 'the Zimbabwean state, on several occasions, adopted a statist approach and marginalised interest groups on indigenisation'.[83] Using the public choice concept, which is premised on the notion 'that people are motivated mainly by self-interest',[84] Ndakaripa suggests that 'business associations [in Zimbabwe took] advantage of their organisation and access to officials and institutions to pester the state to formulate economic

79 T. Madimu, 'Farmers, miners and the state in colonial Zimbabwe (Southern Rhodesia), c.1895–1961' (PhD, Stellenbosch University, 2017); See also T. Madimu, 'Responsible government and miner–farmer relations in Southern Rhodesia, 1923–1945', *South African Historical Journal*, 68, 3 (2016), 366–89.

80 Madimu, 'Farmers, miners and the state in colonial Zimbabwe', 195.

81 M. Ndakaripa, 'State, civil society and the politics of economic indigenisation in Zimbabwe, 1980 to 2016' (PhD, University of the Free State, 2017).

82 J. V. Jesudason, 'Statist democracy and the limits to civil society in Malaysia', *Journal of Commonwealth and Comparative Politics*, 33, 3 (1995), 336.

83 Ndakaripa, 'State, civil society and the politics of economic indigenisation in Zimbabwe', 24.

84 J. S. Shaw, 'Public choice theory', *The Concise Encyclopedia of Economics*, http://www.econlib.org/library/Enc1/PublicChoiceTheory.html, Accessed 26 April 2022, 10:13am.

policies and regulations which [were] tilted in their favour'.[85] This book in part historicises this modus operandi and examines it in the context of relations between the state and industrialists between 1890 and 1979.

The power of organised economic interests in prevailing over the state has received attention elsewhere. For example, Laura Phillips Sawyer analysed the role of the Chamber of Commerce of the USA in mobilising American small businesses and creating an influential fair trade movement in the early twentieth century. To achieve that, Sawyer argues, 'these firms formed trade associations to lobby and litigate to reshape competition policy to their benefit'.[86] The Chamber also 'collaborated with regulators to create codes of fair competition and influenced the administrative state's public-private approach to market regulation'.[87] Such was the influence of the Chamber. Andrew Dilley has made a similar analysis and argument in respect of the Chamber of Commerce in the Commonwealth and British Empire.[88] Taking a cue from these foregoing works, there is utility value in examining the operations of the business associations such as the Chambers of Industry in colonial Zimbabwe and assessing how they lobbied and achieved results for their interests and members, and in so doing shaped the colony's industrial policy.

This book also draws from Belinda Bozzoli's examination of the political nature of the ruling class and its formation as a very useful lens of analysis.[89] Bozzoli explained how various class interests formed and employed various means to express and exert their ideology over the South African state and society. She uses the Gramscian concept of the 'organic intellectual'. Gramsci states that every class creates its own intellectuals that elaborate its ideologies

85 Ndakaripa, 'State, civil society and the politics of economic indigenisation in Zimbabwe', 23.

86 L. Phillips Sawyer, *American Fair Trade: Proprietary Capitalism, Corporatism, and the 'New Competition', 1890–1940* (Cambridge: Cambridge University Press, 2018).

87 *Ibid.*

88 A. Dilley, 'Un-imagining markets: Chambers of Commerce, globalisation and the political economy of the Commonwealth of Nations, 1945–1975', D. Thackeray, A. Thompson, and R. Toye (eds), *Imagining Britain's Economic Future, c.1800–1975: Trade, Consumerism, and Global Markets* (Cham: Palgrave Macmillan, 2018), 253–77.

89 B. Bozzoli, *The Political Nature of a Ruling Class: Capital and Ideology in South Africa 1890–1933* (London: Routledge and Keagan Paul, 1981). 'The book describes both the formation and transformation of South Africa's ruling class, it traces the emergence, interests, ideology and achievements of the mining capitalists, insisting on the 'revolutionary' impact of their dominance and then demonstrates how rapidly this class of imperial capital was challenged and overshadowed by the interests and actions of a commercial and manufacturing national bourgeoisie.' – Review by Colin Bundy in *Journal of African History* (1984).

as it develops.[90] These intellectuals are 'organic' because they identify very strongly with the class, or subclass, whose interests they express. All sections of the capitalist classes that Bozzoli examined (miners, those engaged in commerce, and industrialists) utilised people in the capacities of journalists, speech makers, and writers to exert their ideological influence over the South African state and society. The intellectuals defined and clarified the bourgeoisie's position and standpoints, bridging the 'gap between economic interests and political and ideological realities'.[91] This modus operandi is juxtaposed with Southern Rhodesia's organised industry as an economic interest group in pursuit of secondary industrialisation of the country. This is done by disaggregating organised industry and exploring its composition, functions, and operations as well as its interactions with the various state and government departments. The relationship between organised industry and other economic interest groups is also explored to demonstrate how the pursuit of the goals and objectives of industry impacted on the operations of others. It is also hoped that analysing the power relations and dynamics between the state and industry can help to explain how the manufacturing sector was shaped by interest group politics.

The Evidentiary Base on Secondary Industrialisation

This book draws on documents produced by both industrialists and state officials that historians of industrialisation in Zimbabwe have not accessed before. It is a qualitative study that uses primary material accessed mainly from NAZ, the National Archives of South Africa (NASA), media houses, and the legislative assembly debates. The NAZ holds a number of collections on secondary industry in Southern Rhodesia. The material has information on the state of the sector and statistics on production, employment, and overall contribution to the economy. There are files on specific areas of secondary industries which detail developments in such sectors, for example the steel and textile industries. The debate over tariffs and protection policy in favour of secondary industry features prominently in the archive. The papers of the Chambers of Industry up to independence are also readily accessible in the archive. These papers include minutes, reports, and resolutions of their yearly congresses between 1942 and 1979. The collections also carry contributions from various Chambers affiliated to the ARnI and other invitees, such as government officials and stakeholders from other sectors such as commerce and mining.

I was also privileged to be able to access unprocessed ARnI papers at the records centre at the NAZ. In terms of the access regimes at NAZ, these papers

90 A. Gramsci, *Selections from Prison Notebooks* (London: Lawrence and Wisehart, 1971).

91 Bozzoli, *The Political Nature of a Ruling Class*, 10.

are due to be made available for public use but because of a backlog in the processing, they are not yet accessible. However, I sought special permission from the archive authority, and this was granted. This is the first time that these papers have been used in any academic research. They cover the period from 1964 to 1973 and reveal the constant interactions between the UDI state and industrialists, which hitherto have not been known to researchers, as elaborated in the last sections of Chapters 5 and 6.

Organised industry published a monthly journal, the *Rhodesian Recorder* (available in the NAZ), from 1949 to the 1960s. The journal was a mouthpiece for industrialists and commerce. ARnI's papers and the *Recorder* capture industrialists' voices on many aspects that concerned them. From a careful reading of the *Recorder*, a picture emerged of the development of secondary industry. The aspirations, desires, and demands of industrialists featured in every volume. The government and other interest groups, especially the Chamber of Commerce, were also given space to contribute or respond to issues that were topical concerning secondary industry and the economy in general. Thus, the *Recorder* offered a way to piece together the interaction between industry, other interest groups, and the state.

The National Archives of Zimbabwe also hold other published primary material, primarily official reports, surveys, and position papers by both government and interest groups concerning secondary industry and cognate issues. Statistics on various aspects of Rhodesia, including the manufacturing sector, were published by the Central Statistics Office through either the *Monthly Digest of Statistics* or the *Official Yearbook*. Commissions of inquiry set up by the government also published their findings, which reveal a number of aspects that informed this book. More useful from the commissions' reports were the evidence gathered and the recommendations made. Through their national representative bodies, industrialists published surveys which were crucial in assessing the state of the industrial sector and its position, changes, and developments in relation to the broader economy. Similarly, legislative assembly debates were useful in bringing out the government's voice on industrial aspects. The University of the Free State's International Studies Group (ISG) has a collection of these Hansards dating from 1929 to 1980.

The book has also made use of the Smith Papers. These were accessed from the digital collection at the ISG gathered from the Rhodes University Cory Research Library in Grahamstown, South Africa. The Smith Papers consist of the Rhodesian government white papers, Cabinet minutes, and correspondences, and capture the voice of the government. These were crucial for casting a new light on the decision- and policy-making processes of the Rhodesian Front government during this period and revealing the inside dealings of the government as it sought to maintain power and withstand sanctions. They were also useful for mapping out the government's interactions with interest and pressure groups, an important aspect of the UDI period. Researchers who had previously written about the manufacturing sector during this period did not have access to these papers.

The discussion on trade agreements between South Africa and Southern Rhodesia was informed by material gathered from the NASA in Pretoria. South African newspapers also complemented the archival material. What became clear from the negotiations and the final trade agreements was the feeling of cooperation and competition between the two neighbours. Largely, South Africa prevailed over its weaker neighbour and bullied Southern Rhodesia into agreements which affected the expansion of some of its industrial sectors. But equally, the clothing and textiles industry of Southern Rhodesia enjoyed a favourable market in South Africa as a result of these agreements. Newspapers like the *Rhodesia Herald* and *The Financial Gazette*, and the business journal *Property and Finance* (P&F) were crucial as complementary and alternative sources that bridged gaps where private papers or certain original primary material were unavailable or silent on certain aspects. They were particularly helpful in constructing the discussion in Chapter 6.

The discussion and arguments presented in the chapters that follow were constructed from all the sources mentioned here, and were then corroborated, juxtaposed, and contextualised in debates and conclusions in existing historiography. However, there are particular years in which organised industry did not hold congresses, or records of the proceedings of such gatherings are missing. I tried to remedy these inconsistencies by using either newspapers or the *Recorder*, but still gaps remained. This explains the apparent dearth of the official voice of industrialists in some instances in the book. At the same time, some salient points require attention in a study of this nature. One is the methodological dilemma: the kinds of sources used and the story they tell are very elitist and official. A second point is the ideological implication of this study: it is White settler dominated and capitalist, therefore, tantamount to a full-blown celebration of settler entrepreneurship. Yet that is not the case. By its nature as settler capitalism, the capitalist manufacturing sector was dominated by Whites who, by virtue of colonial privileges, had access to capital and other economic opportunities to the exclusion of other races, especially Black Africans. The latter only mattered to the sector as a source of labour. The effect of White settler dominance on the emergence of Black entrepreneurs is elaborated in the discussion on the post-1979 economy.

Chapter Overview

Chronologically and thematically structured, the book is written over seven chapters. The introduction highlights historiographical issues on secondary industry, presenting themes and concepts which inform the book. Substantive examination of the industrial policy commences in Chapter 1. The chapter discusses the peripheral emergence of secondary industry under the shadow of, and with opposition from, mining and agricultural interests before the Second World War. Chapter 2 examines the outbreak of the Second World War and the changing fortunes it brought for the secondary industry. That development occurred in the face of opposition from other economic interest groups and the state. The development of local secondary industry between 1939 and 1948 is traced in the context of contested policy debates. This discussion terminates in 1948, when Southern Rhodesia signed a Customs Union Agreement with South Africa, which spurred further local industrial development.

Chapter 3 analyses the consolidation of organised industry into a national organisation, the FRI established in 1949, and the politics of this Federation up to 1957, when it amalgamated with other industrialists of the other two federal territories, Northern Rhodesia and Nyasaland, to form the ARNI. This consolidation occurred in the socio-economic and political environment that birthed the CAF in 1953. The establishment of the CAF and other post-war developments are used to assess the relationship between the FRI and the state as well as other economic interest groups and vice-versa. Chapter 4 starts by discussing the establishment of the ARNI in 1957 as a broader industrial organisation for industrialists in the CAF. It details the politics of this organisation, especially the demands and aspirations of Southern Rhodesian industrialists in juxtaposition to those of its counterparts in the northern territories. The chapter also examines interactions with both territorial and federal governments. A discussion on industry's attitude towards the federal dissolution, the new right-wing Rhodesian Front government's policies, and the threat of Unilateral Declaration of Independence (UDI) in 1965 concludes the chapter.

Beginning in 1966, Chapter 5 examines the interaction between the state and industrialists over the administration and implementation of the import control policy and currency allocations – the two principal economic instruments of the UDI regime. This chapter challenges scholars who described organised secondary industry as muzzled and acquiescent to the UDI Rhodesian state. It demonstrates that in the economic sphere, organised industry remained forceful in its pursuit of its interests despite the omnipresence of the state. It underscores Skålnes's notion of societal corporatism to explain the relationship between ARnI and the state during this period. It ends in 1979 with a discussion on the nature and structure of the secondary industry that emerged during UDI, and the industry's position on decolonisation. The book ends with a Conclusion and Epilogue, summarising the relationship between organised industry, the state, and other economic interest groups through emphasising the book's argument and contribution to historiography. It outlines the big ideas and lessons that can be taken away from the book, which can trigger new questions and aspects for further research. A brief discussion of the post-1979 industrialisation trajectory follows this conclusion.

1 The Origins of Secondary Industry: The Teething Years, 1890–1938

The origins and development of secondary industry in Southern Rhodesia between 1890 and 1938 need to be outlined if the clamour and debate over local industry that emerged in the ensuing years of the Second World War are to be understood. While this gestation period of secondary industrial development has received considerable scholarly attention,[1] this chapter discusses in particular the way in which the peripheral emergence of secondary industry amid opposition from mining and agricultural interests during the first forty-eight years of the colony reveals tensions in settler colonialism.

First, there were conflicts between local and national capital and international capital.[2] Local capital, largely comprising rural owner-workers of small and medium-sized mines and farmers, formed the base of the capitalist sector and was committed to the economic development of the country. 'This national character of the white rural bourgeoisie', trenchantly explained Giovanni Arrighi,

1 C. H. Thompson and H. W. Woodruff, *Economic Development in Rhodesia and Nyasaland* (London: Dennis Dobson Ltd, 1953), 161–71; See also G. Arrighi, 'The political economy of Rhodesia', *New Left Review*, 39 (1966), 35–65; I. Phimister, *An Economic and Social History of Zimbabwe: Capital Accumulation and Class Struggle* (London: Longman, 1988), 219–57; E. S. Pangeti, 'The state and manufacturing industry: a study of the state as regulator and entrepreneur in Zimbabwe' (PhD, University of Zimbabwe, 1996); and A. S. Mlambo, E. S. Pangeti, and I. Phimister, *Zimbabwe: A History of Manufacturing, 1890–1995* (Harare: University of Zimbabwe Publications, 2000).

2 For a concise discussion on this, see I. Phimister, 'Accommodating imperialism: the compromise of the settler state in Southern Rhodesia, 1923–1929', *Journal of African History*, 25, 3 (1984), 279–94.

> distinguished Southern Rhodesia from practically all other African colonial territories north of the Limpopo and South of the Sahara, where exploitation of resources was carried out by large-scale international capitalism. In these other territories, where exploitation was based on large-scale mining or plantation or monopoly trade, capitalist interests in the economy were not permanent but lasted until, for example, deposits were exhausted or the raw material was substituted in the industrial process overseas or some more economic source of supply was found.[3]

Second, there was also antagonism within the settler society itself, as reflected by the continuous conflicts among the various interest groups, notably miners, farmers, commerce, and industrialists. These intra-settler relations were crucial in shaping the Rhodesian economy and politics in general and industrial development in particular. Hence, 'the path of capitalist development followed by Southern Rhodesia,' argued Arrighi, 'is intelligible only if due attention is paid to divisions within settler society and between economic sectors'.[4] The conversation over the overall economic trajectory of the colony was underpinned by these differing interests. This marked the beginning of the notion of societal corporatism, as the state and economic interest groups (whose cordiality was indispensable) negotiated, adopted, and implemented policies for the success of the colonial project.[5] The following paragraphs discuss the early foundations of the Rhodesian economy, highlighting the competing views of the different economic sectors and the unfolding societal corporatism as agriculture, commerce, and mining received state recognition and thereby achieved monopoly over industrialists.[6]

Foundations of the Rhodesian Economy

When the British South Africa Company (BSAC) occupied Mashonaland in 1890 and conquered Matabeleland in 1893, its desire was to exploit the envisaged abundant mineral resources. When the expected minerals failed to materialise, the BSAC shifted its attention to the utilisation of the new colony's land resources. The BSAC administration consequently geared its economic

3 G. Arrighi, *The Political Economy of Rhodesia* (The Hague, 1967), 36.

4 I. Phimister, 'Accommodating imperialism: the compromise of the settler state in Southern Rhodesia, 1923–1929,' *Journal of African History*, 25, 3 (1984), 279–94, at p. 1. See also D. J. Murray, *The Governmental System in Southern Rhodesia* (Oxford: Clarendon Press, 1970); P. Mosley, *The Settler Economies: Studies in the Economic History of Kenya and Southern Rhodesia 1900–1963* (Cambridge: Cambridge University Press, 1983).

5 J. Maree, 'Trade unions and corporatism in South Africa,' *Transformation*, 21 (1993), 24–54, at p. 25.

6 *Ibid.*, 26.

policies and political structures towards securing a sound footing for mining and agriculture. Tapiwa Madimu explains that

> numerous mining claims were parcelled out by the BSAC administration. It even encouraged speculation with these mining claims hoping to enjoy maximum profits because it held 50 % share in all mining ventures. Mining therefore, became the initial cornerstone on which the colonial economy was built. Its successful execution became the primary goal of the newly minted Southern Rhodesian State ...[7]

But as the reality of the mining disillusionment set in by 1896, huge tracts of land held in abeyance for speculative purposes immediately became a useful resource for economic advancement. In 1908, the company government reconstituted the Department of Agriculture, which had been part of the Surveyor General Department since 1897. The BSAC also introduced a White Agricultural Policy.[8] In addition to creating wealth for the BSAC and land grant holders, the new policy also became central to the grand political project of luring more White immigrants into the colony. Consequently, the state deliberately promoted the success of agriculture, seeing this as the trump card to creating a permanent White settlement in Southern Rhodesia. Together, therefore, mining and agriculture became the cornerstone of the early economy.

The economy was a typically colonial one. Secondary industry was constantly in the shadow of the mining and agricultural sectors and was so negligible that 'the Colony's official Year Book of 1932 did not even mention the manufacturing industry'.[9] The few incipient industrialists established foundry and engineering firms alongside mining in the short-lived boom between 1894 and 1896.[10] Over the years, concerns derivative of agriculture emerged, notably bacon, butter, cigarettes/tobacco, and grain-milling factories. Broadly speaking, the development of secondary industry flowed along the line of least resistance – that is, simple repair works and first-stage agro-processing.

The incipient industries were boosted by the interruptions caused by the First World War and the Great Depression. Phimister notes that,

> when war broke out in Europe in 1914, the destruction of various international trading relationships and the interruption of others initiated a period

7 T. Madimu 'Farmers, miners and the state in colonial Zimbabwe (Southern Rhodesia), c.1895–1961' (PhD, Stellenbosch University, 2017), 30. See also I. Phimister, 'Rhodes, Rhodesia and the Rand', *Journal of Southern African Studies*, 1, 1 (1974), 77–84.

8 R. Palmer, *Land and Racial Domination in Rhodesia* (London: Heinemann, 1977), 10.

9 Arrighi, 'The political economy of Rhodesia', 37.

10 Phimister, *An Economic and Social History of Zimbabwe*, 239.

> of unprecedented opportunity for southern African secondary industry. Freed from overseas competition, they had domestic and regional markets largely to themselves.[11]

Even then, such opportunities could not inspire any significant shift towards secondary industry. During that temporary reprieve, South African industrial products provided stern competition as industries south of the Limpopo took advantage of the situation and export to their neighbours. The outbreak of the First World War had stimulated the development of manufacturing in South Africa.[12]

Nonetheless, some local industrial expansion took place in Southern Rhodesia. Foundry work was one such sector where expansion was recorded, as 'a great many of the orders in this connection, which in former years have been sent to the Rand [were] now being executed in Salisbury'.[13] This, in part was the beginning of import substitution industrialisation (ISI). As the war ended, some expected slowing of industrial growth, but new stimulus kept the momentum of industrialisation alive: 'Inflation in Europe, limited shipping space and the short supply of manufactured articles all combined to protect local industry in the immediate post-war period', explains Phimister.[14] Rhodesia's inaccessibility offered natural protection. Phimister continues, 'between 1915 and 1918, fertilizer, bacon and vegetable oil factories began production. Maize grinding mills were built in Salisbury and Gwelo, saw mills were started and cattle dipping fluid was manufactured'.[15] Meanwhile, the development of copper mining on the Copperbelt in Northern Rhodesia (from 1926) and Katanga in Belgian Congo also helped to keep incipient factories working. The two mining centres created a market for Southern Rhodesian secondary industry, especially those producing inputs for mining and consumer goods.[16]

Secondary Industry: Early Challenges

The development of secondary industry did not occur without some measure of resistance. The political developments of 1922 and 1923 complicated the situation for industrial development. In 1922, when the BSAC Charter governing the administration of Southern Rhodesia was due to expire, the

11 *Ibid.*, 240.

12 For the impact of this development, see A. Mlombo, 'Settler colonialism and trade in the periphery: customs relations between Southern Rhodesia and South Africa, 1924–1935', *African Economic History*, 47, 1 (2019), 92–115.

13 Phimister, *An Economic and Social History of Zimbabwe*, 241.

14 *Ibid.*

15 *Report of the Director of Agriculture for the Year 1915*, 2–3, 1918, 1. Mlambo, Pangeti, and Phimister, *Zimbabwe: A History of Manufacturing*, 10–15.

16 *Ibid.*

colony faced two options: join the Union of South Africa as a fifth province or pursue self-government. In the referendum held in the same year, White settlers opted for self-governance; this culminated in the establishment of a Responsible Government in 1923. The Responsible Government gave Southern Rhodesia a unique 'self-governing' colonial status wherein it determined its own economic policies with minimal interference from the metropole, except in African and foreign affairs and on matters of currency.[17] With this unique setup and the ability to draw on the skills of its settler population, the colony had the capacity to change its economic trajectory, unlike some other colonies. For nascent industrialists in the colony, however, this advantage was not immediately realised.

The Responsible Government was dominated by settlers with farming interests. For example, by 1924, 'a third of the Members of the Legislative Assembly were farmers, while several others had a direct interest in the farming industry'.[18] With the support of the state, farmers and miners believed in the supremacy of their primary export industries. Merchants profitably surviving on importing and distributing manufactured products to farms and mines voiced their opposition to the development of local industries. They cited increased costs as the trade-off for protecting nascent industries in the colony. For them, encouraging secondary industry at the time would not achieve economies of scale. They worried that products made in this way would be costly and of poor quality.

Following the acceleration of the Great Depression, farmers shifted tack and began to support industrialists. The Great Depression had compounded the crisis for farmers, particularly tobacco and maize producers. In 1928, overproduction of tobacco had saturated the market, resulting in a decline in prices.[19] The onset of the Depression in 1929 had resulted in the loss of export markets for primary commodities and a further slump in prices locally. For farmers, the alternative was to support the development of local industries. The rationale was that local secondary industry would replace the export market lost during the Great Depression. Certainly, the nascent factories required raw materials, which local farmers could supply.

Meanwhile, negotiations over the fate of the 1924 customs agreement with the Union of South Africa were underway. In the history of trade relations

17 C. Palley, *The Constitutional History and Law of Southern Rhodesia, 1888–1965: With Special Reference to Imperial Control* (New York: Oxford University Press, 1966).

18 As quoted in R. Gray, *Two Nations: Aspects of the Development of Race Relations in Rhodesia and Nyasaland* (Oxford: Oxford University Press, 1960), 13.

19 For detailed discussion, see V. E. M. Machingaidze, 'The development of settler capitalist agriculture in Southern Rhodesia with particular reference to the role of the state, 1908–1939' (PhD, School of African and Oriental Studies, University of London, 1980), 182–98.

between Southern Rhodesia and South Africa, between 1899 and 1935, the two countries had maintained the general principle of free exchange of products.[20] Often, the customs and trade agreements worked to the advantage of the Union of South Africa. Conversations around this subject made apparent the place of the manufacturing sector in the Rhodesian economy as well as the general industrial policy. Writing to the treasurer in February 1929, E. C. Baxter, the controller of taxes, noted that the 1924/5 agreement was unsatisfactory and that if another could be negotiated to replace the existing one, it ought to be very different, if it were to meet the needs of the country.[21] Baxter also raised concerns over the protection of the colony's industries. Since South Africa subsidised its local industries and its manufacturing exports entered Southern Rhodesia under preferential duties, it was able to displace other imported articles and locally produced industrial products to the detriment of the country's revenue and trade and industrial development.[22] For this reason, protection of local industries also needed to be considered.

In giving evidence to the Tariff Commission in December 1929, the Bulawayo Chamber of Commerce expressed its opposition to the protection of secondary industries, stating that it increased the cost of doing business.[23] It was, however, agreeable to the duty-free importation of raw materials for industries. At the same time, trade figures between the Union and Southern Rhodesia showed the prosperity of new industries in Southern Rhodesia; this matter took centre stage at the Customs conferences in 1929.[24] In particular, there was a decline in the importation of dairy produce; creameries in the colony were plying a busy trade, and so were sweet factories, suggesting a growth in the manufacturing sector. In addition to this, skewed trade, which saw Southern Rhodesia manufacturers export goods worth £6,000 during the first five months of 1929 against imported goods worth £525,700, emboldened local industrialists in demanding tariff protection that would force the government to adjourn negotiations.[25]

When negotiations for the renewal of the 1925 agreement broke down, Union secondary industries cried foul. The *Rand Daily Mail* reported that 'some of the largest manufacturers recently established here view this break in

20 For detailed discussion of these trade agreements, see A. Mlombo, *Southern Rhodesia–South Africa Relations, 1923–1953: Political, Social and Economic Ties* (Cham: Palgrave Macmillan, 2020), 19–57; and R. Cole, 'The tariff policy of Rhodesia, 1899–1963', *Rhodesian Journal of Economics*, 2, 2 (1968), 28–48, at pp. 28–29.

21 NAZ LE3/1/1, Letter from E. C. Baxter to the Treasurer, 11 February 1929.

22 NAZ S679/15/2, Treasurer's Memorandum to the Prime Minister, 11 January 1928.

23 NAZ S679/15/2, Letter by Bulawayo Chamber of Commerce to the Secretary of Tariff Commission, 16 December 1929.

24 *Rand Daily Mail*, 13 September 1929.

25 *Ibid.*

the negotiations with grave misgivings, and the jeopardizing of a trade of over £3,000,000 will seriously affect all sections of the community'.[26] The break in negotiations was triggered by South Africa's desire to place an embargo on Rhodesian tobacco. In return, Southern Rhodesia demanded a 9% duty on Union manufactured goods entering the country. Crucial here is that high tariffs on manufactured imports were a bargaining point for a larger concession for the tobacco market in South Africa, although in the process local factories would also be protected. Southern Rhodesia ended up settling for 6% duty against Union imports. These concessions and compromises culminated in the completion of the 1930 customs agreement.

This agreement allowed free exchange of goods between the two countries, but only on certain specified products. Article II provided the right of each contracting party to frame its own customs tariff, but Article III compelled Southern Rhodesia to follow the Union should it take action to protect the interests of the nationals in any way. Of particular importance to secondary industry in Southern Rhodesia was Article IV, which provided that

> there shall be a free interchange of the products and manufactures of the Union and of Southern Rhodesia, except that in the event of one party to this Agreement levying an excise duty on any article produced or manufactured in its territory, it shall be entitled to levy a corresponding customs duty on importations into its territory of a like article produced or manufactured in the territory of the other contracting party.[27]

This arrangement was distinctly to the advantage of South Africa, since at the time Southern Rhodesia had a modest manufacturing industry. Thus, this provision stifled factories from continuing to grow in Southern Rhodesia. What was clear from the agreement was the Southern Rhodesian government's attitude towards the protection of local industries. The government did not offer any protection to the emerging local factories, which compromised any sustained secondary industrial development. Contributing to a debate on the agreement in parliament, the country's treasurer argued that it would have been

> foolish for this government or anyone else to have rejected the agreement and cut ourselves off from markets which were open to us. To have done that would have been to sacrifice the interests of the primary producers of this country for the benefit of secondary industries. One has only to look around and see what it [protection] has brought other countries.[28]

26 *Ibid.*

27 NAZ H.Mss LE 3/1/1, Customs Agreement between Southern Rhodesia and the Union of South Africa, Report thereon by the Controller of Customs and Excise and the Government Statistician – The Text of the Agreement, 15 December 1931.

28 Legislative Assembly Debates, 31 March 1930, Cols 410–11; see also, Mlambo, Pangeti, and Phimister, *Zimbabwe: A History of Manufacturing*, 16.

Further castigating the impact of protection of local secondary industry, the treasurer added:

> It has increased the cost of production, and it has made it impossible for them to sell the products of their own countries outside their own borders. Here we are producers of raw materials and we are looking for markets; therefore we want to have as few of these barriers against us as possible … We have to remember that once you put up barriers and walls which may tend to shut out the products of your neighbours, you must also face the other result … [that] may keep your own products within your own country … the protection that local industries seem to desire [was possible] only at the cost of having no agreement at all.[29]

The prime minister, Howard Moffat, made a similar point in his own contribution to the motion: 'Not even the strongest advocate of protection of our products could anticipate that the Union would sign an agreement permitting us to impose taxation on their products while they were not to be allowed to impose any taxation or embargo on our products.'[30]

Three crucial points are worth emphasising from the foregoing remarks. First, the interests of primary producers took precedence in the negotiating of trade agreements, while secondary industry was used as a sacrificial lamb. More tellingly, the lack of protection of local secondary industries by the state hampered their expansion. The state was therefore instrumental in stifling secondary industrial development in the 1920s. Second, South Africa bullied its weaker neighbour into an agreement, because the economy of Southern Rhodesia had not developed significantly enough to provide sufficient bargaining power. Consequently, it succumbed to South Africa's impositions. In doing so, Southern Rhodesia sacrificed the protection of local industries in favour of securing export markets for its primary products, which were seen to be key pillars of the economy at the time.

Commerce and industry disagreed about the implications of this agreement and about their particular interests, which were quite different. Commerce preferred free trade to protection, whereas industry favoured protection. Industrialists viewed the agreement as highly beneficial to South Africa, at the expense of Southern Rhodesia's industries. Reeling from the effects of the Depression, farmers also had similar concerns to the industrialists. Organised agriculture complained that 'the fact remains that the Union market has been further restricted and no corresponding advantage has been obtained for Rhodesian produces.'[31] Tobacco imported into the Union from Southern Rhodesia was limited to a 2,000,000lb weight of the Virginia type

29 Legislative Assembly Debates, 31 March 1930, Cols 410–11.

30 *Ibid.*

31 NASA HEN Vol. No. 3896 Ref. 710, Trade Relations, no date; and NAZ S1246/5/30, Memorandum by the Manager of Neill's Bacon Factory, 21 December 1933.

and 400,000lb of the Turkish type, and such tobacco was not entitled to admission free of duty.[32] These figures were considered small in comparison to the volumes traded in the previous year, 1929, which amounted to 5,833,389lb. Complaining to Prime Minister Moffat in 1930, the Rhodesia Manufacturers Association noted that the agreement 'left the Manufacturers of Southern Rhodesia ... in the old position of having to meet the keenest competition from large and well-established factories in the Union', the effect of which would 'stifle to a considerable extent enterprise in opening up new factories and industries'.[33] This tendency to belittle secondary industry in policy decisions or trade and customs agreement became a huge divisive point, hence the disputes between Southern Rhodesia's commercial and industrial interests over trade policy with South Africa.

Despite the existence of manufacturers' associations – Salisbury Chamber of Industries (SCI), formed in 1921, and Bulawayo Chamber of Industries (BCI), formed 1931 – some manufacturers chose instead to be affiliated with and represented by the Chambers of Commerce. Industrialists felt under-represented by commerce. For example, in memoranda prepared for the government by the Chamber of Commerce in 1933, there was limited coverage of the concerns of industry compared to commerce.[34] Coalescing around the Chambers of Industry in Bulawayo and Salisbury, industry began to demand direct government intervention through protection. In 1933 the SCI wrote to the government, stating that

> the present Customs Agreement between Southern Rhodesia and South Africa affords no protection for the secondary industries of Southern Rhodesia and that the time has arrived when they should be afforded some measure of protection against their more highly industrialised neighbours in the Union of South Africa, by the imposition of tariffs on articles imported from the Union of South Africa when similar articles are manufactured in Southern Rhodesia.[35]

32 NAZ H.Mss LE 3/1/1, Customs Agreement between Southern Rhodesia and The Union of South Africa, Report thereon by the Controller of Customs and Excise and the Government Statistician, 15 December 1931.

33 As cited in Mlambo, Pangeti, and Phimister, *Zimbabwe: A History of Manufacturing*, 15.

34 See, for example, NAZ S679/15/8, Association of Chambers of Commerce of Southern Rhodesia: Memorandum on Customs Agreement with the Union of South Africa, 23 October 1933.

35 NAZ S679/14/4, Salisbury Chamber of Industries: Memorandum on Customs Agreement between Southern Rhodesia and the Union of South Africa as concerns Secondary Industries in Southern Rhodesia, 9 November 1933.

The BCI also supported the idea.[36] Dissatisfied with the agreement, industrialists called for its termination and renegotiation. In its place, 'an Agreement which will afford adequate protection to Rhodesia's secondary industries' was imperative, failing which, 'arrangements [would have to] be immediately made to control our own customs'.[37] The termination of the agreement was justifiable because of the way it was skewed in favour of South Africa. Further, Rhodesian goods were less competitive against the Union's on the domestic market because 'manufacturing costs were higher in Rhodesia than in the Union owing to restricted market for which Rhodesian manufacturers cater, [and] the higher cost of raw materials imported'.[38] Moreover, industrialists argued that 'European wages were considerably higher in Rhodesia than in the Union of South Africa'.[39] In spite of this strong case, the call of the industrialists went unheeded.

Industrialists were neglected because of the dominant sectional interests in the state at the time. Societal corporatism favoured the interests of primary producers and distributors. During this period, Southern Rhodesia's economy depended on the export-oriented primary industries of mining and agriculture. For example, in 1927 mining was the major contributor towards the gross national product, accounting for 21.4%, with agriculture close behind at 19%, while manufacturing contributed only 4.6%.[40] In 1939, the primary exports together contributed 94% of total exports, with gold alone accounting for 60% of this total.[41] This is the classic colonial economic model. Britain and South Africa provided the two most important markets for the products of these two pillars of the settler economy. Agricultural and mining elites, as well as merchant capital (commerce) involved in international trade, wanted to maintain ties with London and Johannesburg, which were the country's key export and financial markets.[42] This found expression through the adoption of the imperial preference policy. As a result, the promotion of secondary industry was looked down upon, and in the broader context the imperial power frowned upon industrialisation in colonies in general.[43]

36 *Ibid.*
37 *Ibid.*
38 NAZ S679/15/4, Memorandum prepared by the Salisbury Chamber of Industries on the Customs Agreement at present existing between the Union of South Africa and Southern Rhodesia; Reasons for Requesting Cancellation, no date.
39 *Ibid.*
40 Pangeti, 'The state and manufacturing', 68.
41 NAZ S482/459/39, Trade of Southern Rhodesia, undated.
42 Phimister, 'Accommodating imperialism'; See also A. Mseba, 'Money and autonomy in a settler colony: the politics of monetary regulation in colonial Zimbabwe, 1930s–1965' in C. Yin Hsu *et al.* (eds), *The Cultural History of Money and Credit: A Global Perspective* (London: Lexington Books, 2016), 133–48, at p. 135.
43 L. J. Butler, 'Industrialisation in late colonial Africa: a British perspective', *Itinerario*, 23 (1999), 123–35.

British officials' remarks concerning the development of manufacturing industries in India during the 1930s testifies to this thinking. Commenting on India's industrialisation, Sir Thomas M. Ainscough (British Senior Trade Commissioner in India) said:

> The policy of maximum industrialization ... must inevitably lead, firstly, to a serious clash of interest with the agricultural element, which constitutes nearly 70 per cent of the population, secondly, to a crisis in India's finances as the Government of India rely upon Customs receipts for some 60 per cent of their revenue, and, lastly, to the collapse of the financial and economic fabric of the Government of India which is dependent upon an excess balance of exports in order to meet India's financial commitments in London (amounting to some Rs.50 to 60 crores per annum) and to maintain the exchange.[44]

For this reason, it was not in the interests of either the colonies or the metropole to promote industrialisation. The agrarian and mining elites in Southern Rhodesia held similar beliefs.

The preference for the export-oriented primary industries of mining and agriculture was routinely affirmed in the recommendations of the state-appointed committees/commissions to undertake investigations into the Rhodesian economy. All these committees recommended that assistance not be given to secondary industries. In 1930, the government of Southern Rhodesia appointed Henry Clay to look into aspects of industrial relations in the colony.[45] Clay presented his findings in 1930. His report downplayed the significance of secondary industry, stating that they were 'dependent for their market on the primary industries, and can only expand if these [agriculture and mining] expand'.[46] The only viable policy for Southern Rhodesia was to concentrate on its comparative advantage of producing primary products for the export market.

Following the Clay Report, the government of Southern Rhodesia commissioned the Max Danziger Committee in 1934 to inquire into the position of the agricultural industry in the colony's economy.[47] During its data collection, the committee asked 'whether it [was] possible to build up a white colony on any other basis other than a white agricultural population', to which it concluded

44 Quoted in S. Akita, 'British economic interests and international order of Asia in the 1930s', in S. Akita and N. J. White (eds), *The International Order of Asia in the 1930s and 1950s* (Farnham: Ashgate Publishing Company, 2010), 17–48, at p. 42.

45 See Government of Southern Rhodesia, *Report on Industrial Relations in Southern Rhodesia* (Salisbury: Government Printers, 1930).

46 *Ibid.*

47 Government of Southern Rhodesia, *Report of the Committee of Inquiry into the Economic Position of the Agricultural Industry of Southern Rhodesia* (Salisbury: Government Printers, 1934); and Pangeti, 'The state and manufacturing', 74.

that a White colony was only possible through promoting a White agricultural population.[48] The Danziger Report was not dissimilar to that produced by Clay, advising that promoting secondary industry in the face of a limited and unreliable local market would result in an increase in the cost of living and cost of production for agriculture.[49] This in turn could lead to food shortages. Meanwhile, local secondary industry could not compete with products from other industrialised countries.[50] Consequently, the Danziger Committee stressed that Southern Rhodesia was best off maximising on its comparative advantage in agricultural exports and making manufactured goods available through imports. Relying on export-oriented primary industries perpetuated Southern Rhodesia's dependency on the imperial centre and South Africa, both of which were politically undesirable for the self-governing colony. In addition, this dependency delayed the adoption of any active policy on secondary industrial development.

Consequently, the Southern Rhodesian parliament began debating about the economic development of the country, and the development of local industries became central to this debate. Contributing to a discussion on the potentialities of the colony, Donald Macintyre (Labour Party) emphasised the establishment of 'any industry in the country that was likely to provide employment for white people'.[51] He gave the examples of asbestos and hide processing as the simplest industries that could be set up. Giving the further example of sugar manufacture, whose raw material was imported from the Sena Estates in Mozambique, Macintyre remarked that if 'we were producing the primary product, we could keep the money in the country and at the same time doing something in the interest of farming and manufacturing community in the country'.[52] He also challenged the notion that only industries using locally produced raw materials should be encouraged. For him it was 'merely the question of whether the hen or egg came first, because if you have the manufacturers in the country, there is an incentive to the local producers, the growers in the country to produce the article necessary for the manufacturing and processing works which have been established'.[53]

Making his contribution, Noaks, MP for Mazowe District, insisted that if any secondary industries were to be established, it should be those based on the country's raw materials. Any other types of secondary industry, he argued,

48 Government of Southern Rhodesia, *Report of the Committee of Inquiry into the Economic Position of the Agricultural Industry of Southern Rhodesia*.

49 See *Ibid.*; and Pangeti, 'The state and manufacturing', 74–75. Interestingly, Danziger would become the future Minister of Finance, under whose remit all industries came.

50 *Ibid.*

51 Legislative Assembly Debates, 27 April 1938, Col. 212.

52 *Ibid.*

53 Legislative Assembly Debates, 27 April 1938, Col. 214.

> are not by themselves making a very great contribution to the wealth or progress of Rhodesia, because they are dependent for their existence, in most cases, either on rebates of duty or difference between the railway rates on raw and manufactured products and in that case, as I say, I do not think they are fulfilling as useful a purpose as would be the establishment of secondary industries based on raw materials actually produced in the country.[54]

The Minister of Finance and Commerce supported Macintyre's sentiments. Drawing from the case of the sugar refinery, he stated that he pushed for its establishment because he believed 'if we could develop a fruit industry and start jam factories or fruit canning factories, one of the necessities would be pure sugar and therefore, I felt that we could not bring the fruit grower and the jam manufacturer together until there was a sugar industry.'[55] The minister also encouraged the support for the establishment of secondary industries: 'Unless all sections of the community go hands in [supporting secondary industry], we will never become a big country and can never hope for the larger population which will undoubtedly result from the development of the country.'[56] He sympathised with industrialists, remarking that they 'worked hard and put in a lot of money before they start reaping any result.' The minister also drew parallels with the Union of South Africa, where industrialists had gone through the similar trajectory.

The desire to see Southern Rhodesia develop pushed the minister to form the Committee on the Economic Development of Southern Rhodesia in 1938.[57] However, the composition of this committee revealed once more the conservative attitude of the state towards secondary industry, because it excluded industrialists from its ranks. Some of its terms of reference were to look into: (i) the establishment and development of secondary industries for the processing of natural products for internal consumption and/or export; (ii) the establishment and development of processing industries making use of imported materials; and (iii) the nature and extent of the assistance to be afforded by the state with a view to the encouragement of new primary and secondary industries, or at least the expansion and development of existing ones.[58] The Economic Development Committee published its findings in 1939, and in its findings and recommendations concerning the terms of reference (i), the committee did not favour the encouragement of the expansion of production by artificial means for industries based on agriculture.

54 *Ibid.*, Col. 222.
55 *Ibid.*, Col. 217.
56 *Ibid.*, Col. 219.
57 NAZ S679/116/22, Southern Rhodesia: Report of the Economic Development Committee, 1939.
58 *Ibid.*

As far as secondary industry based on mining was concerned, no proposal was submitted to the committee for the establishment of any form of industry using any of the minerals produced in the colony. One witness, however, suggested the possibility of an industry in asbestos tiles and sheets based on waste asbestos and cement but the committee's own enquiries brought no fruitful results.[59] In respect of the terms of reference (ii), the committee advised that possibilities existed in the manufacture of fibres, yarns, textiles and apparel, metal manufactures, rubber, and footwear, because these constituted a huge proportion of the country's imports.[60] The high volume of imports of the items mentioned above was an indication that there was a sufficiently high demand for these locally, thus improving the prospects of those concerns manufacturing them. Noteworthy is that before any industry can be established, there must be a volume of demand or prospective demand sufficient to attract the necessary capital and enterprise. The committee's view on the terms of reference (iii) was that private enterprise should be left to its own devices to develop meaningful industries as opportunities arose.[61] Furthermore, the committee expressed that 'it was unnecessary, if not undesirable, for the government to devote funds to hastening such [industrial] development'.[62]

However, the committee remarked that it had been impressed by the readiness with which new industries, given the slightest opportunity, had been established. In light of that, it recommended that industries should continue on that path.[63] The state accepted this advice despite the fact that Southern Rhodesia had neither a textiles sector nor a capital goods sector, both of which present-day economists view as essential building blocks for a secondary industrial sector. On the eve of the Second World War, Southern Rhodesia had 299 factories with a gross output of £5,107,000, employing a total of 17,554 employees of all races and paying wages amounting to £1,254 million per annum.[64] Almost all of these were light consumer goods industries privately owned by domestic White capital, with the exception of the Bata Shoe Company, a local brewery owned by South African Breweries Limited, Fisons Ibatros Fertilisers (Rhodesia) Ltd, and African Explosives and Chemical Industries, among others, which were foreign owned.[65] By contrast, gross output for mining was £7,696,000, and agriculture contributed £3,770,000.[66] These

59 *Ibid.*, 38.
60 *Ibid.*, 34.
61 NAZ S679/116/22, Southern Rhodesia: Report of the Economic Development Committee, 38–40.
62 *Ibid.*
63 *Ibid.*, 38–39.
64 Government of Southern Rhodesia, *Census of Industrial Production, 1938–1962*.
65 Gwande, 'Foreign capital, state and the development of secondary industry in Southern Rhodesia' (MA, University of the Free State, 2015), 15–16.
66 Federation of Rhodesia and Nyasaland, *Census of Industrial Production, 1957–1958*, 4.

industries employed 90,967 and 96,684 workers (of all races), respectively. By the time the war broke out in 1939, Southern Rhodesian factories produced 'butter and cheese, maize meal and wheaten flour, soap and candles, bacon and hams, squashes and minerals [soft drinks] sweets, paints, malt liquors, tobacco, cement and tiles. Smaller industries produce[d] furniture, stationery, biscuits, clothing for the native trade, fertilizers, jams, polishes etc.'[67] Secondary industry was slowly contributing to the gross domestic product (GDP), and thus deserved some attention.

Although successive reports and various interest groups all argued against secondary industry, the commissions had also received representations from witnesses on the need to promote local industries. Giving evidence before the Economic Development Committee, one witness pleaded for 'the establishment of a Board of Trade and Industry or some such organization, whose function would be to advise the government in respect of tariff and other problems connected with the establishment and promotion of trade and secondary industry.'[68] The committee advised that 'the present stage of the colony's industrial development does not appear to warrant the setting up of a permanent Tariff Board or a Board of Trade and Industry.'[69] Instead, the committee proposed that the government should 'nominate a Senior Permanent official to give consideration to proposals requiring government action and to act as the Chairman of the Adhoc Committees [it] suggested, especially in pursuant of the proposals to establishing a textile industry.'[70] Interestingly, the Southern Rhodesian government adopted strikingly similar advice to that given by the Mynors Report on the Question of a Central Bank in 1949, as will be shown later.[71]

Conclusion

The economic and political interests of the successive governments in Southern Rhodesia between 1890 and 1938 shaped the developmental trajectory of the colony. The BSAC, with its interests in mining and later agriculture, meant its policies served to prop up these sectors to the exclusion of manufacturing interests. Its successor government, largely dominated by settler farmers and merchant capital, favoured agricultural development and free trade, both

67 Phimister, *An Economic and Social History of Zimbabwe*, 246.

68 NAZ S679/116/22, Southern Rhodesia: Report of the Economic Development Committee, 40.

69 *Ibid.*

70 *Ibid.*

71 NAZ S2225/4, H.C.B. Mynors, Southern Rhodesia, Report on the Question of a Central Bank, 1949; see also NAZ S2225/4, Memorandum by the Minister of Finance on H. C. B. Mynors' Report on the Question of a Central Bank, 5 March 1949.

of which stifled the emergence of a vibrant manufacturing sector. Farmers, miners, and commerce, with the state's support, believed in the supremacy of the primary exporting industries of agriculture and mining in propelling the economy of Southern Rhodesia. As mentioned earlier, the state blatantly supported mining and agriculture by implementing 'imperial preference'. In this way, it undermined local industries by favouring manufactured imports from other parts of the empire while promoting mining and agricultural exports to the same. It also sacrificed industrial interests in negotiating trade agreements, thus depriving secondary industry of tariff protection.

Further, the various state committees appointed to look into aspects of the economy consistently labelled the importance of the manufacturing sector as secondary to that of mining and agriculture. At best, the policy towards industrial development was conservative. Like a neglected child, secondary industry experienced muted and stunted growth. Societal corporatism, in which farmers' and miners' associations triumphed and received state recognition and support, determined the economic trajectory. Manufacturing associations were not vociferous enough to be heard. However, the outbreak of the Second World War in 1939 rendered any ambivalence towards secondary industrial development untenable. The implications and impact of the war on industrial policy is the subject of the next chapter.

2 'To Industrialise or Not': Economic Interest Groups, the State, and Secondary Industry, 1939–1948

'We must pay due respect and praise to those industrialists who started, with few resources and with very little prospects, the development of secondary industries. They not only faced active opposition in some directions, but they got very little cooperation from the general public, from the merchants or from the government – and very little from politicians. Even today, the position is not such that we can say that the general population, the government or the politicians are fully aware of the importance of the development of secondary industries.'

– J. H. Hendrick Smit, Southern Rhodesian Minister of Finance and Commerce, Address to the Rhodesian Jubilee Industrial Exhibition of the Bulawayo Chamber of Industries, 3 September 1940.

The outbreak of the Second World War in 1939 brought mixed fortunes for Southern Rhodesia. Whereas the colony previously relied largely on imports for manufactured goods, it now turned to local products because of the interruptions in international trade caused by the war. Imports became increasingly unavailable, inducing scarcity and high demand. Shortages stimulated calls for local industry to fill the vacuum. Consequently, an import substitution industrialisation (ISI) drive temporarily developed. However, this impact of the Second World War was not unique to Southern Rhodesia.

It was also felt in some other parts of sub-Saharan Africa.[1] The only exception to this was South Africa, which had a comparatively established secondary industry by the time the war broke out.[2] Not all industrialisation was sparked off by the conditions of the war, however. For example, in British West Africa, Lord William M. Hailey had already recommended in 1938 that Britain allow her dependencies to develop local secondary industries.[3] While these factors are acknowledged, the impact of the war stood out, as it accelerated industrial development.

At the same time, secondary industrial development in colonies such as Kenya and Southern Rhodesia was aided by the greater buying power of their White settler population.[4] Southern Rhodesia had the crucial advantage of being a self-governing colony, a status that gave it some considerable control of the domestic economy. Southern Rhodesia under the Responsible Government was free to manipulate tariffs, something denied to every other colony.[5] Shigeru Akita has observed a similar tendency in British India during the Great Depression, wherein a self-governing India took full advantage of her fiscal independence to promote her industries, which had the effect of elbowing out Britain's efforts to dominate the Indian market.[6] Equally, this autonomy allowed Southern Rhodesia to determine its own economic policies independently of the metropole, except in matters of African affairs, currency, and foreign policy.[7] Its domestic bourgeoisie used the shortages caused by the war

1 For other countries' experiences, see R. C. Riddell (ed.), *Manufacturing Africa: Performance and Prospects of Seven Countries in Sub-Saharan Africa* (London: James Currey, 1990).

2 C. H. Feinstein, *An Economic History of South Africa: Conquest, Discrimination and Development* (Cambridge: Cambridge University Press, 2005); H. S. Jones and A. Muller, *The South African Economy, 1910–90* (London: Palgrave Macmillan, 1992).

3 W. Hailey, *An African Survey: A Study of Problems Arising in Africa South of the Sahara* (London: Oxford University Press, 1938).

4 For comparative studies of the industrialisation experience of other colonies, see A. P. F. Mendes, M. A. Bertella, and R. F. A. P. Teixeira, 'Industrialization in sub-Saharan Africa and import substitution policy', *Brazilian Journal of Political Economy*, 34, 1 (134), 120–38; and Riddell (ed.), *Manufacturing Africa*.

5 For a detailed analysis on how Southern Rhodesia manipulated tariffs, especially with respect to Northern Rhodesia and the Congo, see A. M. Kanduza, *The Political Economy of Underdevelopment in Northern Rhodesia*.

6 S. Akita, 'British economic interests and international order of Asia in the 1930s', in S. Akita and N. J. White (eds), *The International Order of Asia in the 1930s and 1950s* (Farnham: Ashgate Publishing Company, 2010), 17–48, at p. 38.

7 M. M. Burdette, 'Industrial development in Zambia, Zimbabwe and Malawi: the primacy of politics', in Z. A. Konczack *et al.* (eds), *Studies in the Economic History of Southern Africa, Vol. 1: The Frontline States* (London: Frank Cass and Co. Ltd, 1990), 75–126, at p. 75.

to accelerate calls for the development of local industries. This chapter outlines these concerns, as it examines the views of industrialists on one hand and those of farmers, miners, commerce, and the state on the other, regarding the encouragement and development of secondary industry in the country between 1939 and 1948. It elaborates the point captured in the opening quotation of the chapter. By examining the different standpoints of these various interest groups, the chapter scrutinises relationships between these groups and the state in the development of Southern Rhodesia in general and industrial development in particular. It demonstrates how societal corporatism played out during the war.

In what follows, the development of local secondary industry between 1939 and 1948 is traced in the context of contested policy debates. The chapter begins with an analysis of the state and position of secondary industry and its changing fortunes during the war and the immediate aftermath. It also discusses the conditions and factors that affected industrial development during this time. The chapter ends in 1948, when Southern Rhodesia signed a Customs Union Agreement with South Africa, which gave impetus to local industrial development. At the same time, industrialists began to organise themselves into a colony-wide association, eventually establishing this in 1949. To conclude, the chapter analyses the size and structure of the secondary industrial sector that emerged from the developments between 1939 and 1948 and shows the role of industrialists in setting the tone for industrial development vis-à-vis the state and other groups.

The Second World War and Industrial Policy

The outbreak of the Second World War in September 1939 rendered the government's conservative policy towards secondary industry untenable. The war disrupted international trading patterns. Imports (especially of manufactured goods) sharply declined because of hostilities in Europe and North America. Where they were available, the goods were expensive due to the profiteering that characterised the war.[8] Besides, there was no foreign exchange to buy these, and shipping facilities were not available to transport the goods, as priority was given to the war effort. Under these circumstances, the government realised the need to encourage local industrial development. Temporarily during the war, an active and positive policy towards the manufacturing sector emerged.

Meanwhile, the Salisbury Chamber of Industries (SCI) discussed the Economic Development Committee's report, referred to in the previous

8 For more on profiteering during the war see A. G. Buehler, 'The taxation of corporate excess profits in peace and war times', https://scholarship.law.duke.edu/cgi/viewcontent.cgi?article=2017&context=lcp, Accessed 6 August 2018, 5:27pm.

chapter, at a special meeting in early 1940. It strongly condemned the report for its failure to accept the proposal to establish a board of trade.[9] Frustrated by the rejection of their proposal and taking advantage of the shifting government attitude induced by the shortages and high demand during the war, the Chamber, through some of its members who had now joined the government, revived the idea of the board. E. P. Vernall, an industrialist and a member of the SCI, was elected to the legislative assembly for Salisbury Central in 1939 under the United Party. He raised the Chamber's suggestion in Parliament in 1940. Seconded by Macintyre, MP for Bulawayo South and also a businessperson, Vernall moved a motion that a permanent advisory committee be set up to assist in the industrial development of the colony.[10] Out of this motion came the statutory Industrial Development Advisory Committee (IDAC) in 1940.

The legislative debates regarding the motion are very revealing. Vernall pushed for the formation of this board because, in his view, industries had not received the due recognition they deserved from the government. The minister of finance and commerce, J. H. Smit, agreed with Vernall, conceding that 'so far the development of secondary industry in Rhodesia has been mostly through private enterprise'.[11] Smit reiterated his support for secondary industries when he addressed the Rhodesian Jubilee Industrial Exhibition of the Bulawayo Chamber of Industries (BCI) in September 1940. He decried the lack of support for industrial development from parliament and the government because, in his view, 'members of the government had no idea of the importance of industries', but he assured industrialists that in him, 'the industries had a true friend'.[12] Smit pointed to other factors impeding the industrial progress of the country: the conservatism and prejudice of the Rhodesian consumer, and the imperial policy. He explained:

> most people are used to certain brands and articles which they have used for many years ... I know that women are determined to have a particular brand of soap or flour or some other household article. They will not try anything else, even when urged to do so by the shopkeeper.[13]

On the imperial policy, he argued that Southern Rhodesia had been very focused on supplying raw materials to the empire while relying on the secondary industries of Britain. In both cases, the attitude had worked to the detriment of local secondary industries. The positive, however, was that the war was altering the trend.

In 1940, secondary industries were steadily increasing their contribution to national gross domestic product (GDP), as demonstrated by Table 2.1.

9 Legislative Assembly Debates, 1 May 1940, Col. 171.
10 *Ibid.*
11 *Ibid.*, Col. 190.
12 *Rhodesia Herald*, 3 September 1940.
13 *Ibid.*

Table 2.1. Gross value of output in agriculture, mining, and manufacturing, 1938–1940.

Year	Agriculture (£ million)	Mining (£ million)	Manufacturing (£ million)
1938	3.8	7.7	5.1
1939	3.6	8.1	5.4
1940	4.9	9.2	6.3

Source: *Census of Industrial Production*, 1938–1958.

Justifying support for the development of secondary industry, Vernall also pointed to the unfavourable balance of trade with South Africa. In 1934, Rhodesian imports from the Union amounted to £1,748,940 against exports of £423,053. By 1939, the same figures were £2,573,952 against £640,343, creating an adverse balance of £1,933,508.[14] 'Surely,' Vernall argued, 'the industries of this country can make some of these goods instead of having to buy them from the Union.'[15] In his contribution, Macintyre claimed that Southern Rhodesia was the only self-governing colony in the British Empire that did not have an Industrial Development Commission (IDC) of some description to look after trade and commerce generally.[16] Citing the examples of Australia and South Africa, which had the Scientific and Industrial Development Council and Board of Trade and Industries, respectively, he urged parliament to consider setting up such a committee. These departments promoted the development of secondary industry within their own territories. The boards protected industry and supported those industries which the government was satisfied could be made to stand on their own if given a reasonable amount of assistance during their teething years. This was what the envisaged committee in Southern Rhodesia would do.

Although some MPs gave conditional support, others opposed the encouragement of secondary industry. Noaks, a Mazowe MP, established farmer, and member of the Rhodesian Agricultural Union, supported the development of secondary industry, provided it was agro-based.[17] Politically, the Labour Party supported the promotion of secondary industries. Its support was motivated by the self-interest of its constituency, White labour. In 1931, secondary industry employed 2,100 Europeans; in 1936, 2,200; and in 1938, 2,300. For the Labour Party this was a concern, because it showed a very low uptake of White workers into employment. The expansion of secondary industry was,

14 Legislative Assembly Debates, 1 May 1940, Col. 175.
15 *Ibid.*
16 *Ibid.*, Col. 179.
17 *Ibid.*, Col. 175.

therefore, necessary to increase White employment. Furthermore, elements of the Labour Party wanted to establish a central bank to ensure economic and monetary regulation. Incipient industrialists desired the same. Disenchanted by the government's failure to establish the bank, the Labour Party malcontents supported the industrialists' quest for assistance, especially in the creation of a central bank to offer credit to local industries.[18]

There was a convergence of interests. Stronger opposition to the IDAC came from Max Danziger, who chaired the 1934 Committee of Inquiry into the Economic Position of the Agricultural Industry of Southern Rhodesia. He belittled secondary industries; as he bluntly said,

> there is more pathetic faith in the blessed idea of secondary industry. So many people do not hesitate to go to any length almost as long as they can see another secondary industry established in the country. Not sufficient consideration is given to the point as to whether we have enough markets in the country to support the industry or whether such industry is going to be a help to the country or handicap.[19]

Danziger further argued that the country's limited population meant it could not be self-sufficient. For that reason, the country 'cannot possibly substitute for our primary industries the few secondary industry that we can establish in competition with similar industries in England itself'.[20] The doubt expressed by Danziger over the limited internal market was important, as it subsequently became very topical.

Even as these debates raged on, the creation of the IDAC marked the first of the concessions that the government made at the behest of the industrialists' lobbying. However, in this instance, the import supply bottlenecks resulting from the Second World War strengthened the industrialists' position. At the same time, the debate over IDAC revealed the convergence of interests of industrialists, farmers, and labour, which previously were at variance. It suggests that the circumstances of war created a more unified settler economy in Southern Rhodesia. Consequently, IDAC comprised the Salisbury and Bulawayo Chambers of Industry, the Rhodesian Agricultural Union, and the Chamber of Mines. Its mandate was to investigate, recommend, and advise the Minister of Finance, under whose portfolio IDAC was placed, on all aspects of industrial development. In order to help IDAC execute its mandate, parliament, at the insistence of Prime Minister Godfrey Huggins, approved the

18 For a detailed discussion, see A. Mseba, 'Money and autonomy in a settler colony: the politics of monetary regulation in colonial Zimbabwe, 1930s–1965' in C. Yin Hsu *et al.* (eds), *The Cultural History of Money and Credit: A Global Perspective* (London: Lexington Books, 2016), 133–48, at p. 136.

19 Legislative Assembly Debates, 1 May 1940, Col. 192.

20 *Ibid.*, Col. 193.

setting up of a revolving fund in 1941.[21] Start-up funding for industries was crucial for any significant industrial expansion to occur. The fund was for the 'purpose of financing experiments and developing secondary industry, when such experiments and development are recommended by the IDAC and approved by government'.[22] The revolving fund, it was hoped, would operate similarly to the Land Bank, which had successfully supported the expansion of commercial agriculture.

Individual industrialists also petitioned the prime minister to support secondary industry. In a memorandum to the premier, Rhodesian iron and steel works suggested,

> if the government is satisfied that the establishment of factories for the manufacture of articles from iron and steel in Rhodesia is a feasible proposition and that such industries are more likely to be established on a sound economic basis if blast furnaces are erected, then it is clearly the duty of the government either to assist in the establishment of the basic industry or at least to exercise such control as may, in the circumstances, be necessary.[23]

Even commerce supported government intervention to encourage secondary industry. As alluded to earlier, the war induced shortages in the local market due to disruption in international trade, which in turn resulted in most imports being curtailed. In order to survive, traders needed new sources of supply. Rhodesian industry became an immediate alternative. Merchants now looked to local secondary industry to produce and supply manufactured goods to satisfy local demand. Commerce urged the government to assist industrial development by making funds available for IDAC to undertake investigations and recommend the industries that should be developed.[24] The government made £25,000 available to IDAC. It carried out experiments and investigations in, for example, the dehydration of foodstuffs and the distillation of alcohol.[25] The debate over financial assistance actuated the need for a definitive industrial policy and state assistance.

Justifying financial assistance to industries, MP Lister, who linked industrialisation to Southern Rhodesia's grand political project of building a 'white man's country', posited that

> I feel that by establishing secondary industry in the Colony we will eventually be able to encourage a larger European population to settle here,

21 Legislative Assembly Debates, 11 July 1941, Col. 2299.

22 NAZ S932/14, Memorandum on IDAC to the Prime Minister, 1941; and Legislative Assembly Debates, 11 July 1941, Col. 2299.

23 NAZ S915/304/174/1, Riscom, Memoranda and Reports: Memorandum addressed by Rhodesian Iron and Steel Works to the Prime Minister, 17 February 1941.

24 Associated Chambers of Commerce, *Annual Congress*, 5 March 1941.

25 NAZ S104, IDAC's minutes of a meeting held on 28 July 1941.

> because until we can establish such industries, there is not much prospect of this country going ahead rapidly in that respect. We are not likely to get any large influx for European artisans ... unless there are openings for them in this direction and as I say, there is not much outlook for immigration unless we develop our secondary industry in the way which is evidently contemplated in this motion.[26]

Crucial to note from Lister's contribution is how he couched his words within the idea of colonial state making through the promotion of White immigration and settlement. Immigration became a subject of intense discussion between industrialists and state officials.

Before the war, Southern Rhodesia's official policy followed the recommendation given by the Economic Development Committee in 1939 that private enterprise should be left to its own devices to develop meaningful industries as opportunity occurred; in the committee's view, it was undesirable for the government to make funds available for industrial development. However, the war's rapidly changing circumstances did not permit that trajectory; for example, all efforts and investment capital were concentrated towards winning the war, which limited the availability of private capital. With this realisation, IDAC advised the government that 'with private capital for the purpose either short or shy ... it is submitted that the vital requirements of the moment can only be met by active state interest ... actual state intervention, and particularly by the provision of, where necessary, funds by the state for the establishment or expansion of industry'.[27] This was clearly a shift in government policy from leaving industries to their own devices to adopting some qualified intervention. The realities of the war necessitated this shift.

State intervention could be done through

> the establishment of state enterprises directly controlled by the government i.e managed departmentally, ... managed and controlled by a public utility corporation financed by the state or the financing of private enterprises or by direct loans in need or share subscription on the part of the Exchequer or by loans or share subscription on the part of an independent public investment corporation financed or capitalised by the state.[28]

In the end, the state settled for the policy of 'encouraging and assisting private enterprise to carry out the development desired', provided that private enterprise had the capacity and ability and was interested in executing the task to

26 Legislative Assembly Debates, 11 July 1941, Col. 2306.

27 NAZ S482/152/42, Memorandum on Industrial Development in Southern Rhodesia, 1942.

28 *Ibid.*

the benefit of the country.[29] The government of Southern Rhodesia sought to strike some balance between free enterprise and 'measured' state control.

In the context of the war, some measure of control was, however, necessary. Control was introduced through the Excess Profits Tax Act (EPTA) and the Factory Control Regulations. The EPTA had a deterrent effect on profiteering during the scarcities of the war. It was also a method of harnessing the wealth of the country for the war effort and gaining some revenue for the Rhodesian state to 'get on with development'.[30] The factory regulations were to control the setting up of new factories, with workers' health and safety and licensing among their main objectives. The introduction of these measures once again brought to the fore the complex relations between state, industrialists, and other economic interest groups. During the parliamentary debate on the introduction of the EPTA, Noaks, on behalf of the farmers, L. Fereday, on behalf of commerce, and other sympathisers of industry such as Smit, the Minister of Finance and Commerce, opposed it. They feared that the tax would drive out capital and destroy and discourage enterprise.[31]

Moreover, taxation was already a burden, as income tax was still operative and the tobacco sales tax was in place for tobacco producers. Others spoke in support of mining, which they argued had been taxed enough through the gold premiums tax. Ironically, Vernall, an industrialist, and Major Hastings, a firm supporter of private enterprise, supported the tax. For Vernall and other like-minded MPs, the tax was necessary because business could not enjoy profits at the expense of the thousands who were making sacrifices for the country at the war front.[32] However, they qualified their support, noting that in normal times they would have rejected the motion outright, but because of the war, they had to concede.

Factory regulations were introduced on the advice of the IDAC. These were seen as necessary because 'there [was] a growing tendency which [had] become apparent since the outbreak of the war to set up new factories some of which [were] undesirable backyard type'.[33] The haphazard establishment of these factories was likely to compromise the quality of industrial products,

29 *Ibid.*

30 Legislative Assembly Debates, 1 November 1939, Cols 1745–46. For more on the origins, application, and use of the excess profits tax, see Buehler, 'The taxation of corporate excess profits', and D. Johnson, 'The impact of the Second World War on Southern Rhodesia, with special reference to African Labour, 1939–1948' (PhD, SOAS, 1989), 111–14; and D. Johnson, *World War II and the Scramble for Labour in Colonial Zimbabwe, 1939–1948* (Harare: University of Zimbabwe Publications, 2000).

31 Legislative Assembly Debates, 1 November 1939, Cols 1745–46.

32 *Ibid.*, Col. 1755.

33 NAZ S482/458/39, Rhodesian Manufacturing Companies: Letter by the Secretary of Treasury to the Parliament Secretary, 15 September 1941.

thereby failing to meet the legitimate demands of the public. Such an eventuality would affect the interests of old established industries, which in turn would be detrimental to the economic interests of the colony. Even the Associated Chambers of Industries of Rhodesia (ACIR), formed in 1941, supported the regulations, though with some qualification: 'This chamber does not favour the introduction of any system which would restrict the free development of secondary industry, but recognises that indiscriminate expansion would be to the detriment of the country's interests.'[34] The ACIR was, therefore, 'in agreement with licensing of industries as necessary in order to ensure proper control.'[35] It was through the provisions of factory regulations that all new industries were licensed to operate. Licensing afforded the government the power to assess the desirability of a particular industry vis-à-vis the already established ones. Parliament subsequently debated the factory regulations in 1945 and upgraded them to the Factories Act.[36]

Acting on the advice of the IDAC, the state also took over some basic industries. The IDAC recommended to the prime minister that the 'government nationalise basic industries especially those which private enterprise is not willing to take up.'[37] The government took over the iron and steel works at Bulawayo and set up a cotton-spinning mill at Gatooma, both in 1942, and later, in 1944, nationalised a sugar refinery.[38] This was one of the few instances in which the government heeded the IDAC's advice; the majority of its recommendations were ignored. In 1941, the IDAC queried why the country was importing pig iron and steel when the base minerals of the colony offered prospects of starting an iron and steel industry on which other subsidiary industries could depend.[39] Having a functional and expanded iron and steel works was crucial for Southern Rhodesia, since this heavy industry was the basis of all national industrialisation, and without it manufacturing industries would have found it difficult to develop.

34 NAZ S482/458/39, Rhodesian Manufacturing Companies: Record of Proceedings of ACIR Meeting, 26 August 1941.

35 *Ibid.*

36 Legislative Assembly Debates, 25 April 1945, Col. 105.

37 NAZ S106, Letter by the IDAC to the Prime Minister, October 1942.

38 For detailed discussions on the development of these industries, see variously E. S. Pangeti, 'The state and manufacturing industry: a study of the state as regulator and entrepreneur in Zimbabwe' (PhD, University of Zimbabwe, 1996), 173–83; Johnson, 'The impact of the Second World War on Southern Rhodesia', 118–21; A. S. Mlambo and I. Phimister, 'Partly protected: origins and growth of colonial Zimbabwe's textile industry, 1890–1965', *Historia*, 52, 2 (2006), 145–75; and A. S. Mlambo and E. S. Pangeti, *The Political Economy of Sugar Industry in Zimbabwe, 1920–1990* (Harare: University of Zimbabwe Publications, 1996).

39 NAZ S482/152/42, Industrial Development in Southern Rhodesia: Industrial Development Advisory Committee, first report for the year ending 31 December 1941.

The interruptions caused by the war also meant that the country needed its own iron and steel works. Southern Rhodesia already had an iron and steel works in Bulawayo, which was privately owned by domestic capital in partnership with the South African Iron and Steel Corporation (ISCOR). Due to undercapitalisation, the venture could not meet the country's needs. For instance, the minister of mines and public works questioned whether it was in the national interest to leave the industry (iron and steel works) under a private and uncontrolled company that was unable to expand sufficiently to meet the immediate needs of the country or whether it should be acquired by the government.[40] Realising its own funding limitations, the Bulawayo-based company also petitioned the government to develop bigger furnaces to smelt iron ore.[41] The ISCOR was producing steel from scrap metal using a comparatively modern electric furnace and two not-so-modern rolling mills. Its works were not capable of making steel from pig iron. It became necessary for the ISCOR to either cut down production or develop, and in order to develop, a government subsidy was required. The government preferred acquiring the assets of the ISCOR over granting a subsidy. Meanwhile, some engineering firms were complaining that the quality, cost, and supply of steel was uneconomic and poor.[42] It was against this background that the government took over the industry and created the Rhodesia Iron and Steel Commission in 1942.[43]

The IDAC also investigated the possibility of establishing a cotton-spinning industry in the country in 1941. Like the iron and steel industry, cotton spinning was a necessary basic industry important for the establishment of a solid clothing and textile sector in Southern Rhodesia. Consequently, it was crucial that the state set cotton-spinning mills on a sound footing. Several meetings with the Cotton Research and Industry Board throughout 1941 resulted in the granting of a £20,000 loan to the board to set up a textile industry.[44] Some funding also came from the British Cotton Growing Association.[45] Subsequently, a ginnery was established at Gatooma in 1942. It was these mills which

40 NAZ S915/304/174/1, Iron and Steel Industry: Letter to the Minister of Coordination by the Minister of Mines and Public Works, 27 September 1941.

41 NAZ S915/304/174/1, Memorandum Submitted to the Prime Minister by the Rhodesian Iron and Steel Corporation Limited, 30 September 1941.

42 NAZ S482/152/42, Industrial Development in Southern Rhodesia: Industrial Development Advisory Committee, first report for the year ending 31 December 1941.

43 For more on the nationalisation of the iron and steel works, see Pangeti, 'The state and manufacturing industry', 173–77; and Johnson, 'The impact of the Second World War on Southern Rhodesia', 118–21.

44 NAZ S104, Minutes of Meetings dated 19 May 1943. For a detailed study on the development of the textile industry in Southern Rhodesia, see Mlambo and Phimister, 'Partly protected'.

45 Mlambo and Phimister, 'Partly protected', 147.

the government nationalised in 1943. Industrialists and ardent believers of free enterprise resented these take-overs. Government assistance was desired, but not nationalisation or public ownership. The Federated Chamber of Commerce stressed that 'the state should not come into competition with private enterprise and must enjoy no privileges'.[46]

At face value, nationalisation seemed a contradiction to the avowed policy of leaving industries to themselves to develop as opportunity occurred. However, the government argued that state take-overs of basic industries should be seen as complimentary to private enterprise. It qualified that 'where private enterprise is willing to invest, the government should not come into competition with private concerns'.[47] Indeed, these basic industries were of national importance because they formed the basis of industrialisation. Moreover, private capital was not ready to develop these, because they had a longer gestation period before they started generating any return on investment. In addition, private capital, through compulsion and taxation, was aiding the prosecution of the war. What should also be observed is that commerce and industry interests converged in condemning nationalisation.

Administrating the Industry

As the government nationalised sections of the secondary industry, industrialists pushed for improvements in the management of the sector. The government agreed. Towards the end of 1943, the government established the Department of Trade and Commerce with a view to fostering secondary industry in the colony and establishing closer relations with commerce and industry.[48] The new portfolio was put under the administration of Fereday, a businessperson and member of the Chamber of Commerce. Also added to this new department were the Factory Control Regulations, the Weights and Measures Act, the Sugar Prices Order, the Cotton Research and Industry Act, the IDAC, the Industrial Development Act, and the Industrial Alcohol Committee. All were instruments to facilitate the balanced development of industries.

The title 'Trade and Commerce' drew the ire of industrialists, who felt it was not representative enough. Addressing members, the president of the Chambers of Industry said:

> We all wonder, however, why industry was not officially included [in this] portfolio ... why could it not be titled the Department of Industry and Commerce so that Southern Rhodesia as well as our neighbours and our

46 NAZ S106, Letter by Salisbury Chamber of Industries to IDAC Secretary, no date. Quoted in Pangeti, 'The state and manufacturing industry', 79.

47 NAZ S106, Letter by the IDAC to the Prime Minister, October 1942.

48 NAZ S918/3, Commerce and Industries: Department of Commerce and Industries, Evidence to Commission on the Public Service, undated.

> home country might know that industry now forms a definite and most important part of our government programme.[49]

Consequently, and precisely because of these reasons, in October 1944, the name of the department changed from 'Trade and Commerce' to 'Commerce and Industries'. Yet another score for industrialists. However, this happened with the acquiescence of commerce, and this explains why Fereday was appointed head of the department.[50]

Crucially, the government appointed the former Assistant Commissioner of Taxes, A. S. Rowe, as secretary of the department. Rowe became a crucial figure in winning concessions from the Ministry of Finance in terms of customs and tariffs because of his previous attachment with the treasury. With this reorganisation, the Department of Supply, whose function had been to attend to the abnormal wartime needs of commerce and industry, was stripped of its responsibilities, which the government transferred to the new Department of Commerce and Industries. During the transition from wartime to peaceful conditions, this permanent department went on to deal with all industrial aspects.

Changes were also made to the IDAC. The Chamber of Industries was at the forefront in bemoaning the status and capacity of the IDAC in addressing the colony's industrial development. It called for the establishment of a new board of industry. Referring to the IDAC, Stanley Cooke, the president of the ACIR, highlighted that 'the committee [was] only advisory and [was] only part time and [had] no executive power. I therefore urge that a definite department of industry or industrial board be appointed without delay with power to take executive action and to spend funds once approved'.[51] Other evidence suggests that IDAC members resigned because of the limited powers they had and the neglect with which their recommendations were dealt by the government.[52] In response, the government, through the Industrial Development Act, set up the Industrial Development Commission (IDC) in 1944 to replace the IDAC.[53] Whereas the IDAC had been limited to an advisory role, the IDC had the authority to finance new industries and schemes for expansion, and to administrate, organise, and modernise existing industries. The other mandate of the IDC encompassed the coordination of industry, ensuring balanced industrial

49 ACIR, *Report of Proceedings for the Third Annual Meeting*: Presidential Address by Mr Stanley Cooke, 28 September 1944.

50 D. J. Murray, *The Governmental System in Southern Rhodesia* (Oxford: Clarendon Press, 1970), 182–83.

51 ACIR, *Report of Proceedings for the Third Annual Meeting:* Presidential Address by Mr Stanley Cooke, 28 September 1944.

52 Murray, *Governmental System in Southern Rhodesia*, 178.

53 *Industrial Rhodesia: A Record of Industrial Development in Southern* Rhodesia (Salisbury: Rhodesian Publications, 1945), 29.

development in the colony, and overseeing the location of industry and matters of the government's assistance of industry.[54]

The reorganisation of the administration of secondary industry revealed the temporarily positive attitude of the state. Rowe and Fereday, both keen believers in industrial development, assisted the industrialists' push, and so did Prime Minister Huggins. At the same time, the government admitted that since the development of secondary industry was now part of its policy, it was obliged to assist industrialists. Besides, since many of these industries had opportunistically developed during the war, the state acknowledged that 'some if not most of these, [would] need nursing through the post war years and it [was] imperative that the Minister responsible for the economic development of the colony be supplied with the administrative and technical staff necessary to ensure sound development and progress'.[55] Among the prioritised essentials were statistical staff and an economic adviser, because the colony was likely to face the question of the protection of secondary industry. In such an eventuality, the government needed the best economic and statistical advice possible. The IDC was already seeking statistical service from the Department of Commerce and Industries.[56]

The government acknowledged other imperatives, such as the need for a standards bureau, an industrial research laboratory, and a trade representative in London to advertise the possibilities of industrial development and attract capital. The first two were aimed at improving and maintaining the quality of products and investigating new methods of production. The trade representative would also find markets for the produce of the colony and act as a buyer for the various commissions and boards now in existence, as well as for government itself.[57] Matters of taxation and protection of secondary industries also became topical in the management of the sector. The following sections discuss these aspects and other factors of production relevant to industrial growth at the time.

Excess Profits Tax

As industry expanded, so did grievances and demands from economic interest groups. In unison, all the economic interest groups called for the abrogation of the EPT. Even those who had advocated its introduction shifted positions. They pushed for its abolishment through their associations. The president of Salisbury Chamber of Commerce stated, 'I think the colony has been badly let down by the government in this matter of industrial development. I refer

54 *Ibid.*

55 NAZ S918/3, Commerce and Industries: Department of Commerce and Industries, Evidence to Commission on the Public Service, undated.

56 *Ibid.*

57 *Ibid.*

particularly to the urgent representations made by the IDAC and others regarding the detrimental effect the Excess Profits Tax was having upon development.'[58] His sentiments were echoed by the IDAC chairman, who stated that the EPTA stifled the establishment of new industries on any large scale, was already retarding the development of existing and recently established industries, and was an inequitable form of taxation.[59] He explained that industrialists were prepared to contribute to taxes that would finance the successful prosecution of the colony's war effort, but objected to the EPTA's role in furthering inequity.

This objection was born out of the realisation that

> young firms, which have had no time to establish themselves but are growing rapidly, feel the burden of the tax more heavily than old firms which have accumulated large capital reserves out of profits in the past, but may be now in a period of decline. Industry grows out of profits put back into the business ... Excess Profits Tax forbids this growth.[60]

Critics of the excess profits tax (EPT) further noted that it not only severely cut into the industry's ability to finance expansion of its operations, but also stifled reinvestments and improvements by eroding the sector's earnings and capital. But even after the IDAC trenchantly illustrated its case, the state maintained that it was not prepared to repeal the act. Rather, it was prepared to consider exemptions. Industries were, therefore, expected to apply for exemption to the treasury.

The basis for exemption was at the discretion of the state and was underpinned by what it termed 'industries of national importance'. This created another point of collision with industrialists, as the government placed limits on what it considered to be of national importance. For instance, while dismissing an application from the clothing industry seeking relief from the EPT, IDAC adviser, T. C. Lloyd, maintained that the sector was the least deserving in the colony. 'Factories of this type are the poorest employers of European labour, use practically no raw materials of local origin, and enjoy a considerable turnover for the minimum investment of capital. These factories do not appear to me to compare with others which are engaged in essential war work', he elaborated.[61] Yet the Chamber of Industries considered all existing and potential secondary industry to be of national importance. Thus, for them, leaving it to the government to favour the establishment or development of the

58 NAZ S932/14, National Industries: Salisbury Chamber of Commerce: Presidential Address at the 49th Annual General Meeting on 28 June 1943.

59 NAZ S915/40, Excess Profit Tax, 1944–1946, Memorandum to the Minister of Finance by IDAC, 23 December 1942.

60 Quoted in *ibid.*

61 NAZ S915/40, Excess Profit Tax, Letter by T. C. Lloyd, IDAC Technical Adviser, to Acting Secretary of Department of Trade and Commerce, 14 August 1944.

limited few industries considered to be of national importance would preclude the majority of industries from even starting. Even if they were permitted to commence, their efforts would be abortive.

The EPT board's attitude towards industry bred further conflicts among its own members. The negative attitude led to the resignation of its adviser, D. Musgrave. In a letter to Minister Fereday, he wrote, 'I find, by experience, [that] I totally disagree with the Advisory Board on a matter of principle ... in these circumstances, I should be allowed to withdraw from further association with that Board.'[62] Musgrave believed that industry should be encouraged to consolidate its position. To ensure this, industries had to be allowed to reinvest profits, failing which many would be forced to close down, or even liquidate, for lack of capital. The advisory board was, however, opposed to this. Thus, his resignation was not surprising. Doubling as both the EPT board adviser and the chairperson of the IDC, industrial interests were a priority to him: any failure to prioritise them would have triggered such a reaction. Overall, the foregoing EPT discussion is particularly important for two reasons: first, it demonstrates how economic interest groups worked together when their interests converged; second, it demystifies the tendency to present the state's assistance as voluntary and readily rendered.

Protection

If the case of EPT showed the sometimes-cordial relations among the various economic interest groups, protection of industry demonstrates how fraught their relations could be. With expanded powers to coordinate industrial development, the IDC picked up on the need to protect secondary industry. Besides financing industries, industrialists and other state officials encouraged the government to simultaneously offer assistance through other forms. They suggested protection, manufacturing rebates, customs duties and tariffs, trade agreements, and anti-dumping laws as plausible options that the government could pursue. This clamour for protection was not new, however. It started with the emergence of incipient factories in the 1890s, and was protracted through to the Great Depression and the two world wars, but it intensified during the transition to the post-war years.[63] The demand for protection became a crucial determinant shaping the interaction between industrialists, other economic interest groups, and the state throughout the industrialisation of the country. Seeking protection, one company, Rhodesian Plough and Machinery Co. Ltd, petitioned the government, stating that 'protective tariffs similar to those in

62 *Ibid.*, Letter by IDC Chairperson to Minister Fereday, 4 February 1946.

63 For early clamours for protection, see Phimister, *An Economic and Social History of Zimbabwe*, 239–46, and Murray, *Governmental System in Southern Rhodesia*, 174.

the Union of South Africa seem necessary to give effect to the Government's intention to foster the development of sundry industries.'[64]

The Rhodesian Plough and Machinery Co. Ltd's wording of its demand for protection is important for a number of reasons. First, it reveals the South African factor in the Southern Rhodesian economy. In almost all the cases for protection presented to the government, whether individually or through organised interests, there was reference to developments in South Africa.[65] Secondly, the case also shows the organisational status of industrialists. The fact that there existed the ACIR and yet industrialists approached the government individually reveals the organisational limitations of the Chamber at the time. The shortcoming was that the ACIR was almost exclusively an organisation for Salisbury- and Bulawayo-based industrialists. There were yet to be any representative organisations in other towns such as Gwelo, Umtali, Gatooma, or Que Que, where industries were also emerging. Much as there was this organisational limitation, this, however, did not handicap their lobbying. When industrialists could not achieve things individually or through the Chamber directly from the government, they turned to the statutory boards of the IDAC and later the IDC. The statutory boards picked up the industrialists' plea and encouraged the government to consider protecting industries, even if only temporarily.

The government had lukewarmly discussed the IDAC's advice earlier on. Enquiries about state assistance to secondary industry by potential investors laid bare the fact that there was 'no specific instance on record where direct protection through Tariff has been accorded to a budding industry or to one already established.'[66] An attempt to assist industries through protective tariffs was frowned upon in some Cabinet quarters. For instance, the minister of mines and public works expressed his reservations to the premier: 'I was always opposed to the Government's policy of protecting industries by control, subsidies, tariffs and other similar forms,' he stated, further adding, 'attempts have been made to afford protection through income tax. This should not be allowed in any circumstances.'[67] The minister was even blunt on another occasion, when he noted that

> the government has been undeservedly accused of opposition to the establishment of secondary industry. So far the majority of suggested industries that have been submitted to the government may be described as bastard

64 NAZ S482/458/39, Rhodesian Plough and Machinery Co. Ltd: Protection of Native Ploughs, 17 May 1940.

65 See, for example, NAZ S916/20, Protection of Rhodesian Industry, 1945; and ACIR, *Report of Proceedings of the Annual Congresses [Nos 1–5]*, 1942–1946.

66 NAZ S482/101/42, Secondary Industry: Letter to the Minister of Finance and Commerce by the Controller of Customs and Excise, 31 July 1941.

67 *Ibid.*, Letter by the Minister of Mines and Public Works to the Prime Minister on Protection of Local Secondary Industry, 2 December 1943.

> industries which are not worthy of the consideration of the government and if they are established the capital must be found by the public and the geographical protection which they will enjoy should suffice without protection through customs and the like.[68]

He later grudgingly conceded that local industries might need some temporary protection in their teething days.[69] For him, protection was against the spirit of the Atlantic Charter, which promoted trade liberalisation. The Chamber of Industries disagreed with the minister's standpoint. The Atlantic Charter's authors, it argued,

> ought to take note that its terms cannot be applied literally in all cases despite it being a wonderful conception ... for all nations to open wide their doors to the produce of other nations and allow production only in those countries where such production can be effected most cheaply would lead perhaps to a greater disaster than even this last fearful war has proved.[70]

When the IDC replaced the IDAC, it revived the push for protection. 'Vigorous tariff protection [is] wanted if industry is to be substantially stimulated', said G. Musgrave, chairman of the IDC.[71] Acting on the advice of the IDC, the minister of commerce and industries suggested to the premier that secondary industry be protected. He quoted from a South African board of trade and industries report, noting that:

> It is the considered opinion of the Board that if any branch of industry can be established on a sound economic basis with a reasonable measure of protection, such protection should be granted. To overcome initial obstacles the board feels that the protection granted should be high enough to be effective. Once the industry is established and has got over its teething troubles, the protection should be gradually reduced.[124]

Most Rhodesian industrialists demanded and expected a similar attitude from their own government.

68 NAZ S915/304/174/1 Riscom, Memoranda and Reports, Letter to Honourable Minister of Co-ordination by Minister of Mines and Public Works, 27 September 1941.

69 NAZ S482/101/42, Secondary Industry, Letter by the Minister of Mines and Public Works to the Prime Minister: Protection of Local Secondary Industry, 2 December 1943.

70 ACIR, *Report of Proceedings for the Third Annual Meeting*: Presidential Address by Stanley Cooke, 28 September 1944; and also the earlier ACIR, *Report of Proceedings of the Second Annual Meeting*: President's Address by N. A. Phillip, 24 August 1943.

71 *Rhodesia Herald*, 8 November 1945; and also NAZ S482/181/42, IDAC: Industrial Development in Southern Rhodesia: Report by T. C. Lloyd to the IDAC, 1943. NAZ S916/20, Protection of Industry: Minister of Commerce and Industry, Mr Fereday, to the Prime Minister, 1945.

The government put the question of protection up for debate in the legislature in 1945. MP Eastwood, seconded by MP Davies, argued that using customs tariffs to protect secondary industry was undesirable, because tariff protection was insidious to the economy. Instead, they proposed that financial assistance be conditionally granted to the people involved in secondary industry on the basis that such recipients

> submit to a full inspection of their accounts and satisfy the government that (i) the management is operating with efficiency and economy and (ii) that the net profit does not exceed ten per centum on the capital employed in the undertaking after normal allowance for the depreciation and reserves have been made.[72]

Vernall spoke in favour of protection, citing the comparison between Great Britain and America wherein the former temporarily took the free trade route after going off the gold standard in 1931 while the latter, Canada, South Africa, and other European countries imposed trade tariffs and exchange controls.[73] The US, Vernall pointed out, grew her industries to the extent that she began exporting to Great Britain. This later forced Great Britain to protect. The overall point he made was that if Rhodesia were to industrialise, she needed some sort of protection. Vernall further argued that protection was needed because the Union merchants were dumping their jam with extras in order to entice Rhodesian merchants to buy their commodity.[74]

Other interests from the private sector opposed protection. Addressing the Junior Chamber of Commerce in Bulawayo, Balfour Dugmore, the Bulawayo Chamber of Commerce adviser, reflected the general scepticism towards secondary industry. He emphasised that the future of Southern Rhodesia lay not in the establishment of isolated secondary industry, but in the wise exploitation of mining and agriculture. Further, he deprecated the 'present relish' for protection and the 'artificial stimulation of small factories which were glorified in the name of secondary industry'.[75] Clearly, diverse interests were opposed to the protection of secondary industries.

The discussion on protection triggered the appointment of a Commission of Enquiry into the Protection of Secondary Industry in Southern Rhodesia in 1945, under the chairmanship of W. Margolis.[76] The commission published its findings in 1946; two key recommendations are worth noting. First, it advised

72 Legislative Assembly Debates, 4 July 1945, Col. 2274.

73 B. Eichengreen and D. Irwin, 'The slide to protectionism in the Great Depression: who succumbed and why?' *Journal of Economic History*, 70, 4 (2010), 875–77.

74 Legislative Assembly Debates, 4 July 1945, Col. 2279.

75 *Bulawayo Chronicle*, 3 May 1946.

76 *Report of the Commission of Enquiry into the Protection of Secondary Industry in Southern Rhodesia* (Salisbury: Government Printer, 1946); henceforth the Margolis Report.

that 'any assistance given to a particular industry in Southern Rhodesia must be judged in the light of its effects upon the cost structure of those industries producing for export, and cannot on economic grounds be justified if it results in an increase in this cost structure'.[77] Secondly, the commission stated that

> the secondary industries of this colony must for the present be regarded as truly of secondary importance. Their ability to meet the needs of the consumer is restricted largely to consumers within Southern Rhodesia. They are thus dependent upon local consumers, and it would not be in their interests to accept assistance in any manner which might be calculated to be harmful to those very industries upon whom they are dependent for their market.[78]

It justified this position on the basis of the limited contribution made by secondary industries to the country's exports. The contribution of secondary industry to the exports of the country during the war had increased from 8.9% in 1938 to 14.9% in 1944.[79] From the data the commission collected, the antagonistic views among the different interest groups once more became apparent.

The commission noted:

> Whilst the primary industries were prepared to agree that the judicious development of secondary industries in Southern Rhodesia was important to the future welfare of Rhodesia; whilst they were prepared to admit that it might be advisable to protect certain infant industries for a limited period, whilst they agreed that protection against such practices as dumping was necessary, they were yet firm and unanimous in their opposition to any policy which would have the effect of permanently curtailing the economic development and expansion of the primary industries. In certain instances they went so far as to oppose any assistance being granted to secondary industries even if the effect upon the primary industries was of a guaranteed temporary nature.[80]

Representatives of commerce also opposed protection of secondary industry. They feared protection would compromise their long-established profitable trade. Some even refused to give evidence to the commission, while others concluded that 'the commission intended on recommending the imposition of a general tariff on a higher scale, regardless of the interests of the import[er] and of the Colony as a whole'.[81] For a long time, trade and commerce had profitably established themselves in the country. It was, therefore, unsurprising that they opposed the idea of promoting local industries through protection.

77 *Ibid.*, 10.
78 *Ibid.*, 12.
79 *Ibid.*
80 *Ibid.*, 25.
81 *Bulawayo Chronicle*, 5 July 1946.

Taking due cognisance of all evidence, the commission recommended that

> in considering forms of assistance to be applied to any particular branch of industry, account must be taken of the effect of such action upon the costs production of the remaining branches of industry and that for economic reasons no such action should be taken if the effects upon these costs of production is likely to be of a permanent nature.[82]

It further advised that 'having regard to the magnitude of the cost to the consumer of Southern Rhodesia, the government should not for economic reasons embark upon a policy of protecting the local industrialist against external competition purely on the grounds that such a policy would engender certain forms of productive activity in Southern Rhodesia.'[83] It also recommended that controlled assistance and protective duties be granted to given industries for a given period, provided that consumers were safeguarded by granting such aids only to industries which were competitive.[84]

To implement these recommendations, the commission suggested appointing a Tariff Advisory Committee (TAC). Consequently, the government set up the TAC under the chairmanship of the Secretary of the Department of Commerce and Industries in 1947. The TAC's mandate was to receive and investigate all applications for assistance to secondary industry of whatever nature and to recommend to the minister of commerce and industries the extent, if any, to which such assistance should be granted.[85] Further, TAC would also recommend to the minister those commodities for which suspended duties were to be incorporated in the customs tariff of Southern Rhodesia. Granting rebates of duty and reviewing trade relationships with other countries, especially the proposed Customs Union Agreement with South Africa, were also to be the responsibility of the tariff committee. Despite all these concessions, industrialists persisted without a full and definitive protectionist policy. The commission's recommendations still reflected the general belief in primary export industries. To a certain extent, it was also reflective of the influence that interest groups in mining and commerce still had over policy decisions. More tellingly, the adoption of the Margolis Report marked a retreat by the state from the wartime policy and controls.

The government essentially postponed the resolution of problems around industrial development by appointing successive commissions, and following on from the Margolis Report, in 1947 it appointed yet another one: the Development Coordinating Commission (DCC). Chaired by Sir Miles Thomas, a British businessman in the motor industry, member of the British advisory

82 Margolis Report, 37.

83 *Ibid.*, 49.

84 *Ibid.*, 49–58.

85 *Ibid.*, 59–60.

panel on tank production and a later chairperson of the British Overseas Airways Corporation, the DCC was tasked with studying and advising on the necessary methods and priorities:

> To ensure the most rapid development of the colony on sound lines, to effect a rapid increase in European population, to make the best use of water resources both for irrigation and hydro-electric purpose and to expand production and export trade by scientific development of large deposits of coal, iron ore, asbestos and other raw products.[86]

The DCC published yearly reports between 1947 and 1949, but was advisory and non-executive: as such, its recommendations and advice were not binding. The committee assessed the colony's economic development priorities and recommended that improved rail and port facilities were immediately and urgently necessary in order to accelerate coal, chrome, and copper traffic.[87] The commission stated that 'a Central Economic Committee to focus and integrate projects in the Colony and relate them to activities in other Central African territories is urgently needed', and further added that 'improved Commercial contacts with British firms through London [were] essential'.[88]

Other short-term priorities included:

> Continued progress with Kariba hydro-electric generating scheme, establish experimental agricultural plots in the Sabi Valley, quadruple iron and steel production capacity at Que Que, increase capacity at Gatooma to 100,000 spindles and coordinate native cotton growing with animal husbandry, extend subsidy on gold mining, introduce coordination of road and rail freight capacities.[89]

It is worth mentioning that the DCC encouraged development of secondary industries, especially the textiles and cotton piece goods sector and iron and steel production. Despite the non-binding nature of its recommendations, the Southern Rhodesian government took the DCC's advice to promote secondary industry. This decision exposed the inconsistencies in the government's policy towards the development of secondary industry, if judged against its decision to accept the Margolis Commission's recommendations the previous year.

86 NAZ S110, Southern Rhodesia, Development Coordinating Commission, First Interim Report to the Prime Minister of Southern Rhodesia, March 1948.
87 *Ibid.*
88 *Ibid.*
89 *Ibid.*

Factors of Production and Secondary Industry

The previous discussion focused on the government's shifting attitude towards secondary industrial development. At the same time as the government's attitude changed, industrialists demanded that it intervene by granting protection, and this had resulted in the setting up of the Margolis Commission to look into the matter. While overall that commission advised against protection, it did note, however, other critical factors that the government could assist with for the development of secondary industry. 'Development along sound economic lines', noted the commission, 'can ultimately only be obtained by ensuring that the supply of labour, capital and raw materials are being made available to the industrialists in the most efficient manner.'[90] It is to these factors that the following discussion turns.

The committee enquired about the sources of capital. The response was that additional capital could not be obtained in Rhodesia. While indeed some capital could be obtained internally, this was by no means sufficient to meet the total future requirements of the territory. Besides, much of this capital went into a small number of large concerns.[91] The option was therefore to look to outside sources for additional capital needs to finance the smaller firms. To attract such capital, some form of inducement was necessary if local industrialists were to cope with competition from other countries whose industries were backed by big financial investment. One such incentive was the taxation policy. In this regard, the recommendation was a substantial reduction in income and corporate tax and assurance that such a reduction was long term.[92] This suggestion was only implemented vigorously from 1949 onwards, as shall be discussed in Chapter 3.

Another factor that worked against industrial expansion was the limited market. Danziger, farmers, and miners employed the limited market argument as a strong justification for the protracted reluctance to promote industries. All the reports discussed previously raised this point;[93] even industrialists conceded this reality. The internal market could be expanded through

90 Margolis Report, 46.

91 For a detailed discussion on capital flows into the manufacturing sector, see Gwande, 'Foreign capital, state and the development of secondary industry in Southern Rhodesia', and D. G. Clarke, *Foreign Companies and International Investment in Zimbabwe* (Gwelo: Mambo Press, 1980). For a general discussion, see C. Stoneman, 'Foreign capital and the reconstruction of Zimbabwe', *Review of African Political Economy*, 5, 11 (1978), 62–83, and 'Foreign capital and the prospects for Zimbabwe', *World Development*, 4, 1 (1976), 25–58.

92 NAZ S2538/180/57, Investment of Foreign Capital in Southern Rhodesia and the Colonies, 1950.

93 See Danziger Report 1934; Economic Development Committee 1939; Commission of Inquiry into Protection of Secondary Industry; and L. Tow, 'The manufacturing

increasing the White population via immigration or by paying Black African workers living wages. As one industrialist highlighted, 'any prospects of the expansion of industry hinged on making Southern Rhodesia a permanent European settlement and the key to that was immigration.'[94]

This was proved when the establishment of the Empire Air Training Scheme greatly expanded the domestic market. The scheme brought more than 10,000 soldiers into the country, who expanded the local market and increased demand for local manufactured products.[95] It also brought men into the colony who had industry-specific knowledge that had been scarcely available in the country.[96]At the same time, immigration would aid the cause of creating a White man's country. 'We must strongly support our government in its consideration of a large immigration scheme', urged the president of the Chamber of Industries in 1944.[97] He emphasised that his Chamber expected skilled and capitalised immigrants who would contribute to industrial development as either artisans or investors. Another caveat to immigration was that the government had to seriously consider maintaining a reasonable majority of British subjects entering into the colony.[98] In this regard, the industrialists' interests converged with political interests. Thus, immigration and industrialisation were mutual partners and tools for achieving a grand political project.

The other option to deal with the market problem was to lift the industrial colour bar and increase their purchasing power. According to the Minister of Finance, 'an important factor in our future progress is an increase in the spending capacity of the non-Europeans. This is the best way in which to enlarge and establish our internal market.'[99] He further urged skills capacitation for the unskilled, both Europeans and Africans, arguing that 'unless and until we concentrate on these, we stand no chance of becoming industrialised.'[100] Industrialists were the loudest in calling for African advancement. This matter

---

economy of Southern Rhodesia: problems and prospects' (PhD, Columbia University, 1960), 232–49.

94 *Industrial Rhodesia: A Record of Industrial Development*, 17.

95 G. Arrighi, 'The political economy of Rhodesia', *New Left Review*, 39 (1966), 35–65, at pp. 44–45; N. Mlambo, 'Arms production and war supply in Southern Africa, 1939–1945: Limitations of the industrial war effort of South Africa and Zimbabwe during the Second World War' (PhD, University of Cape Town, 2000), 245; see also Johnson, 'The impact of the Second World War on Southern Rhodesia', 118–23..

96 NAZ S482/181/42, Industrial Development in Southern Rhodesia, Report by T. C. Lloyd, IDAC Technical Adviser, January 1943.

97 ACIR, *Report of Proceedings for the Third Annual Meeting*: Presidential Address by Mr Stanley Cooke, 28 September 1944.

98 *Ibid.*

99 NAZ S916/20, Protection of Industry: Minister of Commerce and Industry, Minister Fereday, to the Prime Minister, 1945.

100 *Ibid.*

had topped the agendas of the Chambers of Industry congresses since 1942. Some had even advocated for Black Africans at least having the right to manufacture products to meet their own needs.[101] In 1944, the president of the ACIR suggested that

> one thing that industry must provide for and that is reasonable and gradual is the advancement of the native and the provision of employment at such remuneration that will allow the progressive native to live, feed and house himself suitably. We might again observe that such a provision would soon provide its own reward for industry and commerce, as every native with money in his pocket spends a good portion of that money in the purchase of the extra amenities of life and thus offers to industry the possibility of a great expansion of their markets and for commerce a market for their import goods.[102]

Black Africans were employed in the more rewarding manufacturing sector as permanent staff rather than as casual and migratory workers. Noteworthy here is that resorting to Africans was not a realisation of their skill and abilities but rather a convenient and self-serving manoeuvre by industrialists. The idea found immediate support from Prime Minister Huggins. Addressing delegates at the annual general meeting of the Bulawayo Native Welfare Society in 1946, he said:

> we are rapidly reaching the stage where national economy will no longer permit or support a mode of life for the native based solely on agriculture and the raising of livestock. Every native would have to realise soon that he could not expect to be a farmer in a native area and at the same time supplement his income by labour in industry. He will have to concentrate on one of these two avenues of life.[103]

Permanent industrial employees became permanent urban residents who looked to the products of secondary industries for their livelihoods. African wage employment significantly increased from 254,000 in 1936 to 377,000 in 1946.[104] Of these workers, 31,401 (31,236 males plus 165 females) were employed in secondary industry in 1946. More importantly, the value of wages paid to all workers employed in the manufacturing sector increased from £3,341 million

101 ACIR, *Report of Proceedings of the Second Annual Meeting*: President's Address by Mr N. A. Phillip, 24 August 1943.

102 ACIR, *Report of Proceedings for the Third Annual Meeting*: Presidential Address by Mr Stanley Cooke, 28 September 1944.

103 *Rhodesia Herald*, 25 August 1946. See also L. H. Gann and M. Gelfand, *Huggins of Rhodesia: The Man and His Country* (London: George Allen and Unwin, 1964), 172–79.

104 Stoneman, 'Foreign capital and the prospects for Zimbabwe', 31.

in 1946 to £13,022 million in 1953.[105] The ever-increasing number of Black Africans employed in semi-skilled work in secondary industry translated into increased purchasing power and demand for manufactured products for this section of the population. This in turn offered further investment possibilities to industries catering for these demands.

Much as African advancement expanded the internal market for local industries, it also had other unintended consequences. It caused a shift in the socio-economic order that the state and politicians hoped to achieve in Southern Rhodesia, especially with the promulgation of the Native Urban Areas Act (NUARA) in 1946. The act laid down that employers of 'native' labour must provide, at their own expense, accommodation for their employees and, under certain conditions, for the wives of employees. It also provided that accommodation should be situated on the employer's premises or in an African township. The act came up for discussion at the municipal congress in May 1946. Divergent views were expressed, with Donald Macintyre, now the mayor of Bulawayo, calling it an 'iniquitous measure', while others described the act as 'fundamentally sound and giving greater control over urban natives'.[106] The Salisbury town clerk stated in a memorandum that certain provisions of the NUARA violated the provisions of the Land Apportionment Act (LAA), and would result in large numbers of 'natives' being permitted to put down roots in the European Area.[107]

Two acts, the LAA (1930) and the Industrial Conciliation Act (ICA (1934)), had defined the socio-economic order in the country. The ICA was enacted in 1934 and later amended in 1937. Part of its objective was to prevent Blacks from competing with Whites for skilled jobs in secondary industry, hence the act did not recognise Africans as employees by definition. In the event that Africans were employed, they did not enjoy rights accorded to employees because the ICA excluded them. The LAA, the Magna Carta of White rule in Southern Rhodesia, demarcated land ownership along racial lines. It became the cornerstone of the country's policy regarding Africans, which required Africans to develop separately from Europeans, thereby reducing competition between the two races. Industrial expansion and its attendant African urbanisation necessitated a shift from this status quo. Housing African workers on industrial sites flew in the face of the LAA, which required Blacks to stay in African townships.

The provisions of the NUARA created animosity between industrialists, the central government, and urban municipalities.[108] Municipalities argued

105 C. H. Thompson and H. W. Woodruff, *Economic Development in Rhodesia and Nyasaland* (London: Dennis Dobson Ltd, 1953), 65.

106 *Bulawayo Chronicle*, 31 May 1946.

107 *Ibid.*

108 Chapter 3 in T. O. Ranger, *Bulawayo Burning: The Social History of a Southern African City, 1893–1960* (Woodbridge: James Currey, 2010), clearly articulates the

that it was the responsibility of industrialists to house their workers. Conversely, industrialists argued that municipalities had inherent jurisdiction over urban governance and therefore had the mandate to provide accommodation to urban residents regardless of who employed them.[109] Some industrialists, for example the National Federation of Building Trade Employers, argued that if local authorities could not provide accommodation, they should at least 'allow industrialists to house natives on their industrial sites'.[110] For these industrialists, such an arrangement would reduce transport costs on their part and at the same time lower the government costs of housing Black people working in industry.[111]

African advancement also affected the interests of White labour, miners and farmers, and politicians in general. For farmers and miners, industrialisation, so they argued, would result in labour shortages for their industries. Skilled African labour would now become costly for farmers and miners, who had relied for a long time on this source of cheap labour. To secure and satisfy their labour needs, the Chamber of Industries engaged migrant labour from Nyasaland. Nyasas became preferable because 'the native population generally in Nyasaland is exceptionally well-educated, the proportion of natives with literary and industrial training being well-above that of the neighbouring territories'.[112] The Nyasas were employed under particular terms. It was the Nyasaland government's preferred policy that after two years every Nyasa would have to return home, unless he brought his family to Southern Rhodesia.[113] Additionally, it was compulsory for an employer to deduct five shillings from a Nyasa's monthly wage and send it to Nyasaland, or use the

contradictions and conflicts that emerged between the central government, city councils, and businessmen as a result of industrial expansion and African urbanisation. Although these conflicts were occurring in the 1930s, they continued well into the 1960s.

109 See E. Chipembere, 'Colonial policy and Africans in urban areas, with special focus on housing, Salisbury, 1939–1964' (MPhil, University of Zimbabwe, 2006); *Rhodesian Recorder*, September 1952. This was a long-standing debate between the central government and municipalities which began in the 1930s; see Ranger, *Bulawayo Burning*, 112–17.

110 *Rhodesian Recorder*, September 1952.

111 *Ibid.*

112 Quoted in A. Daimon, '"Ringleaders and troublemakers": Malawian (Nyasa) migrants and transnational labour movements in Southern Africa, c.1910–1960', *Labour History*, 58, 5 (2017), 656–75, at p. 660. See also Z. Groves, 'Urban migrants and religious networks: Malawians in colonial Salisbury, 1920 to 1970', *Journal of Southern African Studies*, 38, 3 (2012), 491–511, at pp. 502–05.

113 A. Daimon, '"Mabhurandaya": The Malawian diaspora in Zimbabwe: 1895 to 2008' (PhD, University of the Free State, 2015), 74–79. See also Z. Groves, *Malawian Migration to Zimbabwe, 1900–1965: Tracing Machona* (Cham: Palgrave Macmillan, 2020).

deferred payment system.[114] It should be noted, however, that this system also applied to farms and mines.

In addition to the 'problematic' African advancement, another way to deal with a limited market was to widen it. Widening the market entailed enlarging the territorial and geographical space within which the manufactured products were sold. This was achieved by forming a closer association with other Central African territories and renegotiating trade agreements. The Chamber of Industries raised these ideas and coincided with other political desires within the territory. For instance, in 1941, Huggins called for closer association with Northern Rhodesia.[115] The Chamber of Industries urged both its members and the government to hasten amalgamation with Northern Rhodesia and Nyasaland.[116] The two territories enjoyed free trade with the Belgian Congo because of the Congo Basin Treaty, and the Chamber suggested that this must now be dispensed with. In its place, the Chamber argued, 'we invite our neighbours, the Belgian Congo, Portuguese East and West Africa to join with us in an industrial and commercial federation of Central African states to give us all the benefits of each other's productions and industries and to help in the development of Central Africa as a whole'.[117] Should this be achieved, the Federation would be extended eastwards to include Tanganyika, Kenya, and Uganda. Such a federation, they hoped, would strengthen their bargaining position in future negotiations with the Union of South Africa.[118] As part of the enormously expanded market created by the envisaged federation, Southern Rhodesia could become a veritable hive of industry. The envisaged federation did not come to fruition. Instead, Southern Rhodesia turned its focus towards its trading relations with the Union of South Africa. It is this subject that the following paragraphs address.

The 1948 Customs Union (Interim) Agreement with the Union of South Africa

Phimister has shown the impact of the Customs Union Agreement on the 'secondary industrialisation of Southern Africa'.[119] However, of interest to this discussion are the negotiations that led towards the agreement, for they reveal the relationship between the government and the economic interest groups. But to be sure, Southern Rhodesia's industrialisation impacted trade relations with

114 *Ibid.*

115 Gann and Gelfand, *Huggins of Rhodesia*, 170, 208–15.

116 ACIR, *Report of Proceedings for the Third Annual Meeting*: Presidential Address by Mr Stanley Cooke, 28 September 1944.

117 *Ibid.*

118 *Ibid.*

119 Phimister, 'Secondary industrialisation in Southern Africa'.

its powerful neighbour. Industrialists had given evidence at the Commission of Inquiry into the Protection of Secondary Industry, discussed earlier, pleading for another look into the existing trade agreements, particularly with the Union of South Africa.

Indeed, the commission recommended renegotiations of trade agreements. Industrialists were, therefore, an interested party in the negotiations. Because of this and for other reasons which will become clearer shortly, talks with the Union commenced. South Africa and Southern Rhodesia had long-standing relations. Between 1910 and 1935, the two neighbours maintained a customs union in which, for the most part, trade relations hinged on a common tariff and some free interchange of products.[120] In 1945, the Southern Rhodesian Department of Commerce and Industries sent out a questionnaire to industrialists regarding the desirability of revising the trade agreement with South Africa. A summary of industrialists' responses to the questionnaire compiled by the IDC showed that 'most of the replies emphasise[d] some disadvantage under which the industry suffers when competing with the Union manufacturers ... the present tariff agreement with the Union is inequitable as far as Rhodesian manufactures are concerned.'[121]

At the same time, the USA was pushing for liberal trade in the post-war period.[122] It encouraged customs unions in place of customs tariffs and preferential trade relations. In line with this, it called for an international trade conference to deal with these aspects. The 1935 South Africa–Southern Rhodesia agreement was seen as more preferential than a customs union.[123] Therefore, the two countries needed to adjust the existing agreement so that it aligned with the proposals being made at an international level.[124] Faced with the dual necessities of aligning future relations to the US proposals and meeting Rhodesian demands, in 1946 the Union government approached the Southern Rhodesian government to discuss the possibility of a new customs union.

120 NASA HEN Vol. No. 3896 Ref. 710, Trade Relations between the Union of South Africa and Southern Rhodesia, 1950; See also Cole, 'The tariff policy of Southern Rhodesia.'

121 NASA HEN Vol. No. 3895 Ref. S710 vol. 6, IDC's T. C. Lloyd comments on Questionnaire to Industries Submitted to the Department of Commerce and Industries, 20 August 1945; and also NASA HEN Vol. No. 3895 Ref. S710 vol. 6, A Survey of the Trade Agreement with the Union by T. C. Lloyd, 4 April 1945.

122 For America's perspectives on international trade, see, for example, R. E. Baldwin, 'The changing nature of U.S. trade policy since World War II,' in R. E. Baldwin and A. O. Krueger (eds), *The Structure and Evolution of Recent U.S. Trade Policy* (Chicago: University of Chicago Press, 1984), 5–32.

123 NASA HEN Vol. No. 3895 Ref. S710 vol. 6, Notes of a meeting of the External Trade Relations Committee held on 16 July 1946.

124 *Ibid.*

During the protracted negotiations, Rhodesia's scepticism regarding its powerful neighbour became apparent. Southern Rhodesia pointed out that its industrialists regarded the Union as a serious threat; thus, the re-establishment of a customs union and the resultant free entry of Union products would hamper the country's own industrial development.[125] Furthermore, the Rhodesian delegation highlighted that Rhodesia was developing along a similar path to the Union and sought to achieve a balanced economy which would, in effect, lessen its dependence on the Union. Rhodesia was also still committed to imperial preference, wishing to retain its trade relations with the United Kingdom and other dominions. The prospects of securing these alternative markets reduced the attractiveness of the market offered by the Union.

Presented with these scenarios, the Union needed to adduce strong arguments as to why it was beneficial for Southern Rhodesia to consider a customs union. The Union government thus argued that 'with a comparatively small European population, the Rhodesian market was too small to allow either the external or internal economies of large scale production to be utilized. A Customs Union would offer a large market which in turn would reduce this disadvantage.'[126] Closely related to this was the possibility of expanded industrial production, which would give encouragement to European immigration into Southern Rhodesia. It is interesting to note that whereas Southern Rhodesia had presented a couple of reasons why it was sceptical of another customs union, South Africa presented nine reasons why Southern Rhodesia needed to join the customs union.[127]

Seeing this as desperation on South Africa's part to have a market north of Limpopo, Southern Rhodesia took advantage and gained a strong bargaining position. For example, Southern Rhodesia demanded that South Africa 'undertakes to give all possible assistance … in accelerating industrialisation.'[128] It further demanded that a classification be made between industries which could be distributed with ease throughout both territories and industries which could advantageously be established in one territory only, with a view to supplying the whole of the Southern African market. It also wished to ascertain the degree of protection against the older established Union industries which would be given to Southern Rhodesian industry during the transitional period.[129]

The Union stood its ground, however. Against these Rhodesian demands, the Union proposed that the customs union should allow for the 'produce or

125 NASA HEN Vol. No. 3895 Ref. S710 vol. 6, Agreed Summary of the Discussions between Officials of the Governments of Southern Rhodesia and the Union of South Africa, 2–4 October 1946.

126 *Ibid.*

127 *Ibid.*

128 NASA HEN Vol. No. 3902 Ref. 710/1, Meeting of the Sub-Committee on Policy held 21 January, 1947.

129 *Ibid.*

manufacture of either territory to be admitted free of customs duties and free of restrictions as to quality and quantity, subject to modifications as may be agreed by both parties'.[130] Both parties, however, compromised and agreed that 'in order to promote conditions which will enable a full Customs Union to be attained, the Union government will co-operate with the government of Southern Rhodesia in a policy of fostering industrial expansion in Southern Rhodesia on sound economic lines'.[131] This clause became Article 4 of the eventual agreement. Further consultations ultimately led to the signing of the Customs Union (Interim) Agreement in 1948, the main purpose of which was set out in the preamble as

> to achieve complete removal of all customs and other trade barriers between the two countries, to re-establish a full and complete Customs Union and to extend such Customs Union to other African States or territories by subsequent agreement with them as a means of contributing to the establishment and maintenance of a high level of production, employment and real income throughout the world and in particular in the territories party to this Agreement.[132]

This preamble was a regurgitation of the principles adopted by the International Trade Organisation Committee, the precursor to the 1947 General Agreement on Tariffs and Trade (GATT). Because South Africa and Southern Rhodesia became signatories to the GATT, they were obliged to assure the other contracting parties that the customs union was not a disguised perpetuation of preferential arrangements between them.

Incorporating the GATT preamble into the agreement was, therefore, a way to gain international acceptability and permission to operate the customs union. The agreement was submitted to the GATT Assembly for assent in 1949, and was indeed approved.[133] The agreement was an interim intended to last five years. Among the provisions of the agreement were that the Union would grant products of Southern Rhodesian origin liberal access to the South African market while allowing Southern Rhodesia to retain protective duties in respect of seventy specified Union-made products.[134] Articles 9 to 12 provided for negotiations on free and restricted entry of goods not specified

130 *Ibid.*

131 NASA HEN Vol. No. 3910 Ref. 710/1/1, Minutes of the First Meeting of the Union–Southern Rhodesian Committee to Carry Out the terms of Clause 3 of the Draft Customs Agreement with Southern Rhodesia, held at Pretoria on 12–13 May 1947.

132 Union of South Africa, *Government Gazette, Notice No. 4059, Customs Union (Interim) Agreement between the Governments of the Union of South Africa and Southern Rhodesia*, 18 November 1948.

133 Cole, 'The tariff policy of Rhodesia', 35.

134 Union of South Africa, *Government Gazette, Notice No. 4059, Customs Union (Interim) Agreement*, Articles 6 and 7.

under articles 6 and 7 into each other's territory. Noteworthy is the sustained South African influence in the Rhodesian economy.

The eventual agreement showed how much Southern Rhodesia depended on South Africa despite both its professed desire for imperial preference and its scepticism of the Union. Indeed, South Africa acknowledged Southern Rhodesia's desire to protect and grow her industries. Thus, it made quite a number of concessions to its weaker neighbour. More importantly, throughout negotiations for this agreement, industrialists in Southern Rhodesia were not consulted, yet the customs union was in part meant to foster industrial development for the colony. Industrialists were incensed by their exclusion from the negotiations, so much so that they never wholly accepted the agreement. Industrialists' ill feelings will be discussed in Chapter 3. In the next section, the focus is on the structure and size of the secondary industries that emerged between 1939 and 1948.

The Post-war Economic Environment and the State of Secondary Industry

Overall, the societal corporatism among the economic interest groups and the state shaped and determined the pace and structure of the secondary industrialisation that emerged during this period. Staggering on with minimal state assistance, be it financial or protection, secondary industry grew in number and value.[135] By 1948, Southern Rhodesia boasted a diversified industrial sector. The major subsectors were food and beverages, tobacco manufacturing, textile and clothing, wood, furniture and fixtures, chemicals and chemical products, rubber, paper, printing and publishing, and metal manufacturing. Of these, food and beverages, textiles and clothing, and metal manufacturing were the biggest contributors to the GDP.[136] These were all basic industries that were key to further industrialisation. Table 2.2 below shows the size of secondary industry by 1948.

The 1948 customs agreement stimulated the clothing and textile industry's export market.[137] Since the agreement only came into operation in 1949, more details and statistical evidence on its impact will be dealt with in the next chapter. Nevertheless, a pointer is necessary here. The Union imported only £65,609 worth of textiles and clothing in 1948, but by the end of 1949, the figure had increased to £988,954.[138] Other exogenous factors eased the market problem. In the post-war period, Britain faced a shortage of the dollars

135 Government of Southern Rhodesia, *Census of Industrial Production, 1938–1948*.
136 Federation of Rhodesia and Nyasaland, *Monthly Digest of Statistics*, 3, 3 June 1954.
137 See Phimister, 'Secondary industrialisation in Southern Africa'; and Mlambo and Phimister, 'Partly protected'.
138 *Commerce*, June 1952.

Table 2.2. Secondary industry expansion in numbers and value, 1938–1948.

Year	Number of establishments	Labour employed	Gross output (£'000)
1938	299	17,554	5,107
1939	294	17,865	5,434
1940	295	20,659	6,297
1941	303	22,334	7,307
1942	296	24,341	8,371
1943	327	26,053	9,458
1944	331	28,668	11,230
1945	382	34,510	14,062
1946	435	39,958	17,264
1947	430	40,684	21,058
1948	473	47,848	25,858

Source: *Census of Industrial Production*, 1938–1962.

needed to import goods. To preserve the dollar reserves it had, Britain looked to its empire for resources.[139] The new inward-looking policy by Britain was a blessing to Southern Rhodesia, especially for its tobacco producers. Southern Rhodesia replaced America as the supplier of tobacco to Britain. The London Agreement of 1947 between Southern Rhodesia tobacco producers and British tobacco manufacturers enabled this.[140] It resulted in an increase in local tobacco production, whose foreign exchange earning capacity was crucial for the secondary industries.

The increase was also accompanied by a corresponding increase in the number of tobacco producers and promoted a high rate of immigration in the post-war years.[141] The influx of European and White immigrants in turn increased internal demand for manufactured products, thereby giving impetus to the development of industries. Meanwhile, there was a huge demand in the USA for Southern Rhodesia's asbestos and chrome in the wake of the Korean War. The two exports became major dollar earners and generated revenue crucial for the importation of industrial machines and other inputs. Labour employment patterns also shifted.[142] By 1948, secondary industry employed

139 For more on this, see P. J. Cain, and A. G. Hopkins, *British Imperialism, 1688–2000* (London: Longman, 2001).

140 For more on the impact of this agreement, see S. Ncube, 'Colonial Zimbabwe's tobacco industry: global, regional and local relations, 1947–1979' (PhD, University of the Free State, 2018).

141 Arrighi, 'The political economy of Rhodesia', 45.

142 See Clarke, 'The political economy of discrimination and underdevelopment in Rhodesia with special reference to African workers'; and Government of Southern Rhodesia, *Census of Industrial Production, 1938–1948*.

46,964 workers compared to the 17,820 it had employed in 1939.[143] Of this figure, 40,818 were Africans and 6,146 Europeans; the corresponding figures for 1939 were 15,048 and 2,772, respectively.[144] Arguably, this shift in the employment of Black workers formed the basis for an African proletariat that was instrumental in the rise of African trade unionism and the labour strike of 1948.[145] More importantly, the expansion of the secondary industries necessitated the formation of a national organisation of industrialists, as eventually happened in 1949.

Conclusion

Competing interests between organised secondary industry, the state, and other economic interest groups shaped secondary industrial development in Southern Rhodesia between 1939 and 1948. The government appointed successive committees to advise on this. Every committee but one advised against the promotion of secondary industry. Mining and agriculture formed the pillars of the economy; hence, their interests took priority over those of secondary industry. The fortunes of the manufacturing sector changed during the Second World War and kept that momentum in the post-war years. However, the sector still faced challenges, stiff opposition and belittlement from the state and other economic interest groups. Nevertheless, industrialists organised themselves into a national association to fight for their interests. This became the modus operandi of secondary industry, as the next chapter will show.

143 Government of Southern Rhodesia, *Census of Industrial Production, 1938–1948*.

144 *Ibid*.

145 See especially P. Harris, 'Industrial workers in Rhodesia, 1946–1972: Working class elites or lumpenproletariat?' *Journal of Southern African Studies*, 1, 2 (1975), 139–61; Gann and Gelfand, *Huggins of Rhodesia*, 186, 200–01; I. Phimister and B. Raftopoulos, '"Kana sora ratswa ngaritswe": African nationalists and Black workers – The 1948 general strike in colonial Zimbabwe', *Journal of Historical Sociology*, 13, 3 (2000), 289–324; and B. Raftopoulos and T. Yoshikuni (eds), *Sites of Struggle: Essays in Zimbabwe's Urban History* (Harare: Weaver Press, 1999).

3 Post-war Industrial Growth, Organised Industry, and the Central African Federation, 1949–1957

This chapter describes Southern Rhodesia's continued post-war industrial expansion, the government's industrial policy, and the consolidation of organised industry into a national association, the Federation of Rhodesian Industries (FRI), established in 1949. It then covers the FRI's politics up to 1957, when it amalgamated with industrialists of the other two federal territories, Northern Rhodesia and Nyasaland. This consolidation occurred in the socio-economic and political environment that 'birthed' the Central African Federation (CAF) in 1953. The post-war environment and the establishment of the CAF were significant in shaping the relationship between the FRI and the state regarding government assistance to secondary industries. The FRI, like its predecessor, was persistent in its pursuit of a definitive industrial policy and government assistance through protective tariffs, among other factors of production. In doing so, it faced a reluctant, if not outright dismissive, state. This apparent arrogance of the state towards secondary industries triggered wide-ranging criticisms from the FRI. All of these dynamics form the core discussion in this chapter.

The chapter begins with an analysis of the impact of the post-war economic environment on the government's industrial policy and industrial expansion. It then examines the consequent transfiguration of the organisational structure of secondary industry. Under the stimulus of continued industrial expansion and due to the desire to achieve more for the country in general and the sector in particular, a colony-wide association of industrialists, the FRI, was formed. The second section goes on to examine the nature, form, and effectiveness of state assistance for secondary industries and the various responses by industrialists thereto, and the last shows the size and the structure of secondary industries that emerged under the existing policy environment.

The chapter concludes that to achieve industrial expansion, industrialists received minimal state assistance and, in fact, largely persevered on their own. Despite the increasing importance of secondary industries to the country and the numerous pleas and proposals from the FRI, the state continued to be a reluctant partner. For instance, by 1957, almost all of industry's requests were yet to be attended to or were completely dismissed by government; even when they did receive attention, it was not satisfactory. Yet, this did not inhibit industrial growth and expansion. In what follows, the discussion turns to how industrial growth and expansion were achieved, notwithstanding the reluctance of the state.

Post-war Industrial Expansion and the Formation of the FRI

To align itself with the economic and industrial expansion after the war, in 1948 the government changed the administrative structure of industry. It disbanded the Industrial Development Commission (IDC) and replaced it with a fully fledged portfolio – the division of trade and industrial development. The IDC's work was continued by a new industries committee, which served

> to investigate applications for assistance to industry other than those falling within the scope of Tariff Advisory Committee, recommend to the Minister what assistance, if any, should be given, keep under review the progress of industries which received unacquitted loans and with the approval of the Minister, to initiate any enquiry or investigation which aims at the development of industry generally.[1]

The government also maintained its policy of 'giving assistance where assistance is needed and for as long as it is necessary in the national interest' and believed that 'inherently, [industry] must be a voluntary and not forced growth'.[2] Therefore, it called upon industry to establish itself.

The state maintained that assistance to industry 'should be given either by rebate of customs duty on imported materials or imposition of a protective customs tariff or the imposition of anti-dumping duty (although this was really never vigorously implemented)'.[3] This applied to an industry as a whole and not a particular firm within an industry. Other forms of government assistance included tax relief, negotiating for export markets, and trade agreements with

1 NAZ F292/1/16/3, Secondary Industry in Southern Rhodesia, May 1953.

2 NAZ S482/134/48, Memorandum on Government's Policy towards Assisting Development of Industries in Southern Rhodesia, 25 January 1949; and NAZ F292/16/3, Secondary Industry in Southern Rhodesia, May 1953.

3 NAZ S482/134/48, Memorandum on Government's Policy towards Assisting Development of Industries in Southern Rhodesia, 25 January 1949.

other countries. In determining which industries warranted assistance, the state prioritised those that utilised local raw materials (as opposed to imported semi-manufactured materials), those that were mechanised, and those whose products enjoyed a stable and sizeable market.[4]

Granting of rebates depended on the protection already afforded to an industry by the duty imposed on imported goods similar to those to be manufactured – that is, the greater the duty on the imported article, the less the rebate on imported raw materials and, conversely, the smaller the duty, the greater the rebate. The period of time the rebate was granted for varied according to industry, the deciding variable being the time needed for that particular industry to be established.[5] Imperial preference was also a determining factor. In some instances, rebate was denied if, for example, the raw material being imported was procurable locally. Manufacturers, therefore, had no freedom to choose the best market from which to buy. Where an industry was assisted through the customs tariff, the Tariff Advisory Committee (TAC) held the mandate to recommend to the government the industries that warranted support. By 1949, customs duty rebates to secondary industries totalled £136,150.[6] Table 3.1 below illustrates the breakdown of the rebates granted. Noteworthy here is that the state officially outlined its industrial policy and the methods of assistance afforded to secondary industry. Despite this well-elaborated policy, industrialists remained unsatisfied; for them, the state policy was cosmetic. Meanwhile, secondary industries registered progressive growth under the stimulus of the 1948 Customs Union Agreement with South Africa, as alluded to in the previous chapter. The next section discusses the impact of the agreement.

The 1948 Customs Union Agreement and Secondary Industries

Aided, partly, by the market and some protection afforded by the Customs Union Agreement, secondary industries expanded in number and value. In 1949, 508 industries had a gross output of £31,300,000. By 1950, the number of secondary industry firms had increased to 648, with a gross output of £42,414,000 and a net output of £19,102,000.[7] According to the *Rhodesian Recorder*, in 1939 the combined output of mining and agriculture was three and half times the gross output of factory industries. By 1949, the products of all secondary industry exceeded the combined gross output of all mining and

4 *Ibid.*
5 *Ibid.*
6 Legislative Assembly Debates, 24 May 1950, Col. 1531.
7 NAZ F292/1/16/3, Secondary Industry in Southern Rhodesia, May 1953; and Federation of Rhodesia and Nyasaland, *Economic Report*, 1955.

Table 3.1. Industries that benefitted from rebates in 1949.

Industrial sector	Rebate value in £
Beer brewing	2,468
Boot and shoe manufacturing	7,652
Brooms and brushware	530
Confectionery	766
Disinfectants and insecticides	854
Fibre suitcases	2,402
Furniture manufacturing	1,069
Hollowware and enamelware	1,352
Iron and steel	818
Paints and colours	323
Paper wares	3,205
Plastic articles	3,038
Polish manufacturing	636
Soap, perfumery and toilet preparations	22,409
Steel windows and doors	2,324
Sugar refining	58,421
Textile manufacturing	25,532

Source: *Legislative Assembly Debates*, 24 May 1950, Col. 1531; and *Rhodesian Recorder*, July 1950.

agriculture by 38%.[8] The expansion continued into the early 1950s. Table 3.2 below demonstrates the importance of secondary industry as an employer, in relation to agriculture and mining.

It is observable from the table that by 1951, secondary industry was the biggest employer of White labour, overtaking mining and agriculture. Although secondary industry used the least Black African labour of the three sectors, its employment figures were not far below those of mining labour. The fact that more than 50,000 African labourers were employed in the manufacturing sector was a significant feat, considering it had employed fewer than 20,000 before 1939. It also reflects how manufacturing was opening up spaces for Africans, thereby promoting African advancement in the colony ahead of mining and agriculture. In terms of value, manufacturing had overtaken mining by a significant margin of £6.7 million by 1951. Though still worth less than European agriculture, manufacturing was showing great expansion. In 1951, manufacturing had a net output of £21.8 million, in comparison to European agriculture's £24.1 million.[9] For agriculture, this figure had actually dropped from £27.1 million in 1950.[10]

8 NAZ F292/1/16/3, Secondary Industry in Southern Rhodesia, May 1953.

9 *Ibid.*

10 *Ibid.*

Table 3.2. European and African labour employed in manufacturing, mining, and European agriculture, 1950–1951.

	Europeans employed		Africans employed		Net output (£ million)	
Sector	**1950**	**1951**	**1950**	**1951**	**1950**	**1951**
Manufacturing	8,845	9,441	53,314	56,748	19.1	21.8
Mining	2,396	2,530	59,548	60,688	13.6	15.1
European agriculture	7,375	7,534	168,997	181,366	27.1	24.1

Source: NAZ F292/1/16/3, Secondary Industry in Southern Rhodesia, May 1953.

Table 3.3. Southern Rhodesia exports (in order of importance) to the Union, 1951–1952.

	Export value in £	
Commodity	**1951**	**1952**
Clothing	2,827,000	2,365,000
Cigarettes	652,000	723,000
Meats (preserved)	413,000	461,000
Sugar (preserved)	403,000	592,000
Jute and hessian (excl. bags)	365,000	172,000
Footwear	340,000	344,000
Cotton piece goods	301,000	239,000
Cotton yarns	226,000	170,000
Asbestos cement manufactures	189,000	264,000
Ground nut oil	180,000	153,000
Wooden furniture	153,000	196,000
Blankets and rugs	142,000	161,000

Source: NAZ F292/1/16/3, Secondary Industry in Southern Rhodesia, May 1953.

Meanwhile, the contribution of secondary industry to the export trade reached substantial proportions. The leading secondary exports in order of importance are shown in Table 3.3 above.

This expansion occurred against the backdrop of the influence of the trade agreement. As the Southern Africa Customs Union Council noted,

> The continued industrial expansion in Southern Rhodesia since the Interim Agreement came into operation cannot be ascribed merely to a fortuitous wave of prosperity during that period, but it is proof that the optimism

> of those who sought, by introducing the agreement, to encourage the development of trade between, and industry, in the two territories, was well founded.[11]

The council visited a number of factories in Salisbury and Bulawayo (in Southern Rhodesia) and the Rand, East Rand, and Pretoria (in South Africa), and 'could not help being profoundly impressed by the immense progress which has been made in industry in the two countries'.[12] The steady growth of industries in Southern Rhodesia warranted a new organisational representative body for the sector, whose formation and *modus operandi* form the subject matter of what follows.

The Federation of Rhodesian Industries

In 1949, industrialists were inspired by the increasing importance of their sector to the country's economy, and the imperative to reflect that growth, to form the FRI. This replaced the narrow old Association of Chambers of Industries of Rhodesia (ACIR), which, according to Sir Malcolm Barrow, the Minister of Home Affairs, was 'not [a] particularly influential body [because] its strength lay in the two Chambers in Salisbury and Bulawayo'.[13] Barrow was himself a founding member of the FRI and had served as the first federal minister of commerce and industries in 1953. He was intimately knowledgeable about industrial development. Even as the FRI came into existence, it complained that not enough firms were members of Chambers of Industry. For instance, out of 700 firms eligible for membership as of January 1950, only 195 firms were members of a Chamber of Industry.[14] The new federation comprised four Chambers: Salisbury, Bulawayo, Gwelo, and Umtali. However, with time, interest in the Federation grew. By 1952, Gatooma Chamber of Industry was formed and became the fifth Chamber. Reflecting on the Federation's growth, in 1953, the FRI president remarked that the 'effectiveness of our organization is illustrated by the steadily increasing membership of constituent Chambers ... several industrial organisations have applied for affiliation ... there is no doubt that the Federation is becoming a widely representative body'.[15]

11 *Rhodesian Recorder*, July 1952; see also A. S. Mlambo, E. S. Pangeti, and I. Phimister, *Zimbabwe: A History of Manufacturing, 1890–1995* (Harare: University of Zimbabwe Publications, 2000), 35–38; and I. Phimister, "Secondary industrialisation in Southern Africa: the 1948 customs agreement between Southern Rhodesia and South Africa', *Journal of Southern African Studies*, 17, 3 (1991), 430–42, at pp. 435–37.

12 *Rhodesian Recorder*, July 1952.

13 Federation of Rhodesian Industries, Final Annual Congress, July 1957.

14 *Rhodesian Recorder*, February 1950.

15 FRI, Annual Congress, July 1953: Presidential Address, 4.

The FRI developed a *modus operandi* of inviting Cabinet ministers, representatives of commerce, other government officials, and many visiting industrialists to its gatherings, in particular its annual congresses. This was in addition to its earlier practice of sponsoring its members to stand as legislative assembly candidates. If the sponsored members won seats, they would be better placed to influence government policy, especially as it related to industrial interests. However, the FRI advice and assistance was not always solicited or taken on by the government. The FRI held its first annual congress in October 1950. It passed a number of resolutions that pertained to industry for onward submission to the government. These included issues such as African housing, road and railway facilities, planning of future industrial development (industrial policy), trade agreements, protective tariffs, and the pricing of raw materials.[16] We will expand on these in subsequent sections.

The FRI undertook a number of initiatives to advance the interests of its members. In its first year of existence, it collaborated with a publishing house, Ramsay Parker Publications, to launch a trade and industry journal, the *Rhodesian Recorder*, to cover and publicise secondary industrial developments. The inaugural FRI president, Stanley Cooke, hailed the *Recorder* as the first journal to represent industrial interests, remarking that it was 'a sign of the times and of the coming of age of industry in Rhodesia'.[17] The premier, Godfrey Huggins, similarly noted that the establishment of the journal by the FRI showed 'the considerable advance made by the secondary industries of Southern Rhodesia in recent years'.[18]

The *Recorder* was a critical advertising medium for the output of Rhodesian factories, for local consumption and export, and for manufacturers outside who wished to enter the Rhodesian market. The value of the journal was lauded by businesspeople. R. Z. Kaufman of Kaufman Sons and Co., a Rhodesian wholesale merchant firm, commented that

> while in Britain, I found the *Rhodesian Recorder* on the desks of many businessmen I visited. In some cases it was open, and I could see that the advertisements and editorial columns had been well pencilled. In thus bringing the potentialities of Rhodesia and the other territories it serves to people overseas, your journal is providing an invaluable service.[19]

Such was the importance of this journal to the publicity of Rhodesian industries.

Locally, the FRI initiated the 'Buy Rhodesia Campaign' to deal with the prejudices against local industries propagated by commerce, local consumers,

16 *Rhodesian Recorder*, November 1950.
17 *Ibid.*, January 1950.
18 *Ibid.*
19 *Ibid.*, January 1951.

and sometimes even government, all of which preferred imports to locally made industrial products. The FRI secretary complained that

> a silly trait that has definitely got to be broken down is the prejudice against reputable Rhodesian products. Twice in one week we have had manufacturers coming into our office telling us that if they put labels on their goods marked 'Made in Rhodesia' they might as well give up trying to sell in the colony. [20]

The intention of the campaign, therefore, was to assure and convince Rhodesians that local industries were able to cater for their requirements. Further, the FRI illustrated the abilities and good quality of Southern Rhodesian products through their acceptability in the export market, wherein up to 85% of the products were absorbed. 'Goods exported are not bought out of sympathy,' the FRI explained, 'but because they [are considered] of good value.'[21] At the time, exports of secondary industries amounted to over £4,000,000 a year; the people purchasing those products could not all have been wrong.

Furthermore, the FRI pressed the government over the 'Buy Rhodesia' principle. The FRI felt that the expansion of Rhodesian secondary industry lacked the encouragement of the government, 'in particular constant support by Ministers in public speeches and public statements and expansion of policy in government departments to buy Rhodesian.'[22] The ill-feeling arose from the government's tendency to award the bulk of its tenders to foreign businesses to the exclusion of local manufacturers. The FRI suggested that the government should increase the percentage of tenders that it held for issue to local industry from 10% to 12.5%. The Minister of Trade and Industrial Development, R. F. Halstead, concurred with industrialists on the 'Buy Rhodesia' campaign. Buying Rhodesian, Halstead suggested, would be a twin solution to address the adverse balance of trade while offering a springboard from which local industries could expand:

> A greater local sale would in the end mean larger production, greater efficiency and lower production costs. The greater the local demand for our own goods, the better able will our manufactures be to compete in the export market. [23]

Citing the examples of Britain and the USA, the largest manufacturing exporters at the time, Halstead acknowledged that their industries had been built up, initially, based on local demand. Thus, a larger and sustained home market was 'the essential basis for a larger export trade. Buying Rhodesian

20 *Rhodesian Recorder*, January 1950.

21 *Ibid.*

22 NAZ F344/39/5/1/50: Federation of Rhodesian Industries: Minutes of a Meeting between FRI and Ministers of Trade and Finance, 6 August 1952.

23 *Rhodesian Recorder*, May 1950.

becomes therefore a factor of untold importance in our industrial development.'[24] The government agreed to inform all its departments of the necessity of purchasing local products and to support local industries through the medium of public ministerial statements on 'Buy Rhodesia'. It resolved that an interdepartmental committee should be set up under the chairman of the tender board to 'look into the whole matter of the buying policy of the government.'[25]

The FRI also pushed hard to secure markets for its members. This was a particular reason for its support of the Federation of Rhodesia and Nyasaland, established later in 1953.[26] In 1950, the FRI's Cooke, made clear his intention to create an organisation to promote amalgamation in Central Africa. Together with Southern Rhodesia's former Minister of Agriculture, F. E. Harris, supported in Northern Rhodesia by Roy Welensky (future prime minister of the Federation of Rhodesia and Nyasaland), formed the United Central Africa Association to campaign for the establishment of a British Central African Dominion, beginning with the federation of the two Rhodesias and Nyasaland in cooperation with Belgium and Portugal.[27] Buttressing the need for a wider market, he commented that 'one of the problems facing Rhodesian industry is that the home market is not large enough to allow production on the same scale as in other industrial countries. If a British Central African Dominion were created, however, this problem would disappear.'[28]

Similarly, the Rhodesia Federated Chamber of Commerce suggested a customs union with Northern Rhodesia and Nyasaland and further suggested that 'an assured future for Southern Rhodesia and economic development of Central Africa territories can only be secured by the closest possible unification of the Central African territories.'[29] It called upon the government to implement their undertakings at the Victoria Falls [in reference to negotiations

24 *Ibid.*

25 NAZ F344/39/5/1/50, Federation of Rhodesian Industries: Cabinet Memorandum on Encouragement of Secondary Industry, 8 August 1952.

26 The literature on the establishment of the federation is voluminous. See variously A. Cohen, *The Politics and Economics of Decolonization in Africa: The Failed Experiment of the Central African Federation* (London: I. B. Tauris Publishers, 2017); P. Murphy, '"Government by blackmail": the origins of the Central African Federation reconsidered', in M. Lynn (ed.), *The British Empire in the 1950s: Retreat or Revival?* (London: Palgrave Macmillan, 2005), 53–76.; R. Hyam, 'The geopolitical origins of the Central African Federation: Britain, Rhodesia and South Africa, 1948–1953', *The Historical Journal*, 30, 1 (1987), 145–72; C. Leys and C. Pratt (eds), *A New Deal in Central Africa* (London: Heinemann, 1960); R. Welensky, *Welensky's 4000 Days: The Life and Death of the Federation of Rhodesia and Nyasaland* (London: Collins, 1964).

27 *Rhodesian Recorder*, November 1950.

28 *Ibid.*

29 *Rhodesian Recorder*, April 1950.

for the establishment of the CAF].' On 1 September 1953, Britain proclaimed the CAF, consisting of Southern Rhodesia, Northern Rhodesia, and Nyasaland, which lasted until 31 December 1963. The formation of the Federation added impetus to calls for a clearly defined industrial policy. The FRI led the way in criticising the government's policy and assistance to secondary industries, to which the following section will now turn.

A Continuing Conundrum: Industrial Challenges

As mentioned earlier, the government's policy was that industry should establish itself voluntarily, with government only giving assistance where necessary or if it was in the national interest to do so. Even when the CAF was established in 1953, it more or less adopted the Southern Rhodesian industrial policy, with minor variation in that the roles of the TAC and the industries committee were consolidated into a newly formed industrial development and research branch. Otherwise, the federal government's policy was that industrial development was 'essentially a field of endeavor for private enterprise', while the government's role was to 'provide the basic facilities on which private enterprise can establish industries ...', and not directly participate in industrial undertakings.[30] Despite this elaborate policy, the government did not fulfil its role to the satisfaction of industrialists, as the following analysis demonstrates. The following paragraphs elaborate the numerous challenges confronting secondary industries, for which they demanded government action.

To begin with, secondary industries endured inadequate transportation facilities, especially rail transport. FRI members persistently complained that Rhodesian industry was forging ahead but inadequate railway facilities hampered progress. Rail transport challenges had resulted in the government nationalising the Rhodesia Railways in 1947, but the problem persisted.[31] D. R. Jackson of the Umtali Chamber of Industry highlighted that many industries were being compelled to operate part-time due to the inability of the railways to meet their requirements. He further commented that 'to be self-supporting, Southern Rhodesia needs many more industries but before we can

30 NAZ S482/134/48, Memorandum on Government's Policy towards Assisting Development of Industries in Southern Rhodesia, 25 January 1949. See also NAZ F292/16/3, Industrial Policy 1953–1963: Memorandum on Industrial Policy, 16 October 1957.

31 For the nationalisation of the Rhodesia Railways, see J. Lunn, *Capital and Labour on the Rhodesian Railway System, 1888–1947* (Oxford: Macmillan Press, 1997), 56–76; A. H. Croxton, *Railways of Rhodesia: The Story of the Beira, Mashonaland and Rhodesia Railways* (Newton Abbot: David & Charles, 1973), 199–206; and I. Phimister, *Wangi Kolia: Coal, Capital and Labour in Colonial Zimbabwe, 1894–1954* (Harare: Baobab Books, 1994), 99–100.

reasonably expect new industries to come here, the government must provide the necessary services and [transport] facilities to enable them to operate.'[32]

In response, Sir Arthur Griffin, the general manager of the Rhodesia Railways, highlighted that one of the main difficulties was that of securing trained staff. Moreover, much of the recruitment was done in the UK, and the success of this was being jeopardised by the shortage of housing in the colony.[33] In addition, the country's immigration laws, which provided that any employer wishing to bring overseas immigrants into the country should pay a guarantee fee ranging between £100 and £300 for each immigrant, compounded the problem. However, after repeated requests from organised industry and commerce for the revision of this unwieldy and costly system of immigration guarantees, the government made two concessions. First, all 'employers [were] free to bring into the colony all the labour they need for commercial and industrial expansion.'[34] Second, employers were 'required to pay only a small insurance premium at the rate of 1% per annum.'[35] The government insisted that the 'immigration guarantees were intended not as a brake on the flow of settlers but to indemnify themselves against the expense of possible repatriation of undesirable immigrants.'[36]

Even as the government dealt with Sir Griffin's complaint of the shortage of skilled personnel by amending the immigration laws, the Gwelo and Umtali Chambers of Industry suggested that 'in view of the inability of the railways to handle the available traffic, the government should give consideration to increasing the number of Road Service permits.'[37] However, the deputy prime minister of the Federation at this time, Sir Roy Welensky, justified the continued use of rail over road based on pricing. Urging industrialists to consider the financial implications of such a switch, he stressed that

> railway rates for such commodities as copper, chrome, coal, cement and maize are low and vary over a long distance haul, from a little under one-half penny to slightly under one penny a ton mile. But the rates quoted by Road Transport Operators are over $4^{1/}{}_{3}$d a ton mile each way, that is nearly 10d. a mile for the return trip ... 8d. a mile when the load is carried in one direction only. This is a great difference.[38]

32 *Rhodesian Recorder*, November 1950; March 1951.

33 *Ibid.*; Lunn, *Capital and Labour on the Rhodesian Railway System*, 77–89; and Croxton, *Railways of Rhodesia*, 208–13.

34 *Rhodesian Recorder*, April 1950.

35 *Ibid.*

36 *Ibid.*

37 *Ibid.*, November 1950.

38 FRI, Annual Congress, November 1954, 4.

Trial runs were undertaken, which attempted to carry large quantities of coal from Wankie to the Copperbelt by road.[39] It became apparent that apart from financial difficulties, as highlighted, there were other major setbacks which could not be lightly set aside. 'For one thing, the roads would not stand the traffic, and for another the weight restrictions on roads and some of the bridges would be a huge limiting factor', explained Welensky.[40] To temporarily reduce the burden on the railways, passenger services were transferred to the road transport system, leaving the railways to focus on cargo deliveries. In spite of this effort, the problem persisted to the extent that Muirhead of Rhodesian Plastics Ltd accused the government of deliberately neglecting transportation facilities to the detriment of industry because it still held the view that 'secondary industry has no future in this country' which reasoning, he argued, was 'a complete fallacy'.[41] This allegation was a clear expression of frustration at the government's lack of support. In contrast to Muirhead's claims, Anthony Croxton explains that Rhodesia Railways had actually undertaken 'modernisation schemes' to cope with the post-war boom.[42]

The challenges for secondary industries were further compounded by the lack of capital; the problem was, however, lessened by the government's cooperation. In 1949 the government launched a booklet to attract capital, entitled *Southern Rhodesia: A Field for Investment*. The government targeted the USA for the circulation of the booklet. Still, one industrialist criticised the booklet as inadequate. He noted that

> where it does fall down is in the impression it conveys that the country needs only a couple more factories to achieve industrial self-sufficiency. It compares this country's present state of development with the middle and south-western US and Canada of 50 or 60 years ago. There are enormous opportunities for industrial expansion in this country but instead of indicating the scope of this expansion, the booklet has unwittingly conveyed the opposite impression and then defeated its own object – to attract dollar investment.[43]

In spite of the criticism, the booklet was well received in America.[44]

At the same time, a high number of immigrants brought in capital and skills which benefitted industry. According to the International Bank for

39 For an in-depth analysis into the problems of coal transportation to the Copperbelt, see Phimister, *Wangi Kolia*, 99–100.

40 FRI, Annual Congress, November 1954, 4.

41 *Ibid.*, July 1953, 17.

42 Croxton, *Railways of Rhodesia*, 208–22.

43 *Rhodesian Recorder*, October 1950.

44 See V. M. Gwande, 'Federation, factories, and foreign capital: economic growth in Southern Rhodesia, 1953–1956', *International Journal of African Historical Studies*, 52, 2 (2019), 231–53, at pp. 248–49.

Reconstruction and Development, European immigration brought in capital ranging between £3 million and £6 million yearly between 1949 and 1952.[45] The 1,606 immigrants who entered Southern Rhodesia during February of 1951 declared capital amounting to £461,834 – the highest amount for any one month since January 1949.[46] During 1950, £3,461,084 was declared by 16,245 immigrants as against £4,068,182 by 1,811 immigrants in 1949. Immigration, therefore, was a stimulating factor in industrial growth, particularly because the majority of these immigrants entered the manufacturing sector.

The establishment of the Federation brought considerable foreign capital into the country. Kirkpatrick, a guest at the FRI congress in 1953, highlighted that during the 'past three years we have been instrumental in injecting something like £3 million into Rhodesian industry and most of that money has gone into the newer and smaller concerns. We are extremely interested to see that Rhodesian industry flourishes and continues to flourish.'[47] However, he warned that capital was becoming one of the scarcest commodities due to competition from Canada and Australia which offered long-term possibilities for investment. The other problem was that UK investors homogenised African problems. 'People in the United Kingdom,' Kirkpatrick elaborated,

> hear of a riot in Durban or some trouble further north, they regard that trouble as a part of the trouble in the whole of Africa ... Africa is regarded as one field for investment and unfortunately, these happenings north and south of us are considered most seriously and are the reason why Africa at the moment is not a popular field of investment.[48]

Despite this spectre of instability, Welensky reported an increase in foreign investment. Southern Rhodesia's efforts were aided by the publication of the Federation's policy with regard to US investors. The federal government welcomed external financial support in its economic development, particularly 'private United States dollar investment.'[49] Furthermore, US capital invested in approved enterprises in the Federation could be remitted to the US at any time subsequent to the initial injection of the dollar capital. This policy was a great advertisement by the Federation to other potential investors. Consequently, investment in private enterprises increased from £1.05 million in 1952 to £3.02 million in 1953 and £5 million in 1954.[50] Investment was forecast to reach

45 World Bank, *The Economy and Development Plans of Southern Rhodesia* (Washington, DC: International Bank for Reconstruction and Development, 1952).

46 *Rhodesian Recorder*, June 1951.

47 FRI, *Annual Congress*, July 1953, 35.

48 *Ibid.*

49 NAZ F184/B/218/01, Federal Information Department: Policy in regard to US Investors, 10 September 1954.

50 FRI, *Annual Congress*, November 1954, 8; and Gwande, 'Foreign capital, state and the development of secondary industry', 73–76.

some £20 million by the end of 1954, excluding inflow into the government, the railways, banks, and other official institutions. Indeed, private investment from abroad for the years 1954 and 1959 was about £123 million, much of it provided by British industrialists.[51]

Local industrialists also joined with other interests to push for the formation of a central bank to provide credit finance for local development. 'In view of the importance of the actions of the banking system and their effects upon the development of the colony', suggested the Central Statistics Office, 'control of the powers of the banking system to create credit is essential.'[52] The two banks in the country, Standard Bank and Barclays, were foreign owned.[53] They kept the bulk of their accumulated funds at their headquarters in Britain and South Africa. Just 50% of their assets were held in local business loans, and these were short-term loans that were considered restrictive and undermining industrial growth. According to Patrick Bond, 'the position of many manufacturers was that finance remained the domain of foreigners who either sent hard-earned Southern Rhodesian money to London and Cape Town or who encouraged excessive luxury goods imports'.[54] These grumblings increasingly showed the need for a central banking system to control the credit system. Presenting the colony's budget in parliament in 1948, the Minister of Finance, Edgar Whitehead, stated boldly that 'it is becoming more evident from day to day that the Colony must control its own monetary system. It is essential that the Colony should maintain the levels of the reserves which back our credit system.'[55]

The need for financial regulation resulted in the commissioning of the Bank of England representative, H. C. B. Mynors, to look into the question of the central bank.[56] Mynors advised against the setting up of a central bank because 'the economy and finance of Southern Rhodesia are so dependent upon external influences that they could not be directed to any extent through

51 G. Rennie, 'Federation: an appraisal', *Investment: British Investment and Industry in Central Africa, Quarterly Review* (1960).

52 As quoted in P. Bond, *Uneven Zimbabwe: A Study of Finance, Development and Underdevelopment* (Trenton, NJ: Africa World Press, 1998), 64.

53 For a *longue durée* examination of the development of the financial and banking system in Southern Rhodesia, see T. Nyamunda, 'Financing rebellion: the Rhodesian state, financial policy and exchange control, 1962–1979' (PhD, University of the Free State, 2015), 24–29.

54 Bond, *Uneven Zimbabwe*, 64.

55 Legislative Assembly Debates, 18 May 1948, Col. 112; and see also Nyamunda, 'Financing rebellion', 38.

56 NAZ S2225/4, Southern Rhodesia: Report on the Question of a Central Bank, January 1949.

the mechanism of a Central Bank'.[57] Southern Rhodesia accepted the advice.[58] Demands for monetary regulation and a central bank continued, however. Industrialists and merchants led the campaign. As Admire Mseba noted: 'Rhodesian industrialists continued to complain that the absence of central bank greatly aggravated capital shortages and seriously retarded the general development of the country'.[59] By 1952, the Southern Rhodesian government warmed up once more to the establishment of a central bank. The creation of the CAF in 1953 and its potential to expand the economy added an impetus to the calls for the Reserve Bank, as it rendered untenable the earlier argument that 'the colony's economy was too small to require the services of a central bank'. Indeed, the CAF established the Central Bank of Rhodesia and Nyasaland in 1956.[60] It is apparent from the creation of the central bank that it 'was set up against the background of continued complaints by industrial and commercial sectors, and by an enlarged economic entity created by the formation of the Federation'.[61]

Industrialists and the government carried out more campaigns to lure in capital, especially from British sources. 'For some time ... [there has been a] need to stimulate British interest in industrial opportunities in Rhodesia, particularly as far as secondary industries and manufacturing are concerned', explained C. J. Hatty.[62] British investment was preferred because it was a way of maintaining ties and showing loyalty to 'home'. In a memorandum to the Cabinet, the Federal Ministry of Commerce and Industry noted Southern Rhodesia's campaigns in the UK to attract investment for industrial expansion.[63] In conjunction with its industrialists, the Southern Rhodesian government engaged the federal trade commissioner in London to approach industrialists in the UK to consider expanding to Southern Rhodesia.

57 *Ibid.*

58 See NAZ S2225/4, Memorandum by the Minister of Finance on H. C. B. Mynors' Report on the Question of a Central Bank, 2 March 1949; and A. Mseba, 'Money and finance in a closed economy: Rhodesia's monetary experience, 1965–1980' (MA, University of Zimbabwe, 2007), 138.

59 Mseba, 'Money and autonomy in a settler colony', 139.

60 For a detailed discussion on the formation of the central bank, see *ibid.*; and Nyamunda, 'Financing rebellion', 38–49.

61 Mseba, 'Money and autonomy in a settler colony', 139.

62 NAZ S3269/34/30, Industrial Booklet: Distribution of Industrial Booklet, 15 December 1955. For information on inflows of capital, see Gwande, 'Federation, factories, and foreign capital: economic growth in Southern Rhodesia'; Stoneman, 'Foreign capital and the prospects for Zimbabwe'; and Bond, *Uneven Zimbabwe*, 73–75.

63 NAZ F292/16/2, Memorandum for Cabinet on Industrial Development by the Minister of Commerce and Industry, 26 August 1955.

The trade commissioner met with the Federation of British Industries (FBI), whose reaction was not, however, encouraging. British industrialists were not easily attracted to expanding their operations in other parts of the Commonwealth, because

> The business offering to United Kingdom industrialists at home and abroad is, in the main, sufficient to absorb their full time energies. There is over employment and yet much to be done to modernise the home industries without thinking of expansion abroad. Many industrialists have experienced bitter disappointments at changes in government policies abroad. They are, therefore, more cautious about accepting promises which might be short-lived. Industrialists are more conscious of the trend towards nationalism in multi-racial communities than possibly ever before.[64]

What also became apparent from the engagement was the lack of information about the Southern Rhodesian government's policy on industrial development.

The federal trade commissioner's observations on the government's industrial policy were indeed correct. Industrialists had consistently and persistently called out the government for the absence of a definitive policy. Contributing to a motion on industrial policy moved by the Salisbury Chamber of Industries (SCI) during the FRI congress in 1953, one industrialist, Poole, exuded the anger and dissatisfaction of industrialists over government industrial policy. He lamented:

> we have lost confidence in any suggestion that the government as a whole, the Cabinet as a whole, appreciates the necessity of the vital part that industry plays, and the necessity for government help in matters of major planning and policy. In the absence of a clearly defined industrial policy, we can only conclude that there is not one ... It is not sufficient merely to quote the statistics of industrial production, compare them with statistics of production of ten years ago and say that we have a successful industrial policy. That is a fallacy.[65]

All twelve contributions made on this resolution concurred with Poole's view, though some qualified their support. L. S. Davies of the Bulawayo Chamber cautioned that the impassioned pleas made for government assistance created a misleading impression that industrialists were like a 'very small child appealing for assistance', yet 'we have become a most lusty child, perhaps in the adolescent stage, and that all we are asking is for a little assistance at high levels which will help to launch us in to manhood'.[66] Nonetheless, the attack on general industrial policy was unanimous. Against the backdrop of this criticism, the FRI urged the federal government to 'recognize in planning

64 *Ibid.*
65 FRI, Annual Congress, July 1953, 8.
66 FRI, Annual Congress, July 1953, 24.

its overall economic policy, the vital part which secondary industry must play in the creation of national wealth and prosperity and to establish and maintain conditions necessary for the continuous expansion of industrial activity.'[67] Others complained of the government's eagerness to accept advice from non-industrialists, who 'tell us how to run our own business having never run one themselves.'[68] The advice referred to here concerned the suggestion that Southern Rhodesia could only encourage and develop those industries which used local raw materials, and not those that needed imported ones. For these industrialists, trying to win the government's support when it readily accepted such advice, as indicated above, was a 'ridiculous waste of time.' [69]

In particular, industrialists wanted an industrial policy that guaranteed protection of secondary industries. They argued that the government gave protection on a selective basis, and that this was inadequate, advancing numerous examples and analogies to demonstrate their case. For instance, the steel industry of Southern Rhodesia complained of competition from the Union. It stated: 'the 25% drop in the sales of the Colony's steel industry was due to unfair competition from the Union.'[70] Consequently, the FRI proposed the adoption of 'a tariff which, allied with control of imports, will afford as much assistance to the development of industries [just] as the similar policy of the Union of South Africa [tariff protection] has afforded to the development of industries in the Union.'[71] Making a case for tariff protection, Poole, for example, also argued that

> our attitude towards world trade seems to me to be odd. We have been told that we must not develop industries which depend on protection for their success, which implies, presumably that any industry locally must be able, without any form of protection whatsoever, to stand on its own feet in the world markets. That I believe is completely useless and futile theory. It is impossible to quote any country in the world, which has managed to survive with an industrial economy based on free trade.[72]

For industrialists, the refusal to grant protection created an impression that the government and other interests did not want 'small industries' in the country because they would demand a measure of protection and were infant industries. Citing the examples of the USA and the UK, one industrialist queried if the government appreciated that '92% of the industries in the UK and a very similar figure in the USA, consist of small concerns employing

67 *Ibid.*, 7.
68 *Ibid.*, July 1953, 9.
69 *Ibid.*, 10.
70 *Rhodesia Herald*, 8 July 1953.
71 FRI, *Annual Congress*, July 1953, 19.
72 *Ibid.*, 9.

under 250 employees [and were] the backbone of industry [there]'.[73] Several of the contributions made during this debate supported the demand for protection. Indeed, the clamour by industrialists was justified, since a protected basic home market was a springboard from which local industries could develop.

Others also questioned the wisdom of joining GATT, given that the country's industrialisation was at such an early stage. In the words of A. E. Abrahamson,

> we are unfortunately placed in the situation where we are a signatory to GATT and I think it is a most unfortunate situation that at such an early stage of our development we should have limitations placed on us as to the extent of tariff protection that we can afford to our various industries. It seems ludicrous in a way that some of the greatest sponsors of GATT are countries which have developed their economies by methods of out and out protection and now that they have developed to the stage where they must trade with the rest of the world, are in the forefront, adopting a big brother attitude to so-called under-developed countries by trying to limit the ability of these countries to protect their own secondary industries.[74]

Responding to this criticism, N. R. Bertram, the Secretary for Commerce and Industry, clarified that by joining GATT the country would derive substantial benefits in the long term. GATT operated on the principle that 'any reduction in Customs tariffs which is obtained by one country in negotiating with another automatically applies to all members of GATT and not to the one party, so to the extent that other countries have achieved reduced tariffs, we benefit'.[75] Due to these anticipated benefits, it was critical that Rhodesian industrialists accepted the GATT. At the FRI congress in 1954, a motion on customs tariffs was tabled once more, wherein the congress 'urged the government to recognize that in a world of managed economies it is folly to imagine that the Federation can make any progress without some form of protection for secondary industry'.[76] Broadly, the same arguments were repeated with minor amendments and additions in subsequent annual congresses and other fora.[77]

Alongside the perpetual debate over the industrial policy and protection, the FRI suggested other forms of assistance and incentives for the expansion of the secondary industries. For instance, they proposed a change in the taxation of companies in the 1950s. Bulawayo industrialists wanted a reduction in company tax from 8s 3d to 5s, in the hope that 'it [would] assist in the formulation of a taxation policy that [would] assist rather than hinder the development

73 *Ibid.*, 20.
74 FRI, *Annual Congress*, July 1953, 22.
75 *Ibid.*, 49.
76 FRI, *Annual Congress*, November 1954, 67.
77 See FRI, *Annual Congress*, October 1955, 60–92.

of industry in the colony'.[78] They further pointed out that the tax that was obtained, made up of income tax of 7s 6d and a gold industry contribution of 9d, with an additional tax on undistributed profits, was only 9d less than in Britain, which was 'a highly socialized state supporting extensive welfare schemes'.[79] This was also compared with South African tax, which comprised 4s plus a provincial rate of 9d (though this differed according to province), which they deemed relatively low.

Industry drew these parallels to demonstrate that Rhodesian business were highly taxed, to its disadvantage. Industrialists, thus, commented that 'the disparity tends to make the Union, on grounds of taxation, more desirable for expansion by the setting up of satellite companies. Companies with interests in both countries may even be tempted to show the greater part of their profits as arising in the Union'.[80] Consequently, they lamented the obtaining of taxation as 'hopelessly wrong, immoral, ill-considered, academic, ponderous, and [with] no logical basis or sequence'.[81] One industrialist gave an analogy to demonstrate his frustrations with the tax system:

> laziness is tax-free, stay in bed long enough, loaf, and introduce a few more tea breaks and your output and profit will be so low that you are untaxable. Speed up, work harder, and better, and your production costs will be lower, your sales will increase, your efficiency will produce a profit and you are damned. Tax assessment is on its way.[82]

The import of this was that Southern Rhodesia punished hard work through onerous taxation.

Organised secondary industry also suggested adjustments to the cost of the raw materials needed by the manufacturing sector. The FRI blamed government for the existing pricing structure because of its actions, which favoured primary producers. While the government could assist primary producers, 'it should not just subsidize primary industries to the pitch where secondary industry cannot use the products of that primary industry. If a primary product cannot be produced economically then I maintain that it should not be produced at all, unless for strategic reasons', considerately argued Hughes in 1953.[83] This matter once more generated a lengthy debate at the FRI's 1954 congress. In his contribution to the motion, Hatty submitted that

> when world prices of certain commodities are fairly high, the products in this country produced here seem to be pitched at the world price and the

78 *Rhodesian Recorder*, July 1950.
79 *Ibid.*
80 *Ibid.*
81 FRI, *Annual Congress*, July 1953, 38.
82 *Ibid.*
83 FRI, *Annual Congress*, July 1953, 15.

> argument is always adduced: 'well, if it will fetch that in the world market it should fetch that locally.' It is a curious thing that when world prices of a particular prime commodity are fairly low, then of course we don't get the price of that same commodity locally very low, but we are then told about the problem of the primary producer in producing it here.[84]

Industrialists were lamenting the policy, which favoured primary producers. For them, it was illogical and futile to rely on primary exports sold in world markets at prices determined by factors beyond the country's control. Instead, it would have been ideal to make affordable the primary products on which secondary industry and possibly tertiary industries were to be based. The overall point was that local industries could process local raw materials but were hampered from doing so by the inhibiting cost structure of these primary products.

Indeed, manufacturers felt the impact of the costly primary products. The case of steel was illustrative of this: 'one steel-consuming business left the country … as a result of giving a high price to primary producer'.[85] In addition to hampering the progress of industrial development, this dynamic had a ripple effect. For instance, it resulted in a loss of employment in secondary industries using steel, a loss of tax on the individual earnings of people employed in the industry, a loss of the confidence of the investing public in any industry consuming steel, and a loss of the skilled immigrants who would have come in to work in these industries. Even more worrying was that it encouraged competition from the Union, a development that placed local manufacturing industries in a very unfavourable position. Such was the net result of pursuing a policy of high prices for the primary producer without due consideration for the secondary manufacturing industry. To this extent, the policy was a complete failure.

In response, the government assured industrialists that they were looking into the matter. Ellman-Brown, the government representative, explained that the government had appointed a steel expert as the general manager and that a new board was put in place after the recommendation from the Commission of Inquiry into the Iron and Steel Industry.[86] He pleaded for patience to 'allow the new board and new staff to stabilize, if not, turn around things'.[87] This subject also revealed the envious attitude of industrialists towards the primary industries, which they viewed as the most favoured sectors. Overall, these exchanges demonstrate the perpetual contestations between the government

84 *Ibid.*, November 1954, 12.

85 *Ibid.*

86 For more information, see Government of Southern Rhodesia, *Report of Commission of Inquiry into the Operations of RISCOM* (Salisbury: Government Printers, 1954).

87 FRI, *Annual Congress*, November 1954, 28.

and industrialists over secondary industry and the frustrations of industrialists in relation to this.

Apart from the challenge of raw materials, secondary industries persistently faced acute shortages of skilled labour. Industrialists believed the answer lay in immigration, hence at their 1953 annual congress they stressed the need to 'foster and encourage large-scale selective immigration of Europeans'.[88] The source target of immigrants was of course Britain. Debating the motion, Abrahamson emphasised that 'the importation of human material should be made as free as possible' and deplored 'any closed shop policy'.[89] He further argued that 'immigration will bring into this part of the world men of ingenuity, men with capital, who will start new ventures to fill the gaps in the productivity of the country, in industry and in all creative endeavor. That is the only way to build the country'.[90] For him, the restrictive or selective policy was likely to deprive the country of White immigrants. Abrahamson's point was consistent with earlier averments on the importance of immigration to the country.

Partly due to the lobbying by industrialists, and partly on its own initiative, the government enacted new immigration laws setting out the selection criteria for immigrants: the Immigration Act (1954) and the Immigration (Selection) Regulations (1954).[91] The criteria included, *inter alia*, that the immigrant '[has] good character, good health, possess[es] capital or income in an amount deemed sufficient by the [selection] Board, has qualifications, education, training or experience likely to render him efficient in the occupation he intends to undertake in the Federation'.[92] In a way, the new immigration laws allowed for the admission of the industry-specific immigrant. Of the 10,700 European immigrants entering the Federation for employment in mining, agriculture, and the manufacturing industry between November 1954 and August 1957, a substantial proportion totalling approximately 7,000 entered the manufacturing industry.[93] These immigrants would have indicated in their application to the selection board the occupation they intended to undertake, hence the huge number that entered manufacturing preferred that sector.

Even as the government made these manoeuvres, its industrial policy came up for discussion again at the 1954 FRI annual congress. Hubert Ponter, the outgoing president of the SCI, complained that the industrial policy of Southern Rhodesia was now unquestionably outmoded and inadequate. 'This policy which has been officially described as the principle of giving assistance where assistance is needed and for as long as it is necessary in the national

88 FRI, *Annual Congress*, July 1953, 41.

89 *Ibid.*

90 *Ibid.*, 42.

91 *Federal Government Notice No. 493*, 22 October 1954.

92 *Ibid.*

93 NAZ F292/16/3, Industry Policy: Association of Rhodesian and Nyasaland Industries – Industrial Charter, undated.

interest, is clearly incompatible with the present and future requirements,' he said.[94] He added:

> beyond certain concessions in the rebate of customs duties to manufacturers, there is but little evidence of positive encouragement to the industries which are making such a vital contribution to the country's economy by the creation of wealth, the maintenance of employment – both European and African – and the expansion of exports.[95]

Consequently, he pleaded for a 'clear appreciation of industry's potentialities coupled with the ability and the will to create conditions in the Federal state which will inspire confidence both in the minds of our own people and in those countries with capital funds for investment.'[96] In addition, the industrialists were infuriated by the absenteeism of the government ministers and officials at their congress, despite an invitation having been sent, which they viewed as a 'sign of lack of co-operation in the Federation.'[97] All that industrialists wanted was a satisfactory and sympathetic industrial policy under which to develop their own businesses. As such, a 'protective' trade agreement with South Africa was seen to be crucial to industrial expansion. We turn to this subject in the next discussion.

Renegotiating the Trade Agreement with South Africa

While the 1948 Customs Union Agreement had initially proved a good stimulus, industrialists from both sides began raising concerns about it. Complaints initially emerged from South Africa. The Transvaal Chamber of Industries complained that certain sections of the agreement were harmful to the Union's manufacturing industry due to the inequitable and economically unsound conditions brought about by the import control.[98] As a result, the Chamber urged the government to take immediate steps to remove the resulting disadvantages, which were jeopardising the continuance of established industries in the Union. According to the Chamber, the clothing industry was hit the hardest by the alleged inequitable competition of the Rhodesian industry. The National Textile Manufacturer's Association of South Africa also weighed in on the matter.[99] This is not surprising, as trade statistics showed

94 *Rhodesian Recorder*, March 1954.
95 *Ibid.*
96 *Ibid.*
97 FRI, *Annual Congress*, November 1954, 80.
98 *Rand Daily Mail*, 30 September 1949.
99 NASA-P HEN Vol. 3907 Ref. 710/1 Vol. 16, Memorandum on the Effects of the Customs Union (Interim) Agreement between the Union of South Africa and Southern Rhodesia on the Textile Industry of the Union of South Africa, 8 July 1953.

that Southern Rhodesian clothing and textile exports more than doubled in the aftermath of the agreement. Recognising this, the Union industrialists were justified in seeking the extension of import control measures to Rhodesia as well as revising the existing tariff system. [100] J. N. Theron, Undersecretary for Commerce and Industries in the Union, however, clarified that the agreement was not merely and purely a trade and economic issue. Rather, the agreement was also 'a matter of major political policy involving the Union's relations with an important Government next door'.[101]

Naturally, these Union protests triggered a reaction from Southern Rhodesian industrialists, who denied that the colony's exports were affecting the Union's garment industry to 'anything like the extent believed'.[102] Instead, they countered that South African goods had always entered Rhodesia and competed with local factories, but they never complained about unfair trading from the Union.[103] The FRI secretary blamed the Union industrialists for causing the competition which they now complained of:

> Personally I have aided more than one [Union company] to open up in the Colony and I have considered it part of our policy to increase, no matter from what quarter it comes, the productive capacity of Rhodesian industry. We are pleased to welcome them and we hope they will long continue with us. These factories are setting up in Bulawayo and more plan to come and they are making clothing, which is being sent down to South Africa. This is greatly to the benefit of Rhodesia and it is adding material to our exports, which are so badly needed. *On what grounds therefore, can the Union manufacturers complain about our increasing exports if they themselves-by their own influx-are largely responsible for the increase?*[104]

For Rhodesian industrialists, their Union counterparts needed not to complain because they contributed to the competition.

If anything, argued the FRI, it was the Rhodesian industrialists' complaints that were warranted because three-quarters of the imports from South Africa entered Southern Rhodesia duty free, while the remaining quarter were admitted at duties considerably lower than the most preferential rates contained in the tariff book. The FRI maintained that the 1948 agreement 'has not only reduced the protective element for Rhodesian industry to insignificance, but has also put the colony in a position where any prospective new class of industry must face completely duty-free competition from South

100 *Rand Daily Mail*, 30 September 1949.
101 *Ibid.*
102 *Rhodesian Recorder*, December 1949.
103 *Ibid.*
104 *Ibid.*, March 1950.

Africa.'[105] Complaints continued at successive gatherings of industrialists. In his presidential address at the FRI annual congress in Bulawayo in 1953, G. A. D. Roberts stated that 'Rhodesian industrialists had completely lost confidence in the ideals of the Customs Union Agreement with South Africa because of South Africa "bypassing" many of its most important objects.'[106] Part of the object of the agreement was to regulate the flow of goods and trade between the parties on a basis of fair and unsubsidised competition. The agreement also provided for Southern Rhodesia's development on a sound economic footing.

However, for FRI, these ideals were, for the most part, by-passed, and this was *ultra vires* the stated purpose of the agreement. In particular, the gravest concern was the Union government's 'complete failure to implement one important article of the agreement – the definition of manufacture – and the result has been a complete loss of confidence in the principle or idea of the Customs Union Agreement.'[107] The FRI vice president, A. H. V. Muirhead, questioned the validity of the customs union. Explaining the very strong feelings held by Rhodesian industrialists about the operation of the agreement, he said, 'in fact, I will go so far as to say that I am not sure that the agreement is in effect a valid operative agreement today, for part of the agreement has never been ratified and brought into operation by the Union Government.'[108] As a result, Rhodesian industrialists recommended that the government should not renew the agreement unless they received a 'similar measure of protection for their industries within the Federal area to that enjoyed by their competitors in the Union.'[109] Although the criticism was aimed at the agreement, it was also a manifestation of the FRI's dissatisfaction over the government's laxity in the implementation of the agreement.

Against this backdrop, the FRI called for the renegotiation of a new trade agreement. In any case, the 1948 agreement was nearing its five-year lapse period. Further, the Federation of Rhodesia and Nyasaland was bound to impact on regional trade, which warranted another look at trading arrangements. The FRI cautioned that 'quite obviously we do need and we must always have neighbourly and brotherly relations with our southern neighbours, but ... we must ensure that in any future negotiation, tariffs or customs union agreements, Rhodesian and Central African interests must be placed in the forefront, for they are virtually the only interests which count.'[110] Furthermore,

105 NAZ F292/14/9/1, Federation of Rhodesian Industries: Memorandum on the Significance of the Federation's Trade Negotiations with South Africa by P. C. Aldridge, 21 October 1954; and also Cole, 'The tariff policy of Rhodesia', 37–39.

106 *Rhodesian Herald*, 9 July 1953; See also *Cape Times*, 9 July 1953; *The Star*, 9 July 1953; and FRI, *Annual Congress* July 1953: Presidential Address, 5.

107 FRI, *Annual Congress*, July 1953: Presidential Address, 5.

108 *Rhodesia Herald*, 10 July 1953.

109 *Ibid.*

110 FRI, *Annual Congress*, July 1953, 23.

it emphasised that any future agreements, while they might be in a spirit of mutual trade, must include provisions to ensure that trade and industry would be carried out on a fair and equitable basis. The government also needed to be wary that agreements were not an end in themselves but were also subject to interpretation and implementation.[111] As such, the government needed to be aggressive regarding the last two. Even a government official agreed, but for different reasons to those of industrialists, that the customs agreement should be discontinued. In response to the demands for the non-renewal of the customs agreement with the Union, Bertram said that 'the existing agreement cannot continue if for no other reason than that it is an agreement one of the parties to which is no longer competent to operate such an agreement. Southern Rhodesia will lose her right to deal with external trade matters for the Federal government.'[112]

In negotiating the trade agreement, some factors needed consideration. For instance, the realignment of the federal tariff was imperative, given the different stages of development in the three federal territories. In the first instance, a tariff is a means of raising revenue for an importing country. Bearing this in mind, Nyasaland, for instance, was entirely an importing country; it was producing raw materials for exports, hence its whole tariff structure was based on raising revenue on certain types of imports in order to pay for the needs of its central government.[113] The situation was different for Northern Rhodesia, and more so for Southern Rhodesia, which had advanced industrially and needed protection for its local industries. So any commission or body that was tasked with negotiating tariff policy and trade relations needed to address the imperative of raising revenue and protecting local industries while also considering Nyasaland's needs.

A Federal Fiscal Commission, formed in 1953, looked into this matter. It then recommended, *inter alia*, that 'a Customs Union should be created between the three territories within one year from the inception of Federation with complete freedom of trade throughout the Federal area in regard to products originating in the three territories. On external goods, there should be a unified general tariff.'[114] Indeed, a uniform tariff among the three federal territories was adopted at the inception of the Federation. More importantly for Southern Rhodesia, the arrangement presented an opportunity to displace South Africa as Northern Rhodesia and Nyasaland's main supplier of manufactured goods. Prior to 1953, both Southern Rhodesia and South Africa exported duty free to the two northern territories, but after the 1955 trade agreement, only Southern Rhodesia could do so. Furthermore, with the new uniform tariff,

111 *Ibid.*
112 *Ibid.*, 46.
113 *Ibid.*, 23.
114 NAZ MS 1199 AEA18/14, South Africa, 1953–1961, Trade Agreements with South Africa, undated, 39.

Southern Rhodesian products became more attractive compared to South African products, which were dutiable.[115] The creation of the Federation of the two Rhodesias and Nyasaland expanded Southern Rhodesia's domestic market, as evidenced by the fact that by 1956 about four-fifths of the manufactured products in the Federation came from Southern Rhodesia.[116]

Another factor to be considered was the Federation's policy of imperial preference. Imperial preference obligated Rhodesians to prioritise Britain and the Commonwealth countries in business transactions, irrespective of the costs. For industrialists, this was a constraint which prevented them from conducting business in the best market and, therefore, a big hindrance to local industries. In this respect, they questioned how this practice was of benefit to industries. Yet, imperial preference was the cornerstone of Southern Rhodesia's most important export – tobacco. Britain was the biggest buyer of Rhodesia's tobacco. Tampering with imperial preference would therefore have adverse implications on tobacco producers, especially in view of the improvement in the UK's dollar situation since the mid-1950s. It became clear to growers that dollar import restrictions could not be sustained in the circumstances. Sooner or later, federal tobacco would have to compete with American and Canadian leaf on its merits, with the imperial preference as the only slight advantage.[117] By virtue of the tobacco industry's strong dependence on the imperial preference, growers would oppose any modifications to the practice. This is particularly so because tobacco growers, through their representative organisation, the Rhodesia Tobacco Association (RTA), were powerful, commanded the government's attention, and were a strong political constituency.[118] Inherent in the imperial preference was also the political relationship between London and Salisbury. On a balance of probabilities, industry was on a wild goose chase.

After lengthy negotiations, in 1955 the Federation and South Africa agreed to a new trade agreement, which replaced the 1948 one. Applying to all three territories of the Federation, the agreement provided, *inter alia*, for

> duty free entry into the Union for 78 Federal items and for a further 91 items if more than 75% of the factory cost accrues in the Federation. If this 75% cannot be obtained, then the items benefit by a considerable reduction

115 Cole, 'The tariff policy of Rhodesia', 37–43.

116 The World Bank, Report No. 6349-ZIM, *Zimbabwe: An Industrial Sector Memorandum*, 4.

117 See S. Ncube, 'Colonial Zimbabwe's tobacco industry: global, regional and local relations, 1947–1979' (PhD, University of the Free State, 2018), 64–70.

118 For more information, see McKenzie, 'Colonial farmers in the governmental system of Colonial Zimbabwe, 1963–1980' (PhD, University of Zimbabwe, 1989); D. J. Murray, *The Governmental System in Southern Rhodesia* (Oxford: Clarendon Press, 1970); and Ncube, 'Colonial Zimbabwe's tobacco industry'.

in the Union's most favoured nation rate, such reduction varying with the percentage added to the factory cost by Federal manufacture.[119]

On the other hand, South Africa was given 'duty free entry on only one tariff item, but [got] preference over all countries except the United Kingdom in all but 39 tariff classifications and further preferences over the United Kingdom in respect of 120 items.'[120] The agreement also granted imperial preference to South Africa. This provision would become one of the reasons advanced by the Federation interest groups to terminate the 1955 trade agreement. Even as these agreements were inked, industrialists persisted with other demands. The following section addresses this.

Relentless Demands, 1955–1957

Meanwhile, in 1955 the federal government yet again stated its trade and industrial policy. The trade and industrial policy of the Federation was embodied in its customs tariff. The general principles behind the tariff were the 'honouring of its existing obligations; the maintenance of an Imperial Preference system with the most favoured nation treatment to members of GATT.'[121] Also embodied in the tariff were the provisions that capital equipment of any nature should be permitted entry into the Federation duty free, subject to the reservation of imperial preference. Raw materials for industry entered free too, except if they were coming from within the Federation, in which case duties charged were of such an order as to not raise the cost of the final product. The government memorandum conceded that industries deserved partial protection. 'Industries should not receive high protection,' explained the memorandum, but the government 'feels that such young industries should not be open to the full blast of abnormal or unfair competition from other countries.'[122]

It was on the basis of that policy that the government granted protection to the Rhodesian Jute Industries of Umtali. Parliament established a select committee in 1956 to look into the position of a customs duty and possible government subsidy on hessian.[123] The company was suffering high duties on its imports from Pakistan and India. As a result, the company product

119 NAZ MS 1199 AEA18/14, South Africa, 1953–1961, South Africa Federated Chamber of Industries, Memorandum on the 1955 Trade Agreement between the Governments of the Union and of the Federation of Rhodesia and Nyasaland, undated. For a greater discussion on the federal tariff structure, see Cole, 'The tariff policy of Rhodesia,' 37–43.

120 *Ibid.*

121 NAZ F292/14/9/1, Industrial Policy Part 2, Trade and Industrial Policy: The Federation of Rhodesia and Nyasaland, 19 April 1955.

122 *Ibid.*

123 Legislative Assembly Debates, 21 March 1956, Col. 2724.

was uncompetitive and almost sank.[124] After some lengthy investigations, the committee recommended that the hessian be protected, and parliament approved this.[125] Leaving the company unprotected had negative ramifications for Umtali. The jute industry had one of the largest factories in the city. It provided livelihoods to about 400 Europeans. The company employed about eighty specialists drawn from Lancashire in the UK. Around 1,700 Africans were also dependent on the factory. The closure of this factory would hit these people hard. The government responded to the plea of Rhodesian Jute Industries because it was one of those cases where it was necessary and in the national interest to give it assistance. It could also be that the government succumbed to the powerful lobbying of the RTA: the colony's tobacco industry was a major consumer of hessian. This matter was an exception, however; in other cases, the government often left industrialists to paddle their own canoe.

The FRI continued to demand assistance from the Southern Rhodesian territorial government. The Southern Rhodesian government succumbed to the industrialists' pressure and escalated the matter to the federal government, which resulted in the appointment of a Cabinet working party in 1956.[126] The federal prime minister, Godfrey Huggins, set up the working party to examine, report, and recommend to the Cabinet the incentives and the structure for industrial development. As it commenced its work, the working party noted the 'absence of a defined policy in regard to tariff assistance', and thus remarked that 'tariff assistance is the most obvious instrument of industrial policy and we consider that in order to remove uncertainty and promote confidence for future investment in the Federation, government's view on tariff assistance should be formulated'.[127]

The demands by the Southern Rhodesian government and the recommendations by the Cabinet working party are worth enumerating. The Southern Rhodesian government claimed that the lack of sufficient local skills and capital made it necessary for the Federation to 'import' new industries; otherwise, the country would lose out if it did not take advantage of the existing opportunity afforded by the interest in the Federation. Furthermore, the two memoranda made frequent reference to efforts in other countries to encourage the establishment of industries, urging the Federation to enter into competition and bid for industries by offering incentives. The working party objected by arguing that 'industrialisation is a continuing process and ... government policy should not be conditioned by an attitude that certain firms must be attracted here

124 *Ibid.*

125 Mlambo and Phimister, 'Partly protected', 159, offer a different account of the Rhodesian jute industry, stating that the sector remained unprotected and actually protested against any relaxation of import controls on cloth.

126 NAZ F292/14/9/1, Industrial Policy Part 2, Report of the Cabinet Working Party of Officials on Incentives and the Structure for Industrial Development, August 1956.

127 *Ibid.*

now or else the opportunity of similar development will be lost forever'.[128] It added that 'every country presents different circumstances and government incentives are only one of the competitive factors influencing an investor'.[129]

The Southern Rhodesia government also desired 'dispersion of industry', which was interpreted to mean 'the encouragement of industry to establish itself in those parts of the Federation where demands on services, particularly municipal, can most easily be met'.[130] Responding to this expectation, the officials pointed out the dangers of using government intervention to achieve such an end, especially in the case of the federal government. For them,

> the danger of exposing government to charges/accusations that one territory or part of one territory [was] being developed at the expense of others [was] real. Nor [was] it desirable that territorial governments, by competing with each other should introduce an artificial factor leading industries to locations where, on economic considerations solely, they would not otherwise establish themselves.[131]

Instead, the working party held that the government's responsibility was to make information fully available to industrialists on the industrial conditions in each centre of the Federation and let them decide where best to set their enterprise.[132] However, this highlighted that it was not averse to competition between municipalities to attract industries.

The working party further recommended that there be no tax exemptions as a means of encouraging the establishment of new industries and no acceleration of wear and tear allowances on new plant and machinery; the existing allowances were considered adequate, and no provisions of capital or loans by any government, federal or territorial, were to afford local industry any preference over and above the existing one. Industrialists also sought the creation of an Industrial Development Corporation (IDC), bureau of standards, information bureau, and board of trade, but the working party dismissed these requests. The overall conclusion drawn from these recommendations was that the 'government should be selective in the encouragement it gives to industry and should consider in each case first the public interest in policy aspects and secondly the industrial or commercial interests involved'.[133] The federal government adopted wholesale the working party's recommendations.

Despite the crushing working party report, the FRI did not give up in its pursuit. Addressing fellow members during the final congress of the FRI in

128 *Ibid.*
129 *Ibid.*
130 *Ibid.*
131 *Ibid.*
132 *Ibid.*
133 *Ibid.*

1957, President Hubert Ponter called for the restructuring of the government machinery:

> We want to see an overhaul of the existing government machinery dealing with trade and industry and with tariffs in particular ... I cannot see why an independent Board of Trade, for which we have appealed for many years, cannot be established. [134]

Similar calls had been made at earlier congresses when industrialists demanded an industrial charter in the form of a board of trade and industry and the replacement of the TAC with a broader, more authoritative body to handle, on a wider plane, issues which affect trade and industry.[135] Bertram concurred with Ponter that it was desirable to set up a legally constituted board of trade and industries, the same as South Africa's one, to advise the government on matters pertaining to operation and development of industry.[136] Despite these pleas, the government did not heed industry's demands.

During the same 1957 congress, the FRI voiced its misgivings at the terms of the 1955 trade agreement with South Africa.[137] While acknowledging the importance of trading with South Africa and other countries, Ponter bemoaned the fact that the trade deal agreed was not best suited for Southern Rhodesia. He blamed the arrogance of federal negotiators which had 'led to the outwitting of the Federation during negotiation of the South African Trade Agreement'.[138] Unlike their South African counterparts, who consulted with South African industrialists, the official federal negotiators rejected 'outside advice' during the talks. Ponter was disappointed that the Federation, 'a young country in which everything depended on economic health and development, allowed large quantities of manufactured goods to enter to the detriment of its own industries'.[139] ACCORN also expressed dismay at the impact of the agreement on the federal economy. Like the FRI, those involved in commerce decried the fact that they 'had little opportunity of influencing the course of negotiations because such negotiations were conducted by government officials on the basis of the new tariff for the Federation which, at that stage, had not been published'.[140]

134 *Rhodesian Recorder*, August 1957.

135 FRI, Annual Congress, November 1954: Presidential Address, 20.

136 *Rhodesian Recorder*, August 1957.

137 *Ibid*. For a South African view of this agreement, see G. F. D. Palmer, 'A note on the trade agreement between the union and the Federation of Rhodesia', *South African Journal of Economics*, 23, 3 (1955), 203–12.

138 *Rhodesian Recorder*, August 1957.

139 *Ibid*.

140 NAZ MS 1199 AEA18/14, South Africa, 1953–1961, Associated Chambers of Commerce Rhodesia and Nyasaland, Memorandum on the South African Agreement, 10 October 1958.

In terms of the agreement's impact on, for instance, the textile industry, the trade statistics are revealing. 'Our textile industry ... which was beginning to obtain the greatest foothold in the Union market prior to the agreement, is subjected to severe restrictions which do not apply in reverse direction', complained Rhodesia's Chambers of Commerce and Industry.[141] Whereas exports of cotton piece goods and clothing from the Federation to the Union in 1954 amounted to some £2.4 million, this dropped to £1.8 million by 1957. Conversely, exports in this period from the Union to the Federation increased from £5.8 million in 1954 to over £7 million in 1957. Similar restrictions were noticeable in the cigarette and tobacco trade. Whereas in 1955 the Union purchased over £2 million worth of Rhodesian unmanufactured tobacco, in 1957 it only took £549,000 worth.

Overall, commerce and industry grumbled that the

> present trade agreement has resulted in the Union of South Africa being granted a preferential position in the Federal market in many respects even greater than the United Kingdom, notwithstanding the fact that the basis of the Federation's tariff is Imperial Preference and that the Federation has particular obligations to the United Kingdom ... Britain is still the Federation's best customer ... is also the source of the majority of our investment capital.[142]

For the Union to be granted more favourable terms than the UK was no small concession, yet the Federation only received a very limited concession in the Union market. Flow of trade progressively favoured the Union, as Table 3.4 below shows.

Table 3.4. Value of exports between the Union of South Africa and the Federation, 1954–1957.

Year	Union to the Federation (£ million)	Federation to the Union (£ million)	Balance of trade (£ million)
1954	43.4	13.7	29.7
1955	45.5	16.7	28.8
1956	53.3	16.6	36.7
1957	60.9	13.6	47.3

Source: NAZ MS1199AEA18/14, South Africa, 1953–1961, Associated Chambers of Commerce of Rhodesia and Nyasaland, Memorandum on the South African Agreement, 10 October 1958).

141 *Ibid.*
142 *Ibid.*

The Chamber of Commerce bluntly stated that it could not support the continuation of the 1955 Trade Agreement with the Union. These grumblings led to the renegotiation of the agreement, which resulted in a new one in 1960.[143] Noteworthy also is the convergence of industrial and commercial interests.

Meanwhile, the demand for the protection of secondary industries persisted. In 1957, industrialists demanded that 'the Federal Government in consultation with organized industry carry out a full investigation into the whole question of protection with a view to the employment of tariffs as an effective instrument for the encouragement and growth of healthy secondary industries.'[144] Abrahamson highlighted that 'the country lost £6,000,000 on maize. Surely it would have been better for the government to encourage and protect a fully integrated industry which could process maize in this country instead of to export millions of tons at a loss!'[145] Other industrialists weighed in with their contributions. L. S. Davies, also from Bulawayo, said 'exclusive protection attracted competitive firms and thus brought down prices.'[146] K. Fiksl of Midlands added that 'there is no country in the world which wants industry and which has no protection.'[147]

Industrialists felt that by insisting on selective protection, the government had failed in its efforts to encourage secondary industry. The state gave minimal and, at best, partial support to secondary industry. One industrialist, Hercules Robinson, testified that he had 'made four separate applications for protection. Each was turned down – each time for different reasons and each time without reference to previous reasons given.'[148] In negotiations, the government would never give the real reasons for a refusal of protection. 'If any are given', he added, 'the reasons would make one either roar with laughter or weep with frustration.'[149] Indeed, the government stuck to its position that industry must establish itself. With minimal and selective support, secondary industries still expanded, as will be seen in the next section.

The Structure and Size of Secondary Industry, 1949–1957

Industrial expansion recorded between 1949 and 1957 is attributable in part to the efforts of private enterprise aided by its representative organisation, in part to the FRI, and in part to other factors against the lack of sympathetic policies from the state. Addressing industrialists at the valedictory congress of the FRI,

143 For more, see Cole, 'The tariff policy of Rhodesia', 42–43.
144 *Rhodesian Recorder*, August 1957.
145 *Ibid.*
146 *Ibid.*
147 *Ibid.*
148 *Rhodesian Recorder*, August 1957.
149 *Ibid.*

Figure 3.1 A photograph showing the industrial expansion of Salisbury, Southern Rhodesia, 1956 (Source: *The Times*, 16 January 1956).

the mayor of Salisbury, Harry Pichanick, acknowledged the impact of private enterprise (industrialists) on the growth of Salisbury. He said,

> Salisbury today has a budget equal to 50% of the total budget of the Colony. It is twice as much now as that of Southern Rhodesia in 1939, and it is growing infinitely faster than the rest of the Federation put together. The funny part is that the City Council is not responsible, and more strangely still, the Southern Rhodesia government is also not responsible, for this state of affairs. You, Sir, that is the people in private enterprise, are responsible, for you have unquestionably built up this City. You have had the courage and the vision, and the enterprise, to pour millions of money into Salisbury, and to show the world this glorious and magnificent city, which has arisen around us.[150]

Figure 3.1 above depicts this industrial expansion.

The government was consistent on its position and role regarding industrial development. In line with its policy of leaving industries to private enterprises, government relinquished control of its investments in secondary industries, as

150 FRI, Final Annual Congress, July 1957.

evidenced by the privatisation of the sugar industry board (1954) and Riscom (1956). The nationalisation of these industries in the 1940s had been justified because it was government policy to take over and establish industries that could not be profitably run by private capital or those of national interest. At the time of privatisation in the late 1950s, it was felt that the industries had been sufficiently developed and could now be passed over into the hands of private capital. In addition, privatisation was necessitated by the failure of the state to either properly manage nationalised industries or adequately fund their operations.

By 1957, the number of industries had increased to 923 from 508 in 1949,[151] and gross output had tripled, from £31,076,000 in 1949 to £104,945,000 in 1957. More tellingly, its 1957 net output of £43,176,000 was almost double the gross output of mining at £25,764,000, and slightly lower than that of agriculture at £45,086,000.[152] Table 3.5 shows the output of the manufacturing sector by 1957.

Table 3.5. Manufacturing industries' output compared with agriculture and mining, 1949–1957.

Year	Net output of manufacturing industries (£'000)	Gross output of agriculture (£'000)	Gross output of minerals (£'000)
1949	14,218	19,050	11,293
1950	19,101	27,110	13,607
1951	21,754	24,360	15,039
1952	24,531	34,010	20,201
1953	26,084	34,220	19,491
1954	-	37,610	18,776
1955	30,378	38,458	20,514
1956	35,814	43,133	23,261
1957	43,176	45,086	25,764

Source: Federation of Rhodesia and Nyasaland, Central African Statistical Office, *Report of the Census of Industrial Production*, 1938–1957.

There was also a tendency for production to be concentrated in the hands of bigger firms. In 1957, 31 firms (3%) (out of a total of 918) with a net output of £250,000 and over produced £18,209,000 (42.2%) of the total net output (£43,166,000) of the manufacturing industries. Table 3.6 shows the distribution of the manufacturing industry by unit output.

151 Government of Southern Rhodesia, *Census of Industrial Production, 1938–1962*, 31.
152 Federation of Rhodesia and Nyasaland, *Census of Industrial Production, 1957–1958*, 4.

Table 3.6. Distribution of manufacturing establishments by value of net output in Southern Rhodesia 1956/1957.

	Establishments		**Net output of each group**	
Range of net output	**Number**	**% of total**	**£'000**	**% of total**
Under £5,000	57	6	61	0.1
£5,000–£10,000	203	22	1,466	3.4
£10,000–£15,000	121	13	1,545	3.6
£15,000–£20,000	71	8	1,321	3.1
£20,000–£30,000	96	11	2,407	5.6
£30,000–£40,000	47	5	1,688	3.9
£40,000–£50,000	40	4	1,886	4.3
£50,000–£100,000	79	9	5,680	13.2
£100,000–£150,000	35	4	4,260	9.9
£150,000–£200,000	14	1	2,469	5.7
£200,000–£250,000	8	1	1,772	4.1
£250,000 and over	31	3	18,209	42.2
Total	918	100	43,166	100.0

Source: Federation of Rhodesia and Nyasaland, Central African Statistical Office, *Report of the Census of Industrial Production*, 1956/1957.

Amid this expansion, there emerged a problem of imbalanced development of secondary industry in the country. Minister of Agriculture, P. B. Fletcher, noted that 'a problem that has been worrying the government for considerable time is over-concentration of industry in the two main centres, Bulawayo and Salisbury'.[153] This needed redress. However, the two major cities possessed great advantages, hence the concentration of industries there. For instance, Bulawayo was directly connected by rail to the export markets in the north and in South Africa. Salisbury was the capital city, the seat of legislature and the heart of the tobacco-growing districts.[154] The other advantage was that, to the manufacturer requiring considerable labour, Salisbury was the initial destination for migrant labourers from Nyasaland. Though untrained and lacking industrial skills, these workers provided Salisbury with a reservoir of labour which was not so easily acquired in some of the other centres.[155] Between them, the cities held the majority of the country's European population, which at the time formed the core of the domestic market.

These advantages notwithstanding, over-concentration deprived other towns and cities of the opportunity to expand on the basis of industrialisation. In addition, this over-concentration flew in the face of the government's

153 *Rhodesian Recorder*, March 1950.

154 *Ibid.*, October 1950.

155 *Ibid.*

vision of balanced development. Decentralisation was, therefore, imperative in the development of the smaller towns.[156] The government took a deliberate policy to build up the other hitherto seemingly neglected towns. Such towns, in order of size, included Umtali, Gwelo, Que Que, and Gatooma. The aim was to establish in these towns ancillary and complementary industries which would promote the development of the towns concerned and level off their inequality with Salisbury and Bulawayo.[157] Partly because of this, the government established a dehydration factory and Jute Industries at Umtali, steelworks at Que Que, and the Cotton Research Board's ginnery and spinning mill at Gatooma. In addition, decentralisation allowed undeveloped communities to share some of the amenities of urban life and counteracted the city-to-city migration. To an extent, this spirit was also engendered by the establishment of the Federation. In 1956, parliament appointed a Select Committee on Decentralisation.[158] The committee endorsed decentralisation but advised that the government should establish an economic coordinating council to deal with the practicalities of decentralisation. The council never came into being, and decentralisation remained unimplemented and a contested policy, as will be shown in Chapters 5 and 6.

At a federal level, industrial expansion took place in Southern Rhodesia rather than in the other two northern territories. This trajectory had implications on the organisational structure and abilities of the FRI. In 1953, the mayor of Bulawayo, J. H. Butcher, encouraged the FRI to expand into the Federation.[159] In 1954, the Chambers of Commerce of the three federal territories formed the Federal Council for Commerce. It invited industrialists to join the council, but this invitation was rejected, as industrialists desired to form their own organisation. Subsequently, negotiations among industrial interests of the three territories resulted in an agreement to form a Federal Council for Industry in 1955.[160] It consisted of the Association of Chambers of Commerce and Industry of Northern Rhodesia, the Federation of Rhodesian Industries (FRI), and the Nyasaland Chamber of Commerce and Industry.

156 This logic is well captured in the debate on the location of a third spinning mill for the Cotton Research and Industry Board. See, especially, P. Nyambara, 'The politics of locating the third spinning mill in Southern Rhodesia, 1951–1953', *Historia*, 59, 2 (2014), 46–68.

157 *Rhodesian Recorder*, October 1950.

158 See NAZ F292/16/14, Decentralisation of Industries: Memorandum on Distribution of Industry, 11 April 1957; and Federation of Rhodesia and Nyasaland, *Federal Assembly Report of the Select Committee on Decentralisation*, 6 August 1957.

159 FRI, *Annual Congress*, July 1953: Mayoral Address by Councillor J. H. Butcher, 1.

160 NAZ F292/14/9/1, FRI: Letter by FRI Secretary to Secretary for Commerce and Industry, N. R. Bertram, 16 July 1954.

The council championed the interests of industrialists in the territories, but in reality it was mostly utilised by the Southern Rhodesian industrialists, because

> in the two northern territories development of secondary industries had not reached the level that it had in Southern Rhodesia and also because existing organisations in these territories covered both the field of industry and commerce and there were practical difficulties in the way of separating the two functions.[161]

Reflecting on the council, Sir Malcolm Barrow, the Minister of Home Affairs, said 'its weakness lay in the very fact that it was an organisation resting on three independent and administratively unconnected pillars. The spirit of co-operation and goodwill was always present but such a body could never have been a permanent one.'[162] The council, therefore, was circumscribed in its function. Crucially, however, this council formed the basis of the formation of the Association of Rhodesia and Nyasaland Industries (ARNI), which will be discussed in the next chapter.

Conclusion

This chapter has discussed the sustained industrial expansion between 1949 and 1957 under the stimulus of a number of factors: the post-war economic environment, the impact of the 1948 customs agreement, the establishment of the Federation of Rhodesia and Nyasaland, and, more importantly, the relentless efforts of industrialists. Buoyed by the increasing importance of their sector and the quest to advance their interests, industrialists formed a national association in 1949, the FRI. The FRI proved a useful vehicle through which the industrialists could engage the state in seeking assistance for the expansion of secondary industries. In spite of several pleas, the government rarely conceded to the FRI's lobbying. Instead, it stuck to its avowed policy of leaving industries to paddle their own canoe, with the state only offering assistance where necessary. Without the state's guaranteed protection and other forms of support, secondary industries nonetheless expanded both in number and value. Having grown in number from 508 in 1949 to 923 in 1957, secondary industries had surpassed mining's net output and were catching up with agriculture.

161 FRI, *Final Annual Congress*, July 1957.
162 *Ibid.*

4 Secondary Industry, Changing Economic Fortunes, and Central African Decolonisation, 1957–1965

This chapter discusses the establishment of the Association of Rhodesian and Nyasaland Industries (ARNI) in 1957 as an organisation that could speak for industrialists throughout the Federation of Rhodesia and Nyasaland. It details the politics of the ARNI, especially the demands and aspirations of Southern Rhodesian industrialists as they interacted with territorial and federal governments as well as their Northern Rhodesian and Nyasaland counterparts vis-à-vis other economic interest groups. The formation of the ARNI happened in a fast-changing economic and political space in British Central Africa. The Federation suffered an economic recession from late 1956 following a fall in the price of copper, the linchpin of the federal economy, on the global market. From 1957, African nationalism in the Rhodesias and Nyasaland grew, resulting in frequent protests and states of emergency. In 1962, general elections in Southern Rhodesia brought in a new right-wing government under the Rhodesian Front. This political and economic situation resulted in the dissolution of the Federation in 1963, paving the way to the independence of Zambia and Malawi in 1964, while Southern Rhodesia continued under a White minority government that proclaimed a Unilateral Declaration of Independence (UDI) from Britain in 1965. The following pages give an overview of how the ARNI manoeuvred itself in this changing economic situation and during decolonisation. It further assesses how the dissolution of the Federation reconfigured trading relations among three territories and the implications of this on industrial development.

The discussion begins with the transition from the Federation of Rhodesian Industries (FRI), the predecessor to the ARNI. The second section analyses the existing economic and policy environment and the ARNI's perspectives and responses on these. The next part discusses the road towards decolonisation and how the ARNI positioned itself under the circumstances. Lastly, the chapter examines the structure of secondary industry and its position in the economy. Broadly, the chapter maintains that industrialists managed with minimal state support. Other economic interest groups, in particular commerce, remained somewhat unsupportive of industrial development.

From the FRI to ARNI

The ARNI, established in 1957, succeeded the FRI, which until then had represented only the interests of industrialists in Southern Rhodesia. During the final congress of the FRI on 18 July 1957, Sir Malcolm Barrow, the Minister of Home Affairs (and former Minister of Commerce and Industry), urged industrialists to expand their membership to reflect the geopolitics of the Federation. 'It is important', he said, 'that Federal Industrialists should have an organisation in which they can speak as industrialists.'[1] However, he qualified his call, noting that he was not encouraging industrialists to break away from organisations to which they already belonged, such as organised commerce. Many, both in Southern Rhodesia and in the two northern territories, were members of Chambers of Commerce and associations of commerce and industry, respectively. In Southern Rhodesia, some 40% of the members in the Chamber of Commerce were industrialists.[2] If anything, for Barrow, the presence of industrialists in a Chamber of Commerce was a way of achieving cooperation between commerce and industry, itself an imperative for industrial expansion. That cooperation was necessary, as will become more evident in this chapter.

After Barrow's call – indeed, the next day – industrialists debated the idea of creating a federal-wide body. Seconded by C. H. Targett, A. E. Abrahamson of Bulawayo Chamber of Industries (BCI) moved a motion for the establishment of a federal-wide organisation under the new title of 'the Association of Rhodesia and Nyasaland Industries' and a revised constitution. He argued that it was 'in keeping with the spirit of progress of the country and making the industrialist alive to the totality of industry within the Federation'.[3] All contributions to the motion supported the establishment of the ARNI. M. Rabb from Northern Rhodesia also assured the meeting that 'Northern Rhodesian industry stood four-square behind the new Federal organisation for the

1 FRI, *Final Annual Congress*, 18 July 1957.

2 *Ibid.*

3 NAZ F292/14/9/1, Industrial Policy Part 2, ARNI Proceedings of Inaugural Meeting, 19 July 1957.

industry'.[4] The Northern Rhodesian Association of Chambers of Commerce similarly supported the motion. It stated that 'industry in Northern Rhodesia, for many years, was linked to the organisation for commerce because a separate industrial body was not warranted', but now 'industry in Northern Rhodesia would benefit immensely from the new Federal industrial organisation.'[5]

The ARNI came to life, with Abrahamson elected its inaugural president. Its objectives were:

> the promotion and protection of the interests of industrialists and manufacturers, encouragement, assistance and promotion of the organization of industries, representing the views of manufacturers and industrialists to, and cooperating with governments, local authorities and other institutions on matters directly or indirectly affecting industry, and printing, publishing or supporting any magazine, periodical, brochure or publication seen to be consistent with ARNI's objectives.[6]

The membership of the ARNI comprised manufacturing firms, which ordinarily were members of a Chamber of Industry. However, because of the paucity of manufacturers in Northern Rhodesia and Nyasaland, industrialists found it impracticable to establish separate Chambers of Industry in the two northern territories. The ARNI made a constitutional provision for the admission of individual manufacturing firms as direct members.[7] Also, there were many firms in the Federation which, though not engaged in manufacturing, nevertheless had a vital interest in the industry's activities. These included commercial banks, industrial consultants, the copper mining groups, and finance houses, as well as employers' associations in various subsectors. The ARNI sometimes admitted these institutions as associate members. It is also crucial to note that although by this time the ARNI broadly represented all federal industrialists, the core members of its constituent Chambers remained those from Southern Rhodesia, namely Salisbury, Bulawayo, Midlands, and Umtali: it was itself a reflection of the skewed industrial development in the Federation. To reflect the more extensive representation, the ARNI focused particular attention on enrolling new members from across the Federation during 1959, and it appointed a public relations officer for this express purpose. The ARNI reported that the campaign met with marked success and approximately 'one hundred new members were enrolled since the public relations officer took up office [in 1959]'.[8]

4 *Ibid.*
5 *Ibid.*
6 NAZ F292/14/9/1, Industrial Policy Part 2, ARNI Proceedings of Inaugural Meeting, 19 July 1957.
7 ARNI, *Review of the Presidential Year*, 1959/60.
8 *Ibid.*

Prominent among critical services afforded by the ARNI to members were assistance on matters such as the submission of applications for tariff protection, rebates, and suspension of duties, applications for dumping duties, and applications for import and export permits. The ARNI further assisted with information and advice on export markets and the location of suitable agents, in addition to investigating trade licensing problems, the interpretation of labour and other regulations, the location of sources or raw materials, and the investigation of railway problems. It also introduced other initiatives such as the launch of a *Register of Manufacturers*, which was later superseded by an annual industrial register. This served as an advertising medium for manufacturers and a reference book for consumers. Its distribution areas included the federal and territorial government offices, the offices of high commissioners and trade commissioners abroad, and the representative offices of foreign governments in the Federation, business houses, and municipalities.[9] These places were strategic in publicising industrialists' activities and reaching out to potential partners, investors, and consumers.

The ARNI also expanded the 'Buy Rhodesian' campaign to the 'Buy Federal' campaign, to encompass all three territories. The ARNI successfully advocated local preferences in government purchasing patterns. To show its commitment to supporting local manufacturers, the government undertook to shoulder the costs for the 'Buy Federal' campaign. Both the federal government and the ARNI agreed to circulate a 'housewives' guide', showing consumer products made in the Federation.[10] These rare moments of cooperation notwithstanding, the government and industrialists often clashed, as is discussed below, over the overall industrial policy.

The Struggle Continues: The ARNI, the Government, and Industrial Policy

From late 1956, the federal economy suffered a decline because the price of copper, the mainstay of the economy, collapsed on the international market.[11] Disturbed by the slowing rate of development of the Federation's economy during 1957, the ARNI and other employer organisations approached the new federal prime minister, Roy Welensky, advocating a policy of industrialisation. In an industrial charter to Welensky, the ARNI called for the creation of a climate to which private enterprise could be attracted and within which it could flourish. The responsibility for the creation of such a conducive atmosphere

9 ARNI, *Report for the Presidential Year*, 1962/1963.

10 Southern Rhodesia Legislative Assembly Debate, 6 September 1961, Col. 2210.

11 For detailed discussion on this, see A. Cohen, *The Politics and Economics of Decolonization in Africa: The Failed Experiment of the Central African Federation* (London: I. B. Tauris Publishers, 2017).

fell mainly on the federal government, because the portfolio of commerce and industry came under its umbrella. However, because of the governmental structure of the Federation, other factors of production lay within the sphere of territorial governments and even local authorities. Consequently, the ARNI emphasised the 'necessity for close collaboration between all forms of government and industry'.[12] Welensky responded that 'a policy of industrialisation pursued as a matter of urgency, *regardless of the purely economic aspect*, could not command government's support'.[13]

Responses in other government quarters echoed the prime minister's office. R. M. Taylor, Secretary to the Federal Treasury, shared his thoughts with T. S. Bell of the Ministry of Commerce and Industry over the demands enumerated by the ARNI. Acknowledging the vital role manufacturing could play in the expansion of the economy, he warned industrialists 'not to over-state their case' and the government 'not to be bamboozled by the extravagance of [the industrialists'] phraseology'.[14] Taylor disagreed with industrialists that the expansion of the economy was only achievable through the manufacturing industry in preference to other forms of production. He even mocked that manufacturers 'beat up their drum without due regard to facts'. Taylor demonstrated statistically that, in order of importance to the Rhodesian economy, manufacturing, with average annual earnings of £1,072, came fourth, after mining (£1,219), building and construction (£1,168) and transport (£1,100).[15] About 121 in every 1,000 gainfully employed Europeans worked in manufacturing in 1956, compared to 149 in every 1,000 in 1951. Secondary industry absorbed less labour force, and for that reason the manufacturing industry was not as crucial as it portrayed itself. The decline demonstrated by Taylor, however, reflected the economic recession of the time and not the pattern of industrial growth. To even further dampen the spirit of industrialists, Taylor invoked the Marxist analogy that the creation of an industrial proletariat worsened relations between the 'have' and 'have-not', concluding that the Federation needed to avoid a similar fate.[16]

The government officials' dim view towards industry angered organised secondary industry. At the ARNI 1958 congress, industrialists tore into government's industrial policy. Gordon Harper of the Salisbury Chamber of Industries

12 NAZ F292/14/9/1, Industrial Policy Part 2, ARNI, An Industrial Charter, November 1957.

13 NAZ F292/14/9/1, Industrial Policy Part 2, ARNI, Note of a meeting between the Prime Minister, the Minister of Finance, and Representatives of the ARNI, 7 November 1957.

14 *Ibid.*, ARNI, Letter by Secretary to the Federal Treasury, R. M. Taylor, to T. S. Bell, Secretary to the Federal Ministry of Commerce and Industry, 13 November 1957.

15 Cited in *ibid.*

16 NAZ F292/14/9/1, Industrial Policy Part 2, ARNI, Letter by Secretary to the Federal Treasury, R. M. Taylor, to T. S. Bell, Secretary to the Federal Ministry of Commerce and Industry, 13 November 1957.

(SCI) decried the dilatory treatment of industrialists' request: 'if we approach the government for help ... we are wasting time ... if a firm is making a loss, it is told that it is uneconomic and should not have started in any case'.[17] Van De Bergh of the Central African Textile Manufacturers' Association (CATMA) weighed in, emphasising 'the need for a changed attitude because no matter how well-worded industrial policies may be, they will be meaningless without the determination and goodwill of the government to implement them'.[18] Citing the finance minister's views on import control and the credit squeeze, which, he argued, indicated the minister's general attitude towards industry, he complained that because of proximity, big business received a sympathetic ear from the government, while 'applications from smaller concerns are not expeditiously handled ... it seems that the Federal government cannot be persuaded to act unless there is pressure (attracting to ARNI the label of a pressure group)'.[19] Concurring with van De Bergh, K. W. Spilhaus urged the government to 'appreciate the importance of favourable treatment for the small man [because he was] the foundation of industrial development'.[20] For M. Rabb, who represented the Northern Rhodesian industrialists, most of the industrialists' difficulties stemmed from the absence of any clear governmental policy. Consequently, he said, 'the government must declare itself – whatever the declared policy may be'. Clearly, what was presented as the government's policy did not impress the industrialists.

To further press its case, the ARNI presented secondary industrialisation as a means of dealing with the potentially explosive sociological, political, and economic problems facing the Federation. This narrative emphasised the interplay between population increase, unemployment, and industrial development. There was also unanimity that industrial expansion was the panacea for dealing with both high population and unemployment. The ARNI had made this point clearly in its industrial charter in 1957. It stated:

> While it is most necessary that primary production should expand, it is incapable by comparison with the manufacturing industry of absorbing employees, whether white or black, at a sufficiently rapid rate. Again, the manufacturing industry is the most effective channel for absorbing employees, both white and black, into the economy of the country and of paying a level of wages well above those applicable in the primary industries.[21]

17 *Rhodesian Recorder*, November 1958.
18 *Ibid.*
19 *Ibid.*
20 *Ibid.*
21 NAZ F292/14/9/1, Industrial Policy Part 2, ARNI, An Industrial Charter, November 1957.

Since 1954, employment in agriculture had increased by 12% and decreased in mining by 14%, while employment in manufacturing had increased by 23%.[22] A predominantly agricultural and mining economy, then, could only offer a limited solution to the problem of unemployment.

Left unchecked, that trend posed a threat to the colony's stability. Consequently, finding a solution to the unemployment problem ceased to be exclusively an economic matter, becoming a socio-political one as well. Seeking the government's cooperation on the subject, the ARNI pleaded that

> the increasing African population not continue to live under a system of peasant agriculture ... the disparity in living standards between black and white is a fertile breeding ground for domestic and racial disturbances. It is a matter of urgency, therefore, that steps should be taken to provide opportunities for employment in manufacturing industry both for a larger European population and for the African people in particular.[23]

J. de Haas, ARNI vice president, repeatedly cautioned that 'if racial harmony and the policy of partnership are to become facts, and not just election slogans, full employment must be assured.'[24] For the ARNI, the government should, therefore, foster industrial development, because it was the quickest way to avert this problem.

Fostering manufacturing growth required some measure of protection. However, varying views on industrial protection exposed the different hopes and expectations of government and industrialists over the path of industrial development. This was once more laid bare at their meeting in 1958 to discuss the Review of Industrial Policy. At the meeting, attendees enquired about the government's protective assistance to potential industrialists intending to enter the Federation, to which the minister replied that 'any firm setting up an assembly plant in the Federation must, in order to claim assistance, have long term intentions and provide proof of them by considerable initial capital investment and output.'[25] The minister further advised that it could not promise a particular scale of protection to a firm in advance: the firm needed to be in production first. De Haas of the ARNI, however, warned that no foreign industrialist would bring considerable capital into the Federation without a guarantee of some sort of protection.[26] The minister's response received heavy criticism from the ARNI, forcing him to clarify that the Review of Industrial

22 NAZ MS 1201/A.44/1, ARNI Reports, 1959–1960, Committee on Policy – Underdeveloped Countries: Industrialisation in Underdeveloped Countries, undated

23 *Ibid.*

24 *Bulawayo Chronicle*, 12 November 1958.

25 NAZ MS 1201/EA1, Minutes of a Meeting between the Minister of Commerce and Industry and Reps of the ARNI held on 17 April 1958.

26 *Ibid.*

Policy was not meant to keep industry out of the Federation, but was simply aimed at 'offering less attraction to the less desirable industries'. The government overlooked that a desirable industry deserved protection and that government needed to indicate a comprehensive policy to protect such industry.

At the same meeting, the ARNI called for a review of imperial preferences for imports, particularly from the UK. The minister justified this by stating that the UK reciprocated by granting concessions to Southern Rhodesia for observing imperial preference. Another official added that the value of the UK preference for federal tobacco approximately equalled the federal preference for UK-manufactured goods. The ARNI refuted the explanation, noting that imperial preference in Southern Rhodesia was sentimental and not on a *quid pro quo* basis.[27] The matter came up again at the ARNI 1958 congress, where it was argued that

> the whole emphasis [on imperial preference and tariffs] often seemed to be solely on the selling of more tobacco. Although industry supports any stimulation of exports, [industry] cannot continue indefinitely to be sacrificed 'at the altar of tobacco'. [Industry] cannot develop if foreign countries are given concessions for their manufactured goods in return for their purchases of tobacco.[28]

More tellingly, industrialists demanded protection, even if it meant sacrificing long-standing trade policies. 'It really is very extraordinary that the Federal Government gives the benefit of every doubt to the foreign manufacturer but treats Federal industry with the greatest suspicion', fumed Hercules Robinson of the SCI when he introduced the motion on tariff protection at the congress.[29] Tariffs are generally designed to raise revenue, to encourage imports from certain selected countries, or to protect existing domestic industries and to encourage new ones. The federal tariff structure, therefore, should have reflected whether or not it wished to become industrialised. Yet, it retained a tariff structure, which did nothing to achieve that aim, argued Robinson.[30] Under a four-column tariff, about 80% of imports came from countries to which the lowest rates of duty (5.83%) applied. These imports had the consequential effect of competing with, if not outcompeting, local manufactured products.

Industrialists expected the tariff wall to be high, protecting local infant industries from the long-established industries of the Western world. This was even particularly crucial for the Federation, given that other industrialising countries such as

27 *Ibid.*
28 *Rhodesian Recorder*, September 1958.
29 *Ibid.*
30 *Ibid.*

> America maintained tariffs at an average of about 12%. Australia's barrier was far higher (at between 30 and 40%), Israel totally prohibited the import of any goods produced locally, the Belgian Congo recently raised its tariff to protect its industries and South Africa, with an average tariff of just under 8%, gave additional and far more effective protection through import control, a double protection also practiced by Australia, New Zealand and many other countries.[31]

Indeed, the federal tariff was inadequate for the necessary encouragement of industrial development.

However, industrialists' impassioned plea for protection attracted opposing responses from the Associated Chambers of Commerce of Rhodesia and Nyasaland (ACCORN). Formed in 1957, the ACCORN claimed to be 'an organisation dedicated to preserving an economic system based on the principles of private enterprise and free competition ... [that would] attack any action on the part of government or individual which might adversely affect such interests'.[32] The subject of free competition differentiated the ACCORN from the ARNI. The ARNI ardently believed in protection as opposed to free competition. The ACCORN also believed in the supremacy of the primary industries of mining and agriculture. For these reasons, commerce and industry consistently clashed. To begin with, the ACCORN was cautious over the promotion of secondary industry. At its 1958 congress, it expressed that the Federation was still dependent on primary industry, which for a long time to come would remain its chief source of revenue, especially from the exports of minerals, tobacco, and tea. Thus, 'in fostering secondary industry, we must not lose sight of the vital part which primary industry plays in our economy', advised the ACCORN.[33]

ACCORN's sentiments created an impression among industrialists that commerce was against secondary industry. The ACCORN president, H. A. Krikler, sought to clarify the situation:

> the opinion appears to be fairly widely held that [ACCORN] is opposed to any form of protection. This is not the case. Commerce is fully aware of the importance of a healthy and virile secondary industry and will support any reasonable measures introduced to foster the growth of industries of significant benefit to the country's economy.[34]

Even as ACCORN made this clarification, it still reiterated its opposition to the use of embargoes and quantitative restrictions to promote secondary industries. Its major concern was that such an approach led to inefficiency through

31 *Ibid.*
32 ACCORN, *Minutes and Proceedings of the First Annual Congress*, April 1958.
33 *Ibid.*
34 *Ibid.*

lack of competition and to price structures which would place an unfair burden on other sectors of the economy. ACCORN believed that the judicious use of customs tariffs best supported secondary industry.

Supporting the ACCORN's view, Harry Oppenheimer, the chairman of Anglo American Corporation – one of the biggest conglomerates in the country – was also more circumspect and cautious in the protection of industry. Addressing the ACCORN congress in 1959, he guardedly suggested the following:

> Of course, the government can encourage industry directly by way of tariffs. I would say there is a particularly strong case for assistance in infant industries in that way in a new and developing country, but in giving tariff protection, you have to be rather careful ... in a country such as this, it is plain that secondary industry, unlike the big primary mining industry, will, in the majority of cases, be producing for the local market and not for export. If by means of tariffs you cause industries to start at the price of raising the whole cost of living in the territory, then the advantages of the new industry will be offset by a falling in the standard of living of the people. Another thing is that if by means of tariffs, you raise the whole price structure unreasonably, you would be faced very quickly with balance of payments difficulties. Therefore I say by all means let us protect our infant industries, but let us be careful to see that this protection is only given to such industries as can, after a reasonable period, stand on their own feet.[35]

The Ndola (Northern Rhodesia) Chamber of ACCORN repeated the same point on another occasion, where it argued that 'the present government policy of encouraging secondary industry by tariff protection is pushing up the cost of living in the two northern territories without any resultant benefits because industrial development is almost confined to Southern Rhodesia.'[36]

Aware of the simmering tensions between commerce and industry over the assistance to be afforded to industrialists, Oppenheimer encouraged closer cooperation. Addressing the ACCORN's congress in 1959, he recommended that the interests of commerce and industry be harmonised so that

> the possibilities of conflict between commerce and industry should not be allowed to develop as they do from time to time in other countries ... commerce [should] naturally do all it can to increase the sale of Rhodesian manufactured goods, and that is highly desirable ... all that is a very excellent thing.[37]

H. A. Krikler, the ACCORN president, acknowledged the need to assist secondary industry. Addressing his members at the congress, he conceded that

35 ACCORN, *Minutes and Proceedings of Second Annual Congress*, Ndola, 1959.

36 See *Rhodesia Herald*, 23 October 1959, and ACCORN, *Programme and Agenda*, 1963.

37 *Ibid.*, 1959.

'with the growing importance of secondary industry in the Federation it is understandable, indeed inevitable that the Chambers of Commerce should pay increasing attention to this important section of business activity'.[38]

Even as he made this concession, Krikler still expressed commerce's reservations over industrial protection. He continued,

> The exclusion or the tempering of external competition by protection is not the only or the most important means by which secondary industry can be encouraged to establish and develop within the Federation. The all-important thing is to create and maintain within the country a favourable climate for investment, and particularly for investment in secondary industry.[39]

Krikler further said that the emphasis on industry should not reach the 'proportions of an obsession'.[40] For this, he criticised the government for lacking a clear policy for economic development in general and industrial development in particular. Explaining the importance of a clear policy, he said 'cooperation will be more readily and more intelligently given if we know that we are working within the framework of a definite plan and if we know what that plan is'.[41]

The need for a close working relationship was more imminent during that time, when the Federation was facing an economic recession. Welensky also urged the Chambers of Mines, Commerce, and Industry to work together. In particular, he invited them to arrange exchange visits with trade missions from other countries, all in support of industrial development.[42] Alongside Welensky's intervention were other attempts at cooperation. In late 1959, the ARNI, in association with ACCORN, the Chamber of Mines, the Federation of Civil Engineering Contractors, the National Federation of Building Trade Employers, and the Rhodesia National Farmers Union (RNFU), submitted proposals to the federal government for the establishment of an economic development advisory council. The prime purpose of such a council was to bring together under one body representatives of the four governments of the Federation and the five main sections of the economy, namely agriculture, building and construction, commerce, the manufacturing industry, and mining. Underlying this plan was the hope that the combined knowledge and experience of these institutions could be applied to devising ways and means of renewing and expanding the Federation's economic development.[43]

38 ACCORN, *Minutes and Proceedings of Second Annual Congress*, 1959.
39 *Ibid.*
40 *Ibid.*
41 *Ibid.*
42 NAZ MS 1198 AEA2/1, Letter by Chamber of Mines of Rhodesia to ARNI Economist, 10 July 1959.
43 ARNI, *Review of the Presidential Year*, 1959/60.

Calls for harmonious relations between the ACCORN and the ARNI gained momentum as Barrow urged commerce to support the local manufacturing industry through buying locally. Opening the ACCORN congress, he remarked that,

> to a very great extent, the development of secondary industry in the Federation must be directed towards production for the domestic market. If such development is to be successful, it must clearly involve changes in the existing supply patterns, as domestic manufactures replace imported goods. Such changes are without doubt inconvenient for those traders who have hitherto handled the displaced imports. Commercial relationships, often of very long-standing, must be disrupted. But, given the willingness to change with the times, not only must commerce as a whole gain by such developments, but individual firms must each gain themselves ... I think that there is still considerable room for a greater part to be played by commerce in the promotion of the Federal industry and particularly the manufacturing industry.[44]

The ACCORN's attitude towards the secondary industry demonstrates how, even as late as the 1950s, industrial development was yet accepted as an essential sector of the Rhodesian economy that could assist in the country's overall development. Sentiments still existed that for developing countries such as Rhodesia and Nyasaland, the maintenance and expansion of both agriculture and mining were essential, for these were fields in which the country enjoyed a comparative advantage. Industrialists, therefore, had to fight for the state's attention, lest they remained secondary in importance to primary industry and commerce.

Due to the persistent demand for a clear industrial policy and state assistance, the federal government appointed a Committee of Enquiry into Manufacturing Industry in 1958.[45]Also known as the Committee on Industrial Policy, it existed for two years and presented its report to parliament in 1960. Its terms of reference were to investigate and report on the opportunity and need for further development of manufacturing industry in the Federation, having regard to 'social and economic conditions; to the relationship of the development of manufacturing industry to other sectors of the economy, and to the policies and incentives, if any, aimed at securing such growth which should be adopted by the Federal government'.[46] The committee also had to consider whether the development of any specific classes of industry deserved preference. However, it could not recommend any specific assistance to be accorded in any individual case.

44 ACCORN, *Minutes of the Proceedings of the Annual Congress*, 1960.
45 NAZ F187/E/598/02, Committee of Enquiry into the Manufacturing Industry, 1958.
46 Southern Rhodesia, Legislative Assembly Debate, 29 June 1959, Col. 942.

The role of the manufacturing industry in dealing with high unemployment afflicting the Federation at that time was a recurring theme in the evidence submitted before the committee. Statistical evidence showed that the manufacturing sector had absorbed a considerable number of job seekers. According to the ARNI, 'not only was the rate of African labour absorption greater in the manufacturing industry than any other directly productive sector, but it was also greater in terms of the numbers of Africans absorbed'.[47] So far as European employment was concerned, the absorption rate in the manufacturing industry also outstripped the rate in any other sector. In 1958, European employment increased by approximately 8,800, but African employment suffered a setback, with its employment figure reduced by 3,900.[48] In 1959 African employment increased by 6,600 over the previous year, while European employment increased by only 1,350.[49] Between 1954 and 1959, there was a significant increase in agriculture, mining, and manufacturing. European employment in this period rose from 4,800 to 5,400 in agriculture, from 9,600 to 10,500 in mining, and from 12,000 to 18,500 in manufacturing.[50] Despite the manufacturing industry's high rate of expansion, it only contributed about 10% of the gross domestic product (GDP). Between 1955 and 1960, the manufacturing industry absorbed 12,400 immigrants, in comparison to 3,000 for agriculture and 3,400 for mining. The manufacturing industry absorbed 25% of immigrant labourers, compared with 6% for agriculture and 7% for mining.[51] All indications pointed to the fact that only increased industrial development could absorb the surplus labour force. Yet, the government seemed reluctant to encourage the development of secondary industry. These findings caused ARNI to demand that the government develop a definitive industrial policy.

There were also calls to have balanced industrial development. Industrial units tended to be concentrated in the big cities of Salisbury and Bulawayo and later in Umtali and Gwelo. With the establishment of the Federation, industrial development was concentrated in Southern Rhodesia, to the detriment of the other two federal territories. For this reason, the Commercial and Industrial Association of Northern Rhodesia called for 'more emphasis on decentralisation and intending industrialists must be encouraged to look beyond Salisbury, Bulawayo and Umtali for industrial sites'.[52] It further submitted that 'the apparently increasing tendency to regard Salisbury as the Federation

47 NAZ MS 1200/A.50, Unemployment Conference: Memorandum on Industry and Employment, by P. C. Aldridge, ARNI Director, 3 May 1961.

48 *Ibid.*

49 *Ibid.*

50 *Ibid.*

51 *Ibid.*

52 NAZ F187/E/598/02, Committee of Enquiry into the Manufacturing Industry, Letter by the Commercial and Industrial Association of Northern Rhodesia to the Committee Secretary, 24 August 1959.

is unhealthy, and a threat to the whole economic future and stability of the country'.[56] Even as it called for decentralisation, it noted that the Federation relied almost entirely on two or three primary products (tobacco, copper, and gold), the market prices of which fluctuated considerably and the control of which lay outside the Federation. Precisely because of that, diversification of the economy was imperative, and industrialisation was key to that.

As the Committee on Industrial Policy carried out its work, the ARNI was expressing to the government its dissatisfaction with the Tariff Advisory Committee (TAC) as a means of making investigations and recommendations into applications for customs tariff protection and similar forms of assistance for industry. The ARNI felt that a body more fully representative of industrial and commercial interests should be set up to replace the TAC, which thus far had comprised officials of the federal public service exclusively. Therefore, it advocated the establishment of a board of trade similar to the one in the Union of South Africa.[53] A proposal in favour of a board of trade was also a subject of a motion adopted by the federal assembly in 1959.[54] In moving the motion, parliament envisaged the creation of an autonomous body such as a statutory board or commission performing two functions. The first would deal with questions concerning tariffs and rebates, drawbacks, and trade agreements, and the second, the development and creation of new industries in particular and the introduction of incentives to attract industrial investors to the Federation in general. Concerns over tariff protection and the board of trade at the same time triggered the conversation on trade agreements. The following paragraphs briefly focus on trade agreements. Due to space constraints, this discussion deliberately excludes the trade agreements entered into between the Federation and Japan and Portugal.

The 1960 Trade Agreement

In June 1959 Sir Roy Welensky made a statement in parliament regarding the termination of the 1955 trade agreement with the Union of South Africa. In terms of article 16 of that trade agreement, the deal was due for either termination or renegotiation on 30 June 1960. If it continued, it would be subject to twelve months' notice on either side. The federal government examined the practical effects of the agreement, including the sizeable adverse balance of trade that the Federation had had with the Union of South Africa. 'We concluded that Agreement is no longer beneficial to the Federation and it would be likely to operate increasingly to our disadvantage in the future', said Welensky,

53 ARNI, *Review of the Presidential Year*, 1959/60.
54 Legislative Assembly Debates, 19 November 1959. Cols 3852–72.

adding that 'we decided that it would be in our best interests not to continue the agreement in its present form.'[55]

The ARNI made a detailed study of the effects of that agreement on local industrial development. In the course of its review, the ARNI sought the views of all member firms and presented these to the federal government. The ACCORN also showed considerable interest in the new trading relationship that could be negotiated with South Africa. Consequently, the ARNI and ACCORN held joint meetings wherein they unanimously agreed that 'the present agreement should be terminated but replaced with a new Agreement'.[56] Broadly, industrialists felt that the federal government should negotiate preferential access to the Union market for those federal manufacturers who had previously enjoyed tariff concessions in that market. Furthermore, it urged that the tariff concessions heretofore enjoyed by South Africa be substantially reduced to afford local manufacturers a better opportunity of exploiting the domestic market.[57]

The new trade agreement, which came into operation on 1 July 1960, gave no tariff concessions to South African manufacturers, with the almost inevitable result that federal manufacturers lost a substantial measure of their concessions in the South African market. The essence of this agreement was that for the most part the Federation admitted South African products at column C (preferential) rates of duty.[58] At the same time, South Africa granted a limited range of federal products with specific reductions on South Africa's intermediate rates of duty. It was due to terminate on 30 June 1965.[59] While federal manufacturers, who were concerned mainly with the domestic market, were more than satisfied with the terms of the new agreement, local industries, who had virtually lost their export markets, were naturally perturbed. Those adversely affected were mainly the textile, clothing, and footwear industries. The ARNI joined these groups in making representations to the government to urge the adoption of measures designed to afford them greater protection

55 Legislative Assembly Debates, 24 June 1959, Col. 878.

56 NAZ MS 1199/18/4, ARNI, Trade Agreement with South Africa, Report of a Joint Meeting between ARNI and ACCORN on the South African Trade Agreement held on 7 April 1959.

57 ARNI, *Review of the Presidential Year*, 1959/60.

58 Tariffs or duties charged on imports were categorised into four columns, A to D. Column A tariffs applied to countries grouped as 'Others', Column B applied to 'Most-favoured – nations', Column C was for 'Dominions', and, lastly, Column D applied to 'United Kingdom and Colonies'. Preference applied in descending order: countries classified under D enjoyed preferential treatment (i.e. no duties or very low duties), and those in Column A attracted the highest tariffs.

59 For a detailed analysis of the provisions of the 1960 Trade Agreement, see R. Cole, 'The tariff policy of Rhodesia, 1899–1963', *Rhodesian Journal of Economics*, 2, 2 (1968), 28–48, at p. 42.

in the domestic market to offset their diminishing export opportunities. Tariff protection, however, remained elusive. Indeed, industry was partly protected.[60]

Renewed Complaints and Demands

As the government signed the 1960 trade agreement, it also pronounced, in line with the proposals by the ARNI, that it would introduce a board of trade to replace the TAC. Responding to questions in parliament, the Minister of Commerce and Industry, Owen, explained the government decision: 'The government choice lay between the establishment of an autonomous body which it would delegate its responsibilities for industrial development or the retention of the responsibilities by performing the services through a strengthened Ministry of Commerce and Industry. The government has decided in favour of the latter', he said.[61] The strengthening of the ministry entailed the reorganisation of the industries branch. The envisioned industries branch was to comprise two sections, a tariff section and a new industries section, each under the control of a senior official.

The tariff section examined all applications for assistance from industry, consulted other ministries or governments, visited applicants' factories, called for evidence from all interested persons, and reached conclusions within the broad outline of government industrial policy. Members of the tariff section could then form the nucleus of the board of trade, or tariff board, should the government at a future date decide to have one. The new industries section, dealing with the development of industry, concentrated its efforts on compiling an outline of industrial development, preparing material for distribution to investors, establishing regional industrial development committees, reviewing incentives, and generally providing an efficient and imaginative service for the expansion of manufacturing industry in all its forms. These actions did nothing to appease industrialists, who continued to call for the establishment of a fully independent board of trade with executive powers.

In November 1960, parliament tabled the report of the Committee on Industrial Policy. Members of parliament picked up on some concerns raised by witnesses at the committee's inquiry. In particular, they placed great emphasis on the issue of decentralisation, reiterating that the 'manufacturing industry was being attracted to too few places in the Federation ... Southern Rhodesia was securing more than its fair share of new enterprises, while within Southern Rhodesia ... Salisbury (to some extent Bulawayo) was benefitting at

60 A. S. Mlambo and I. Phimister, 'Partly protected: origins and growth of colonial Zimbabwe's textile industry, 1890–1965', *Historia*, 52, 2 (2006), 145–75, reaches a similar conclusion.

61 Legislative Assembly Debates, 4 July 1960, Col. 981.

the expense of the other municipalities'.[62] Despite these representations, this trend did not alter, but rather continued until the break-up of the Federation. Other members opined that responding to the report was also an opportunity for the government to re-state its industrial policy. This was especially imperative because the report rehashed that 'the role of Government is essentially that of providing the necessary basic services or infrastructure, and to create a general climate conducive to private investment from both internal and external sources'.[63] This incensed one member of parliament, P. Staub, who dismissed the report as of little value to the government because it did 'not give any guidance to government on a new policy, nor [did] it say anything that the government [was] not already doing ... the report [was] money not very well spent.'[64]

Following the report, the ARNI also published its *Blueprint of an Industrial Policy* in 1961, which emphasised the need for favourable government policy.[65] The ARNI later met with the new Minister of Commerce and Industry, J. A. Clark, who clarified the federal government's industrial strategy. The federal government accepted the necessity of economic planning and was in favour of the broader use of the customs tariff to stimulate industrial production. It was, however, opposed to the utilisation of import control on any scale for fostering industrial development, mainly because, apart from in exceptional circumstances, this form of control conflicted with the Federation's obligations under the GATT.[66] Industrialists also received valuable support from an African trade union, the Trades Union Congress, in 1961. Headed by Reuben Jamela, this delivered a memorandum emphasising that the organisation 'wished to see industrial prosperity in the country and wished for further protection for industry and a bold and progressive policy of industrialisation'.[67]

Similarly, in 1962, three key Southern Rhodesian government officials, namely Premier Edgar Whitehead, Minister of Treasury C. J. Hatty, and Minister of Labour A. E. Abrahamson, publicly emphasised the necessity of stimulating industrial development through tariff protection or import controls. Speaking in the legislative assembly on 17 July 1962, Welensky highlighted the necessity for Southern Rhodesia to have a significant drive to help secondary industry and expansion. He followed up these statements with a public speech on 9 August 1962, when he outlined the support given by the federal government to the manufacturing industry. 'My government's policy', he explained,

62 Southern Rhodesia, *Legislative Assembly Debate*, 9 November 1960, Col. 3966.

63 *Ibid.*, Col. 3948.

64 *Ibid.*, Col. 3969.

65 ARNI, *Blueprint of an Industrial Policy*, 1961.

66 ARNI, *Review of the Presidential Year*, 1961/62.

67 *Rhodesia Herald*, 18 August 1961.

> has always been to give protection wherever it can be shown that protection will benefit the country. In present circumstances, and particularly in view of what I have been saying about unemployment, I am willing to go further and say tonight, where it can be shown that employment will benefit from the extension of protection, my government will accept that as a strong argument for extending protection.[68]

Despite these half-hearted concessions, the government still had a lot to do in introducing a more active industrial policy. This was illustrated by the fact that this matter topped the list at the ARNI's annual congress in 1962, where it resolved to use tariff protection and import control as mechanisms for the promotion of industrial development and expansion.[69] Two more pronouncements in 1962 further confirmed the unreliability of the government in the eyes of industrialists.

First, in June 1962, the federal government published a policy statement entitled 'Federal Government Economic Policy: Principles' in conjunction with its development plan for 1962/65. As regards secondary industry, the statement made a guarded admission that 'certain types of manufacturing might be useful'.[70] The ARNI expressed its disappointment with the policy report:

> We expected something good. What did we get? A wordy conglomeration of nebulous observations and unsubstantiated opinions that appear to have been phrased to avoid any definite commitment whatsoever, prefaced by the classic piece of defeatism that all economic progress must await the improvement of political conditions. Now we know why the Federal Government has shown such a maidenly reluctance to publish its economic policy before. It has not got one.[71]

Second, the publication of the Phillips Report in 1962 added to industrialists' ill feelings towards government policy. The Southern Rhodesian government had appointed an *Advisory Committee on the Development of the Economic Resources of Southern Rhodesia, with Special Reference to African Agriculture* in 1961, chaired by W. Phillips.[72] It tabled its findings in 1962. The committee highlighted that the export-oriented primary industries remained the mainstay of the economy. These industries, it concluded, 'provided the greatest proportion of the output of the country ... the foreign exchange

68 ARNI, *Review of the Presidential Year*, 1961/62.

69 NAZ MS 1198 E.A.4/4 Protection of Industry, Resolution by the Salisbury Chamber of Industries, 1962.

70 *Rhodesian Recorder*, June 1962.

71 *Ibid.*, and also ARNI, *Record of Proceedings of Sixth Annual Congress*, 1962.

72 Government of Southern Rhodesia, *Report of the Advisory Committee on the Development of the Economic Resources of Southern Rhodesia, with Special Reference to African Agriculture* (Salisbury: Government Publishers, 1962).

earnings necessary to finance the imports of consumer goods, raw materials and capital equipment required to sustain the expansion of domestic industries and the standard of life of the population.'[73] The Phillips Report further warned that a policy of increased self-sufficiency, which increased the costs of the export industries and undercut their capacity to compete in world markets, would result in a slackening in the growth rate of the economy, if not an actual decline in incomes. This conclusion was strikingly similar to the ones reached by previous committees of the 1930s and 1945.

The committee's attitude towards the manufacturing industry disturbed industrialists. Lampooning the report, the ARNI's Chegwidden noted that by stressing the overriding importance of exports to the economy of the colony,

> the Phillips Report had unhesitatingly supported the old archaic views that national income of the Rhodesian people depended upon the successful exploitation of the comparative advantage obtainable by concentrating their productive efforts on exports of primary products in return for which they were able to import manufactured goods that could either not be produced in Rhodesia at all or whose production locally would be so expensive as to yield a very much smaller quantity of goods than could be purchased for the same effort devoted to the production of exports.[74]

In 1945, industrialists had accepted that, at the time, hardly anyone could challenge this attitude because the miners, farmers, and merchants were the most powerful elements in society. But that, as late as 1962, the government still accepted such advice worried them. In listening to such advice, to industrialists, the government reinforced its long-held view that secondary industry was hardly worth fostering at all.

Towards Decolonisation: Politics, Economic Crisis, and Industrial Development

As alluded to earlier, from late 1956 onwards, the Federation faced its most serious economic crisis, when copper prices slumped on the global market. As the copper mining industry was the backbone of the federal economy, its decline had a multiplier effect. At the same time, the heightened African opposition to

73 *Ibid.*, 358–59; See also E. S. Pangeti, 'The state and manufacturing industry: a study of the state as regulator and entrepreneur in Zimbabwe' (PhD, University of Zimbabwe, 1996), 106; and A. S. Mlambo, E. S. Pangeti, and I. Phimister, *Zimbabwe: A History of Manufacturing, 1890–1995* (Harare: University of Zimbabwe Publications, 2000), 45–48.

74 ARNI, *Record of Proceedings of Sixth Annual Congress*, 1962.

the Federation added to the spectre of economic gloom.[75] This was exacerbated by the intensification of the implementation of the Native Land Husbandry Act of 1951 (NLHA).[76] Both African resistance to the Federation and the application of NLHA 'led to a reduction in employment opportunities, and large numbers of Africans who had formerly derived a part of their income from the land now found themselves not only unemployed but landless'.[77] For Southern Rhodesian African nationalists,

> Any act whose effects undermine the security of our small land rights ... dispossess us of our little wealth in the form of cattle, disperse us from our ancestral homes in the reserves and reduce us to the status of vagabonds and as a source of cheap labour for the farmers, miners and industrialists – such an Act will turn the African people against society to the detriment of the peace and progress of this country.[78]

The threat began to manifest itself by 1958, when African protests and political mobilisation in the three federal territories increased. These political developments resulted in states of emergency in 1959, as well as investigations into the future of the Federation.[79] All of this had economic consequences. The immediate effect was a slowdown in the Federation's economic advance and a lack of confidence from overseas investors.[80] The feeling was that the Federation was collapsing and that, because of this, it was not worth giving financial support. American investors quite openly expressed their preference for an investment climate underpinned by 'a settled, stable government, through which a suitable legal framework has been created'.[81] They prioritised investment in areas where there was a 'steady increase in the earning capacity of the

75 For more, see A. Cohen, *The Politics and Economics of Decolonisation in Central Africa*.

76 The objectives of this statute were to stem the fragmentation of the land and to promote good farming habits, making the right to cultivate land conditional upon the observance of sound methods of husbandry. In doing so, it sought to create a loyal urban and rural African middle class, satisfying at the same time the country's need for the rapid expansion of secondary industry by denying urban workers access to farmland. This expectation, however, was not fulfilled. See also I. Phimister, 'Rethinking the reserves: Southern Rhodesia's Land Husbandry Act reviewed', *Journal of Southern African Studies*, 19, 2 (1993), 225–39.

77 Gloria C. Passmore, 'Historical rationale of the policy of community development in the African rural areas', *Zambezia*, II, i (1971), 63.

78 Cited in Phimister, 'Rethinking the reserves, 227–28.

79 *Rhodesia Herald*, 3 June 1959. See also Cohen, *The Politics and Economics of Decolonisation in Central Africa*.

80 *Rhodesia Herald*, 3 June 1959.

81 *Ibid.*, 16 September 1959.

indigenous population.'[82] The Federation in general, and Southern Rhodesia in particular, was not such a place during this time.

Despite the discouraging political environment, the Governor of the Bank of Rhodesia and Nyasaland, A. P. Grafftey-Smith, remained optimistic. In 1959, he said that despite a slowdown in the flow of private capital to the Federation, its economy was healthier than in 1958. The inflow of private capital to the Federation in 1959 was between £12 and £15 million, and there was still a favourable balance on visible trade of £35 million for the first nine months of 1959.[83] In addition, international companies were making inquiries and others were applying for permission to operate in the Federation.[84] The British Motor Corporation, the Ford Motor Company, and the Rootes Group all established assembly plants in Southern Rhodesia in 1960. Also, the number of industries rose from 1,000 in 1955 to well over 1,300 in 1960, while in the same period gross output increased from £94 million to about £150 million, despite the unsettled political situation.[85] At the same time, in 1960, the South African government relaxed restrictions on the flow of capital to the Federation. According to the Minister of Finance, Donald Macintyre, money was expected to come from the Union for purposes like 'direct investment in either new or existing businesses in the Federation, the purchase of equity shares and the purchase of physical assets such as office blocks.'[86]

The political climate in the Federation and the region worsened in 1960–1961. Agitation by African nationalists now threatened to derail industrial development. For them, among other factors, the state of industrial development in the country was used as the justification for denying political power to Black Africans. Joshua Nkomo, one of the nationalist leaders, said the British government had told him that 'they were not prepared to hand over the country to inexperienced people because it was a highly industrialised country.'[87] He thus warned, 'if industry stands in the way of democracy, we shall set it aside.'[88] However, he qualified this by stating that he was not against industrialists but 'could not stand an obstacle for the sake of a few people who want to make money.'[89] Nkomo's warning caught the attention of the ARNI; this prompted this body to seek an audience with him, hoping to 'put across to him the

82 *Ibid.*
83 *Rhodesia Herald*, 18 November 1959.
84 See reports in the *Rhodesia Herald*, 24 June and 11 August 1960; and NAZ MS 1198 EA6/3, Letter by Leonard Tow to ARNI, 17 June 1960.
85 NAZ MS 1198 EA6, Overseas Investments, 1957–1962: Memorandum on Investment and Development in Industry, undated.
86 *Rhodesia Herald*, 15 January 1960.
87 *The Sunday Mail*, 20 August 1961.
88 *Ibid.*
89 *Ibid.*

significance of industrial development to the African in particular'.[135] The details of the eventual meeting were, however, not made public.

In 1961, the Secretary to the Federal Treasury also enumerated other series of events, creating anxieties among investors. The Sharpeville massacres occurred in the Union of South Africa in 1960 and Belgian Congo became independent the same year, while in Southern Rhodesia riots broke out in African townships. Furthermore, the Advisory Commission on the Review of the Constitution of the Federation of Rhodesia and Nyasaland (the Monckton Commission) was published, giving the right to secede to all territories of the Federation. All these events impacted the level of confidence in the Federation, such that, as the treasury noted, 'no major project financed by private capital from overseas has been announced'. [90] Business leaders in the Federation also remarked that the ensuing recession was attributable to the parallel political trouble and the uncertainty hanging over the Federation, resulting in the 'stepped flight of capital ... a move, which has increased public distrust [while] many Europeans are pessimistic about finding a way out of the recession and openly talk of union with South Africa as the only hope'.[91] Domestic investors became sceptical as their confidence was shaken by this 'unsettled political situation ... to such an extent that [they] tended to remove [their] capital elsewhere'.[92] The treasury felt it necessary to curb any significant residential capital outflows because had any such likely movement happened on a grander scale, 'the Federal economy would have been irreparably harmed, with increased unemployment following a sharp decline in economic activity'.[93]

To curb the potential flight that could have emanated from these fears, the federal government introduced the Exchange Control (Temporary Measures) Act 1961. This was temporary in nature, and the measures applied to domestic capital and not outside investors, who were 'free to enter and leave the Federation at any time, subject only to the technical requirements of passing through the control machinery to ensure that it is non-resident monies'.[94] The Ministry of Finance, however, annually renewed the control measures until the dissolution of the Federation in 1963. Even Southern Rhodesia adopted a similar approach, and this became the cornerstone of economic policy during the UDI, as will be discussed in a later section.

Business took a keener interest in the political developments in the country. 'Financial, commercial and industrial circles in Salisbury', reported the *Rhodesia Herald* in February 1961, were 'studying in detail the decisions

90 A. Mseba, 'Money and finance in a closed economy: Rhodesia's monetary experience, 1965–1980' (MA, University of Zimbabwe, 2007), 32.

91 Africa Institute Bulletin, 9 March 1961.

92 Mseba, 'Money and finance in a closed economy', 32.

93 *Ibid.*

94 *Ibid.*

of the Southern Rhodesia Constitution Conference and their possible implications.'[95] However, the spokespersons for all significant bodies but the ARNI declared that it was too early to formulate ideas on the effects the decisions were likely to have. For the ARNI's president, 'any settlement of Southern Rhodesia's problems was bound to have a favourable reaction in industry and the flow of overseas capital into the country'.[96] The BCI shared this optimism when it reported that 'major plans for the expansion of Bulawayo's industry lie "pigeon-holed" in the offices of several firms – awaiting the outcome of the referendum and a more settled political situation'.[97] The ARNI president expressed similar optimism in 1962 when he said:

> although the political changes are not yet finalised and the full effect on the economy cannot be seen, the outlook is by no means dismal. I think it is going to prove right that stability, resulting from changes which have taken place, will provide a sounder basis for industry than the uncertainty of the past few years, whatever the details of the changes may prove to be.[98]

As negotiations for the dissolution of the Federation gathered pace from 1962, so industrialists became increasingly alarmed. Writing to the British Secretary of State for Central Africa, R. A. Butler, the ARNI president said:

> My association representing the manufacturing industry in the Rhodesias and Nyasaland earnestly appeals for the preservation of strong and enduring economic links between Rhodesias as essential means of avoiding impediment to long term industrial development in both territories and creation of unnecessary additional unemployment among all races. Continued economic association is imperative for ensuring the maximum growth of the economy in future years to the benefit of all.[99]

More than this, industrialists, especially from Southern Rhodesia, feared the loss of the lucrative domestic market afforded by the Federation.

The ARNI studied how the economic problems likely to arise as a result of the dissolution would affect manufacturers. It was apparent for various reasons, not least financial ones, that the separate territories wished to resume

95 *Rhodesia Herald*, 9 February 1961.
96 *Ibid.*
97 *Ibid.*, 26 April 1961.
98 ARNI, *Report for the Presidential Year*, 1962/1963; and also an essay by Professor W. L. Taylor of the University College of Rhodesia and Nyasaland published in the *Rhodesian Recorder*, July 1962, wherein he argued that 'the tough conflicts in the political and economic spheres and the relentless onset of economic decline will slowly precipitate a fumbling and groping movement towards solutions which offer prospects for ultimate success, over the long haul'.
99 NAZ MS 1198 EA/4, Memo by P. C. Aldridge to the Office of the Rhodesian Prime Minister, 25 March 1963.

their powers of imposing customs tariffs and subjecting inter-territorial trade to restrictions. During the ten years of the Federation's existence, its trade statistics were kept on a federal basis. No information regarding inter-territorial trade was available – information which was vital to the ARNI in assessing the possible effects of dissolution on its members, and information which the three territorial governments also needed to carry out their examination of the probable consequences of dissolution on their economies.[100] Those predictions that were made were at best generalisations.

In 1962, an election in Southern Rhodesia ushered in a new government under the Rhodesian Front party led by Winston Field. The Rhodesian Front was a right-wing party that perceived the Rhodesian business community to be its most prominent and potentially threatening antagonist because of its assumed closer political links with the United Federal Party. According to Rowe, 'the Rhodesian Front immediately began using the power of office to systematically undermine the foundations of business influence. It stripped the business community's representative associations of their role in administering government policy.'[101] In light of that, it was important for the ARNI to ascertain the views of the new government and its policy concerning industrial development, protection, and other aspects of the economy. The ARNI put before the Rhodesian Front government the matters it had discussed with its predecessor. The new prime minister, Field, stated soon after he took office that he was 'an old-fashioned protectionist.'[102] Field and his ministers used the same phrase on various occasions. Industry, therefore, felt that the protectionist policy, so essential to a developing country and adopted, albeit somewhat reluctantly and half-heartedly, by the federal government, would be embraced in Southern Rhodesia when the territory resumed full fiscal powers from 1 January 1964.

At the same time, encouraging developments took place. First, the new prime minister split the portfolios of the Minister of Mines and Industrial Development into two, the latter becoming the Ministry of Trade, Industry and Development. Secondly, the new Minister of Industry, G. W. Rudland, introduced a new policy when he moved for the second reading of the Industrial Development Bill that would later become the Industrial Development Act 1963, which birthed the Industrial Development Corporation (IDC).[103] Government

100 ARNI, *Report for the Presidential Year*, 1962/1963.

101 D. M. Rowe, *Manipulating the Market: Understanding Economic Sanctions, Institutional Change and the Political Unity of White Rhodesia* (Chicago: Chicago University Press, 2001), 106.

102 ARNI, *Report for the Presidential Year*, 1962/1963.

103 The IDC was a wholly owned state holding company created by Act of Parliament in 1963, with initial nominal capital of $10 million, divided into 5 million shares of $2 each. It was established to invest in economic enterprises and assist with its expert services in the promotion of objects which the government decided to be in

policy, Rudland stated, was designed to achieve two results: 'to put to work the machines and men that were idle because of the present slackness of local business and to create new enterprises and new jobs to renew the expansion of which the economy was capable.'[104] It satisfied industrialists to find that the minister's full statement contained many points that the ARNI had impressed upon both the federal and territorial governments for a long time; it was 'encouraging to feel that the representations [were] not in vain.'[105] Industrialists also raised questions concerning the steps the government would take to protect the market for Southern Rhodesian manufactured goods after federal dissolution. In a parliamentary statement Rudland added, 'government will pursue its expressed policy of external trade representation in every country where markets exist or are likely to exist for goods manufactured in Southern Rhodesia. The government will seek to enter into reciprocal trade agreements with neighbouring territories.'[106]

Consequently, the Southern Rhodesian government moved to negotiate a new trade agreement to replace the 1960 one. The ARNI's view on renegotiation insisted on the retention of the existing levels of protection against South African competition. 'This seems to be of prime importance bearing in mind the break-up of the Federation and the limitations of the domestic market, which now consists of Southern Rhodesia alone', justified industrialists.[107] They further clarified that South Africa consistently maintained that it was not opposed to the protection of the Southern Rhodesian industry; rather, all it sought was parity of tariff treatment with the UK. In that respect, it was deemed feasible to select specific classes of goods not produced locally, which could form the subject of a reciprocal tariff concession to South Africa.[162] This resulted in the negotiation of a new agreement in 1964.

Reconfiguring Trade Relations

In August 1964, industrialists met with the Minister of Trade, Industry and Development to discuss the approach to the negotiations of the trade agreement. Meanwhile, the ARNI changed its name to the Association of Rhodesian Industries (ARnI) to reflect its geographical representation following the dissolution of the Federation. The ARnI now only represented industrial interests

the national interest. For more on the IDC, see Pangeti, 'The state and manufacturing', 201–13, and the *Rhodesian Recorder*, October 1963.

104 ARNI, *Report for the Presidential Year*, 1962/1963.

105 *Ibid.*

106 Legislative Assembly Debates, 1 March 1963, Col. 1195.

107 NAZ [R]ecords [C]entre, [L]ocation. C21.6.9R, [B]ox 141849, Commerce and Industry, 1963–1972: ARNI, A Memorandum for members of the Economic Affairs Committee by P. Aldridge, 29 May 1964.

in Southern Rhodesia. At the meeting, Chegwidden, of the ARnI, pointed out that the association had already expressed that the prospects for developing the export of manufactured goods to South Africa were necessarily limited, but its immediate concern was import controls.[108] The ARnI felt it was important that this matter be dealt with, because in all previous agreements with South Africa, special provisions had been made, but these had precluded the imposition of import controls. In response, the minister said that he was loath to include a requirement for import controls in any new agreement because what was needed was an expansion of trade between the two countries. 'It was not in South Africa's interest to see the Southern Rhodesian industry closed down,' the minister continued. 'There was a tremendous feeling of goodwill in South Africa towards Southern Rhodesia.'[109] The minister's response was a surprise: it appeared he vouched for South Africa more than his own industrialists.

An even more seemingly dismissive response came when Chegwidden raised the subject of consultation. Citing the example of South Africa, wherein in the previous trade agreement negotiations, representatives of private organisations in South Africa were closely consulted at all stages, he grumbled that 'the representatives of organised industry in Southern Rhodesia had been ignored or simply not consulted at all.'[110] The ARnI wished its government would adopt similar methods to South Africa. Chegwidden thus enquired on whether the representatives of the organised industry would be consulted in the impending negotiations, to which the reply was 'this was a matter which must be left to officials to decide at their discretion.'[111] The minister's response carried undertones of disinterest in an otherwise crucial matter raised by the ARnI. Industry often received such treatment from the executive.

Eventually, on 30 November 1964, Southern Rhodesia and South Africa signed a new trade agreement, which came into effect on 1 December 1964. The agreement would become crucial in sanctions-busting and the survival of the Rhodesian economy during the UDI period.[112] It provided for preferential tariff treatment of trade in both directions between the two countries. According to Rudland, 'the new agreement reflects the determination of both governments to bring about a considerable expansion in trade and the closest possible economic relationships between the two countries.'[113] Broadly speaking, the

108 NAZ RC, L. C21.6.9R, B141849, Commerce and Industry, 1963–1972: ARNI, Notes of a Meeting with the Minister of Trade, Industry and Development on 13 August 1964.

109 *Ibid.*

110 *Ibid.*

111 *Ibid.*

112 Mlambo, Pangeti, and Phimister, *Zimbabwe: A History of Manufacturing*, 54–55.

113 NAZ MS1199/18/4, ARNI, Trade Agreement with South Africa, Statement by the Minister of Trade, Industry and Development on the Signing of the South African Trade Agreement, 30 November 1964.

concessions in both directions that were provided for in the 1960 agreement were retained. The exception was that a wide range of South African goods would now enjoy increased tariff preferences; in some cases, the special preferences extended to Britain and, in other instances, preferences between those enjoyed by Britain and the general Commonwealth preferences.[114] Among the items to which these new preferences applied were specified manufactured foodstuffs, blankets, carpets, ladies' stockings, household linen, woollen equipment, specific glassware and chinaware, clothing footwear, and jewellery. Meanwhile, a wide range of Rhodesian products would enjoy duty-free entry into South Africa or entry at preferential rates. Overall, about 75% of all Rhodesian manufactured exports went to South Africa under this agreement. As Pangeti observed, 'this was a significant percentage of Rhodesian trade, and, under sanctions, this Agreement was to turn South Africa into Rhodesia's lifeline, providing market, source of investment capital and much-needed transit trade routes'.[115]

The break-up of the Federation also actuated discussions on trade arrangements with Northern Rhodesia. On the dissolution of the Central African Federation (CAF), the three separate territories agreed to adopt their own customs tariffs, which were similar to the federal ones in structure and the level of duties. This implied that in trade between Northern Rhodesia and Southern Rhodesia, the manufactured goods of the one territory would be admitted into the other territory at no, or the lowest, rates of duty. Southern Rhodesia announced, however, that for a short while, the duties on Northern Rhodesian manufactured goods would be suspended, thereby permitting importation into Southern Rhodesia free of duty. Conversely, Northern Rhodesia agreed to suspend most of the duties on Southern Rhodesian manufactured products, but where Northern Rhodesia considered it necessary to retain a measure of protection of their factories, it could do so. Broadly speaking, the trading arrangement between the two countries consisted solely of governmental decisions duly gazetted to suspend duties, and no official instrument purporting to represent a trade agreement existed. When asked about the prospects of a trade agreement with Northern Rhodesia, Aldridge, director of the ARnI, explained that 'so far as can be ascertained the Southern Rhodesian government does not appear to have exercised any initiative in approaching the Northern Rhodesia government in connection with the negotiation of a formal trade agreement'.[116]

Some Rhodesian industrialists raised concerns over this arrangement. Aldridge reported that complaints reached him regarding the 'unfair'

114 *Ibid.*

115 Mlambo, Pangeti, and Phimister, *Zimbabwe: A History of Manufacturing*, 55.

116 NAZ RC, L. C21.6.9R, B141849, Commerce and Industry, 1963–1972: ARNI, A Memorandum for Members of the Economic Affairs Committee by P. Aldridge, 29 May 1964.

arrangement that saw certain Southern Rhodesian manufactured products bearing customs duty when imported into Northern Rhodesia while no customs duties were levied on any Northern Rhodesian products imported into Southern Rhodesia.[117] For this reason, Aldridge urged the ARnI's Economic Affairs Committee to seek clarification on the Southern Rhodesian policy or attitude towards Northern Rhodesia on future trade relations. However, he cautioned that

> in cases where particular Southern Rhodesian manufacturers can show that their export trade to Northern Rhodesia is being impeded by the imposition of duties, then I recommend that ARNI should assist by suggesting that the Southern Rhodesia government should consider tactfully taking up particular cases with the Northern Rhodesia government. I see no purpose, however, in presenting a generalised case based on an attempt to secure reciprocal free trade.[118]

Just like the case of South Africa, the future trading relationship with Northern Rhodesia came up for discussion when an ARnI delegation met the minister in August 1964. Chipman of the ARnI highlighted that 'there appeared to be an attitude on the part of certain businessmen in the North in favour of breaking the trading relationship with Southern Rhodesia'.[119] In his response, the minister acknowledged that he was 'well aware of this and it appears to be a popular line of thought on certain quarters for various reasons', but that he did not think this attitude had any real significance.[120] Although the thought did not prevail then, political developments – that is, Zambia's attainment of independence in 1964 and the UDI in 1965 – affected the trade relations.

The Threat and Implications of UDI

As industrialists engaged the government over industrial policy, political developments in the country posed a new challenge. Following the federal dissolution, the Rhodesian Front government in Southern Rhodesia engaged in negotiations for independence, under a White minority rule, with Britain.[121]

117 *Ibid.*

118 *Ibid.*

119 *Ibid.*, ARNI, Notes of a Meeting with the Minister of Trade, Industry and Development on 13 August 1964.

120 *Ibid.*

121 For details of these discussions, see L. White, *Unpopular Sovereignty: Rhodesian Independence and African Decolonization* (Chicago: University of Chicago Press, 2015); A. S. Mlambo, 'From the Second World War to UDI, 1940–1965', in B. Raftopoulos and A. S. Mlambo (eds), *Becoming Zimbabwe: A History from the Pre-colonial Period to 2008* (Harare: Weaver Press, 2009), 75–114; F. Clements, *Rhodesia: The Road to Collision* (London: Pall Mall Press, 1969); and L. Bowman,

When these negotiations collapsed, the Rhodesian Front government threatened a UDI. On 29 June 1964, the ARnI's president stated that 'any precipitate action which might fan the flame of hostility towards Southern Rhodesia and prejudice neighbouring markets for our manufactured goods and world markets for our primary products would be disastrous to the Southern Rhodesian economy.'[122] By October 1964, those fears appeared imminent. The threat of UDI invited Britain's pronouncements. On 27 October 1964, the British prime minister, Harold Wilson, issued a statement against a UDI by the Rhodesian government. Wilson warned that a UDI would be 'an open act of defiance and rebellion [which was] treasonable.'[123] More threateningly, it stated that

> an illegal declaration of independence in Southern Rhodesia would bring to end relationships between her and Britain, would cut her off from the rest of Commonwealth, from most foreign governments and international organisations, would inflict disastrous economic damage on her and would leave her isolated and virtually friendless in a largely hostile continent.[124]

Because of the gravity of the economic consequences mentioned in the statement, Rhodesian industrialists, understandably, reacted. The ARnI executive met to assess the implications of UDI and the British declaration. It was apparent at the meeting that the manufacturing industry in Southern Rhodesia had been capitalised and developed based on the former federal market. The assessment also revealed that the gross output of the Rhodesian industry 'in 1964 was estimated at £170 million, of which exports were expected at £45 million. Of this amount, Zambia would absorb almost £30 million worth of manufactured exports, while Malawi would take £4 million and South Africa about £6 million.'[125] Because of this reality, if Rhodesia found herself outside the Commonwealth, duties on Rhodesian products would automatically be subjected to a non-preferential higher rate of duty – assuming trade was permitted to continue in the usual way.

The meeting also unanimously called for an immediate response to the British government's pronouncement. Accordingly, the ARnI stuck its neck out and cautioned that

---

Politics in Rhodesia: White Power in an African State (Cambridge, MA: Harvard University Press, 1973).

122 As quoted in ARNI News Bulletin No. 14/64, 29 October 1964.

123 NAZ RC, L. C21.6.9R, B141849, Commerce and Industry, 1963–1972: Statement of Views of British Government on a Unilateral Declaration of Independence in Southern Rhodesia, 27 October 1964.

124 *Ibid.*

125 ARNI News Bulletin No. 14/64, 29 October 1964.

> while recognising that independence for the country is the ultimate aim of all, ARnI feels that the point of no return in negotiations has not yet been reached … the effect of such a step [UDI] on the industrial sector of the Rhodesian economy would be catastrophic, resulting in widespread unemployment at every level consequent upon the loss of markets and a slowing down of the economy generally.[126]

Through the statement, the ARnI also suggested a meeting of all economic interest groups to discuss the impending threat. On 29 October 1964, the representatives of the RNFU, Rhodesia Tobacco Association, Tobacco Trade Association of Rhodesia, National Coordinating Council of the Clothing Industry of Southern Rhodesia, CATMA, and the Rhodesian Society of Accountants attended a meeting with ARnI. From the meeting came public statements condemning any UDI.

However, when the Southern Rhodesian government eventually proclaimed the UDI on 11 November 1965, industrialists changed tack. One newspaper reported that 'industrialists in Rhodesia are preparing to go on a war footing in a determined effort to counteract the effects of [potential] sanctions'.[127] For Rowe, all the influence industrialists had previously exerted on the government dissipated once the UDI was announced and industrialists became acquiescent.[128] Even more, the UDI brought the government into the economic sphere much more actively. Political and economic conditions dictated that the government became interventionist. Free enterprise was on the back foot. One way the government did this was through its import control policy.

Import Control Policy

The government of Southern Rhodesia introduced an import control policy to hedge its foreign exchange reserves. Import control, however, had been used since 1947, although this was limited to dollar imports. This mainly applied to products that could be produced in Rhodesia. It was also in the context of the post-war dollar crisis that engulfed Britain. The remaining dollar import controls were removed in November 1959.[129] However, in 1961, the federal government introduced yet other controls, namely Exchange Control (Temporary Measures), to regulate capital flows, which had the same effect of reserving foreign exchange. In 1964, these measures were upgraded to the Southern Rhodesia Exchange Control Act. The act gave powers to the Reserve Bank

126 NAZ RC, L. C21.6.9R, B141849, Commerce and Industry, 1963–1972: ARnI, Statement Issued by the Association of Rhodesian Industries, 27 October 1964.

127 *Herald Africa News Service*, November 1965.

128 Rowe, *Manipulating the Market*, 106–09; and Phimister and Gwande, 'Secondary industry and settler colonialism', 85–112.

129 Legislative Assembly Debates, 18 August 1959, Col. 3696.

governor to oversee: (i) the prohibition or restriction of dealings in or possession of any gold, currency, or securities; (ii) the prohibition or restriction of the importation into and exportation from Rhodesia of any property; and (iii) the prohibition or restriction of any dealing in or concerning any property with persons resident outside Rhodesia.[130] It further provided for the control of imports and exports from Rhodesia and the transfer or settlement of property, payments, and transactions concerning debts.[131]

An import control system (ICS) accompanied the Exchange Control Act. On 3 November 1965, the Minister of Finance, John Wrathall, in consultation with the Governor of the Reserve Bank of Rhodesia, Noel Bruce, and the Minister of Commerce and Industry, G. W. Rudland, intensified an ICS of goods into Rhodesia with effect from 4 November 1965. This was prompted by the realisation that 'indenting for goods at an abnormally high level has created a contingent liability for payments which, if allowed to materialise could well have a serious effect on our external reserves' and therefore 'timely and precautionary action is being taken to limit the strain on our reserves and to restore the situation.'[132]

Consequently, imports now required an import licence and prior approval from the government. Worth noting, however, is that the ICS intended to save the foreign currency and not to assist the local manufacturing industry. Any benefits to industry that accrued were incidental. If anything, the ICS with the accompanying foreign currency control initially stifled the manufacturing industry. Given the abruptness with which the government announced control measures, the authorities had to clarify the effect of the measures on imports already ordered or in transit. In that respect, 'foreign currency to meet the cost of goods shipped or railed up to and including midnight 3 November will be provided by banks against relevant shipping and railing documents, in such cases no import licence will be required, [but] all other goods, not shipped or railed, by midnight (3 November) will require an import license', clarified the ministry.[133]

In 1965 the government announced new regulations, the Control of Goods [Import] Regulations, to augment terms of the Control of Goods Act (1954).[134] After the UDI, the Minister of Commerce and Industry issued a statement reiterating that 'the restrictions on imports will have to be intensified.'[135] This followed Britain's imposition of sanctions in response to the UDI. In light of

130 Southern Rhodesia, Exchange Control Act, No. 62, 1964.

131 *Ibid.*

132 NAZ MS1198, Import Control Policy: ARNI News Bulletin, 4 November 1965.

133 *Ibid.*

134 *Rhodesia Government Notice No. 721A, Control of Goods (Import) Regulations,* 1965.

135 NAZ MS1198, Import Control Policy: Statement by the Hon. G. W. Rudland, 12 November 1965.

this, he advised that the licensing system that had been put in place earlier would be invalidated in order to deal with changed circumstances because of sanctions. The minister, therefore, pleaded with the business community to 'accept the inconvenience suffered gracefully' after the disruption caused by the invalidation of licences they had acquired.[136] He also emphasised that under sanctions, 'we can spend only what we earn'.

The severity and duration of the controls depended upon the impact of the sanctions imposed on Southern Rhodesia. The government impressed upon business that 'the immediate issues confronting us are our ability to secure adequate supplies of essential commodities, our ability to earn foreign currency to pay for these supplies and our ability to sustain economic activity'.[137] Naturally, ARnI had to respond to this government plea. It set up a special committee known as the ARnI Import/Export Coordinating Committee, to keep under review national policy and administration relating to imports and exports and to make representations to the proper authorities directly, whenever the occasion required.[138] Stressing that ARnI was a non-political association of industrialists whose principal objective was the development of manufacturing industry in Rhodesia, it stated: 'now that the die was cast and independence declared, the sentiment of the organisation will solidly support a policy designed to mitigate the impact of economic sanctions'.[139] It undertook to conserve foreign exchange by curtailing imports and replacing such imports, where practicable and desirable, by expanding or creating the means of producing the goods concerned within Rhodesia, and to earn foreign exchange by vigorously searching for more markets and promoting manufactured goods for export by fiscal or other means of production.

The foregoing principles were the mainspring of the new government policy in the economic field. To give effect to these principles, the ARnI advised that the system of import quotas (control) on a commodity basis needed some adjustments. The allocation system operated in the following manner. The Associated Chambers of Commerce of Rhodesia (ACCOR), the successor to ACCORN, undertook administrative responsibility for currency allocations to importers. Commodities of a similar nature were grouped together, and importers of such items formed a merchant group. These groups then appointed an allocations committee. For applications received in this way, if the amount of currency available for each tariff item was known, the committee apportioned the amount among the applicants. The basis of allocation depended on the committee.

136 *Ibid.*
137 *Ibid.*
138 Ibid, ARNI News Bulletin, 17 November 1965.
139 Ibid, Memorandum by the ARnI Import/Export Coordinating Committee, December 1965.

However, the ARnI complained about this arrangement. It sought a meeting with the Minister of Finance and the Minister of Commerce and Industry and his secretary. It pleaded that the system of groups should be reviewed to ensure that,

> in the national interest, manufacturers are in a position in future quota periods to secure their allocations of capital goods and materials for industrial use, whether such items are imported direct, or by merchants or agents and the handling of all currency requirements for industry by ARnI.[140]

The ARnI still complained that the ACCOR seemed to have continued with the same allocating powers despite the agreement that allocation for industry should be left to the ARnI. It further highlighted that the application of the quota need not be universal. For instance, merchants, agents, and wholesalers could not, as a class, be treated separately from the clients whose needs they existed to satisfy.[141] The logic ought to have been that the merchant or wholesaler would operate as an importer to the extent that his clients entrusted him with the task of obtaining their permitted imports.

The grouping of commodities created tension between the ARnI and its members. For example, a company called Consolidated Lighting complained to the ARnI that its

> manufacturing and assembling interests are prejudiced and not protected by being tied to a merchant group body, we are convinced that a continuation of this arrangement can only affect us detrimentally in the manufacture and assembly of light fittings for the local and export markets.[142]

The Bulawayo Chamber of Industries (BCI) also registered its displeasure. In a letter to the ARnI, it wrote:

> the present system of controlling imports demonstrates masterly incompetence and a quite naïve ignorance of the needs of business. It is now seven weeks since import control was introduced, and despite assurances, a large number of manufacturers are still not aware of the allocations, which have been made to them. The government system of Groups, classified by customs tariffs, cannot continue. The glaring omissions from the Group schedules have had very clear reactions: the first has been the gross overloading of the General Group 17; the second has been to arouse the hostility of industrialists towards ARnI. The majority of manufacturers, with whom

140 Ibid, Letter by Aldridge to the Secretary of Commerce and Industry, 18 November 1965.

141 Ibid, Memorandum by the ARnI Import/Export Coordinating Committee, December 1965.

142 *Ibid.*, Letter by Consolidated Lighting to the ARnI, 29 December 1965.

we had to deal in Bulawayo, were no doubt as confused, upset and even angry, as were their Salisbury counterparts. [143]

The BCI suggested an overhaul of the existing allocation or grouping system. The obtaining system made a manufacturer dependent on several committees, thereby delaying, if not neglecting, the fulfilment of his domestic needs. Instead, 'a system based upon industrial sectors [with] a committee composed of manufacturers in allied areas is an excellent one. Each sector should be well defined, and no manufacturer should be governed by more than one allocating committee.'[144] The ARnI's Chegwidden concurred with this suggestion. He remarked,

> If the government considers it vital that allocations are made on an item by item basis, then at least let them consult the expert, the man whose business it is and let him compile tariff lists. If the Rhodesian industry is to survive then, manufacturers must feel that the government is making some effort on their behalf. If industry feels that besides fighting the rest of the world, it is also required to fight against its bureaucratic procedures, then the game is lost before it has properly started.[145]

Despite all the grumbling, however, all the industrialists agreed that

> we are now, all of us, engaged in a battle for our economic survival. We shall be successful in this in proportion to the extent to which we abandon previous laissez-faire attitudes and engage in vigorous planning. If we win, and we must win, we may well emerge from the struggle with a far stronger and more closely integrated economy than ever before.[146]

Meanwhile, in controlling imports, the Rhodesian government abolished the imperial preference for goods formerly traded with the UK and the Channel Islands. In any case, the imperial preference was now academic, since sanctions had stopped any formal or official trade between Southern Rhodesia and the UK. Besides import control, currency controls and allocations intensified after the UDI. From 15 November 1965, the ARnI assumed the task of handling currency allocations connected with the importation of all materials for manufacturing, processing, and assembling industries.[147] The impact of import

143 *Ibid.*, Bulawayo Chamber of Industries Memo on Import Control Measures, 23 December 1965.

144 *Ibid.*

145 NAZ MS1198, Import Control Policy: Memorandum by Sir Thomas Chegwidden on ARnI Import–Export Committee, 22 November 1965; and *ibid.*, Statement by P. C. Aldridge on Import control, Policy and Administration, 23 November 1965.

146 *Ibid.*, Memorandum by Sir Thomas Chegwidden on ARnI Import–Export Committee, 22 November 1965.

147 *Rhodesian Herald*, 15 November 1965.

and currency control on the economy in general and secondary industry in particular shall be explored in detail in the next chapter. For now, the following section examines manufacturing growth under the political and economic environment obtaining between 1957 and 1965.

Manufacturing Growth, 1957–1965

Even as Southern Rhodesia went through economic and political turmoil, the manufacturing sector grew in both number and value, as shown in Table 4.1 below.

Table 4.1. Manufacturing sector 1958–1962.

Years	Number of units	Gross output (£' 000)	Net output (£' 000)	Total wages and salaries paid (£' 000)
1958	973	109,194	44,661	23,625
1959	967	120,067	48,830	24,746
1960	975	129,059	50,892	25,504
1961	1,029	141,661	55,997	28,517
1962	1,043	148,704	59,630	31,051

Source: *Census of Industrial Production*, 1938–1962.

The contribution of manufacturing to the economy had increased to such an extent that it surpassed mining by a great margin, and was closing in on agriculture. Considering that agriculture's contribution included both European and African output, manufacturing was arguably the most significant contributor to the national GDP. Table 4.2 below shows the contribution of agriculture, mining, and manufacturing sectors to the country's GDP.

Table 4.2. Contribution to the National GDP: Manufacturing, agriculture, and mining, 1957–1965 (£ millions).

Sector	1957	1958	1959	1960	1961	1962	1963	1964	1965
Agriculture	47.0	46.7	50.8	51.9	62.3	62.5	64.2	69.3	66.7
Mining and quarrying	17.5	17.6	17.2	19.1	18.7	17.0	15.8	19.0	23.1
Manufacturing	35.8	38.8	41.8	44.9	49.2	52.1	53.8	59.1	66.1

Source: *Economic Survey of Rhodesia for 1966.*

Another essential feature of the manufacturing industry during this time was the extent of foreign ownership and control of industrial production. A survey by the Central Statistics Office in 1963 revealed that out of 420 firms surveyed, 147 were either branches or subsidiaries of a big foreign corporation.[148] Of that figure, 72 were controlled from within South Africa. 'Branches, subsidiaries, and associates of foreign companies earned just under 67 percent of the total recorded net operating profits and were responsible for 72 percent of the total recorded capital formation', revealed the survey.[149] Industrial production also increasingly became monopolistic. Approximately 146 large firms (those with a gross output of £250,000 or more) produced 76.2% of all industrial production in 1963, whereas 592 smaller firms (those with a gross output of £40,000 or less) accounted for only 5.2% of the production.[150]

Conclusion

This chapter has demonstrated the continued contestations and shifts in the relationship between the government and industrialists. The industrialists' representative organisation expanded from the FRI to the ARNI, encompassing all three territories in the CAF. The industrialists hoped that this strength in numbers would be met by sympathetic recognition from the government. But it did not move the state to adopt an active industrial policy as expected. Secondary industry remained partly protected, was not consulted in negotiations for trade agreements, and was still seen as of secondary importance, as seen in the Phillips Report in 1962.

The federal dissolution in 1963 worsened the Southern Rhodesian industrialists' situation. They lost free access to their former domestic market of the two northern territories. Even worse, Southern Rhodesia declared independence unilaterally in 1965. This UDI invited sanctions from Britain and other countries under the resolution of the United Nations. Declared a rebel country, Southern Rhodesia was ostracised from the Commonwealth and other traditional markets and trading partners, thus compounding the market crisis

148 Central Statistics Office, *Report on the Results of the National Income and Balance of Payments Questionnaire Sent to Companies Operating in Malawi, Rhodesia and Zambia in 1963* (Salisbury: Government Printers, 1964); and Clarke, 'The political economy of discrimination and underdevelopment with special reference to African workers, 1940–1973', 140–43.

149 *Report on the Results of the National Income and Balance of Payments Questionnaire Sent to Companies Operating in Malawi, Rhodesia and Zambia in 1963*, as cited in Phimister and Gwande, 'Secondary industry and settler colonialism: Southern Rhodesia before and after UDI', 95.

150 Government of Southern Rhodesia, *Census of Industrial Production, 1938–1963*; and Phimister and Gwande, 'Secondary industry and settler colonialism: Southern Rhodesia before and after UDI', 94.

for Rhodesia. This initially caused panic among industrialists. However, the adoption by the government of a new economic policy underpinned by import control proved an unintended boon for the manufacturing industry. The effect of the UDI on economic policy forms the theme of the next chapter.

5 Industrialising under Sanctions: Organised Industry and the State during UDI, 1966–1979

Existing conventional wisdom on the Rhodesian economy during UDI posits that the state muzzled organised secondary industry, which became acquiescent.[1] This assertion captures developments on the political front. However, this chapter shows that in the economic sphere, industrialists remained forceful in pursuit of their interests. They manipulated the state's overreliance on the manufacturing sector to provide employment and consumer goods vis-à-vis sanctions. The chapter also revisits the accepted belief that UDI was the period of high import substitution industrialisation (ISI) and economic nationalism. In this vein, it examines the interaction between the state and industrialists over the administration and implementation of the import control policy and currency allocations – the two major economic instruments of the UDI regime. The chapter suggests that Tor Skålnes's notion of societal corporatism – the changing role of interest groups and their relationship with the state, as well as their collaboration in a broader sense – may be a more useful way to understand the relationship between the ARnI and the state during this period.[2]

In addition, the chapter analyses the numerous interactions between the state and industrialists over several challenges affecting the economy in

1 D. M. Rowe, *Manipulating the Market: Understanding Economic Sanctions, Institutional Change and the Political Unity of White Rhodesia* (Chicago: Chicago University Press, 2001), 106–30; and P. Bond, *Uneven Zimbabwe: A Study of Finance, Development and Underdevelopment* (Trenton, NJ: Africa World Press, 1998), 122–23.

2 T. Skålnes, *The Politics of Economic Reform in Zimbabwe: Continuity and Change in Development* (London: Macmillan Press, 1995).

general and the manufacturing sector in particular. Both the Rhodesian war of liberation and the constitutional negotiations with Britain attracted comments from the industrialists, and as such warrant examination. The chapter begins in 1966 with the imposition of sanctions by both Britain and the United Nations (UN), which necessitated the introduction of a new economic policy. It then moves on to examine the implementation of the economic policies, the challenges faced, and industry's views on decolonisation and African majority rule. It ends in 1979, with a discussion on the nature, pattern, and structure of secondary industry that emerged during UDI.

UDI, Economic Policy, and State–Industry Relations

The UDI in November 1965 had huge economic and political consequences for Rhodesia. Following the White rebellion, Britain and the UN imposed economic sanctions on Rhodesia. The sanctions were applied piecemeal. Britain initially introduced financial sanctions from 12 November 1965 to 16 December 1966.[3] British embargoes were also imposed on Rhodesian tobacco, sugar, and other products, and Rhodesia's Commonwealth trading preferences were suspended, as was the country's access to the London capital markets.[4] These actions were followed by UN selective mandatory sanctions. After the rejection of Tiger Talk proposals on Rhodesia's 'return to legality' in December 1966 by Smith's Cabinet, the British Foreign Secretary, George Brown, travelled to the US to push for a UN Security Council resolution calling for comprehensive mandatory sanctions on Rhodesia. The Security Council resolved that 'the internal situation in Rhodesia constituted a threat to international peace and security, and invoked Chapter VII of the UN Charter to impose economic sanctions'.[5] With the concurrence of Britain, in May 1968 the UN extended mandatory sanctions to all commodities for Rhodesia, including oil. The implication of such a development could have been economic disaster for the belligerent state. 'Sanctions were designed to create a major economic slowdown, high unemployment, reduce incomes, prompt disinvestment of capital and generally stimulate a depression to rapidly and bloodlessly

3 See T. Nyamunda, 'Financing rebellion: the Rhodesian state, financial policy and exchange control, 1962–1979' (PhD, University of the Free State, 2015), 97–111, for detailed analysis of these financial sanctions.

4 Nyamunda, 'Financing rebellion', 97–111.

5 For a detailed discussion, see A. S. Mlambo, '"Honoured more in the breach than in the observance": economic sanctions on Rhodesia and international response, 1965 to 1979', *South African Historical Journal*, 71, 3 (2019), 371–93; R. Coggins, 'Wilson and Rhodesia: UDI and British policy towards Africa', *Contemporary British History*, 20, 3 (2006), 363–81.

force Rhodesia back to legality', so that 'in a matter of weeks and not months', the rebellion could end.[6]

Rhodesia, therefore, reconfigured its economic policies to deal with the emerging potentially harsh economic environment of sanctions and isolation. Confronted by this reality, industrialists shifted from their pre-UDI opposition and began to concur with the state, supporting economic realignment.[7] At the centre of the new economic policy were two instruments: import control and currency allocations. While these principles applied to the whole economy, they weighed most heavily on industry and commerce. The government tried to reduce the impact of sanctions on industry by conserving foreign exchange through reducing imports and improving local sourcing of consumables and goods and increasing employment levels.[8] In December 1965, the Ministry of Commerce and Industry set up the Industrial Tariff Committee and the Industrial Projects Committee. The latter's purpose was to save foreign exchange by closely examining all applications for industrial projects and avoiding duplication and waste of any foreign exchange involved. Under the new system of control, 'it [was] now necessary for any industrialist or prospective industrialist who require[d] an import allocation for plant or initial stocks of imported raw materials to make special application to the Ministry'.[9]

The Industrial Projects Committee, which included representatives from the Treasury and Reserve Bank of Rhodesia, received and considered applications. Where necessary, the committee co-opted representatives of other ministries affected by particular projects. The committee took into account the following main considerations for each application: the net foreign exchange benefit; the extent of any foreign investment in the project and the form thereof; the profitability of the project and the benefit to the economy; the extent and conditions relating to any payments of royalties or rent; the ability to manufacture at competitive prices and to acceptable standards; the

6 C. P. Watts, *Rhodesia's Unilateral Declaration of Independence: An International History* (New York: Palgrave Macmillan, 2012), 24. Coggins, 'Wilson and Rhodesia: UDI and British policy towards Africa', 271.

7 I. Phimister and V. M. Gwande, 'Secondary industry and settler colonialism: Southern Rhodesia before and after the Unilateral Declaration of Independence', *African Economic History*, 45, 2 (2017), 85–112, at pp. 96–102.

8 NAZ RC, L. C21.6.9R, B141849, Commerce and Industry, 1963–1972, ARnI: Notes for Discussion with the Ministry of Commerce and Industry, March 1966.

9 B. H. Mussett, Minister of Commerce and Industry, 'Government industrial policy – Its Aims and Objects in Promoting the Development of Secondary Industry', Paper presented at a Symposium Sponsored by the Rhodesian Economic Society on Industry in Rhodesia, 11–12 June 1969; and also NAZ S3285/9/40, Minister of Commerce & Industry Speeches: Opening Address by the Minister of Commerce and Industry at the Umtali Rhodesian Institute Of Management, 12 November 1975.

effect on government revenue, etc.[10] The committee also adopted a 'first come, first served' basis in handling industrial project applications. Even as the government made these changes, D. V. Divett, the ARnI president, emphasised the need for a new look at Rhodesia's industrial structure and the essentiality of relations with neighbouring territories to sustain the economy. This was particularly important because the old international trade patterns were gone, and so was the Zambian market. Thus, it was vital for Rhodesia to find compensatory outlets and to arrive at new economic alignments.[11]

The introduction of close control over industrial development and expansion had long been 'foreign' to Rhodesian economic philosophy. Ordinarily, secondary industry opposed government interference and control in its sphere and the economy in general. However, the ARnI went along with it at this juncture. It did so for two reasons. First, the imposition of sanctions necessitated closer planning and coordination to create a proper balance between the economic sectors, thus enabling smooth functioning of the economy. Second, the use of import control in planning was also a method of protecting local industry. Debating at the ARnI's tenth annual congress, Chipman, a long-serving member of the association, active since 1949, 'was particularly gratified to know that at long last a policy which used to be considered rather suspect had now been adopted as an instrument of government policy' to assist industrial development.[12] Meanwhile, much as the introduction and adoption of import control as a policy instrument was welcomed, its operative longevity became a contentious subject between the ARnI and the government. Because of the centrality of import control, it warrants a closer examination, and as such the discussion will now turn to this.

Planning and Administering Industrial Development under Siege

On 7 March 1966, the Ministry of Commerce and Industry released a memorandum explaining its position on the use of import control as an instrument of industrial policy. It stated upfront that 'it has been the policy of the government to use the customs tariff and not Import Controls, as the means of affording protection to domestic industry against external competition. This remains the basic policy of the government.'[13] Customs tariffs were preferable to import controls because they enabled 'the margin of protection to be set at a predetermined limit in monetary or percentage terms, leaving domestic

10 Mussett, 'Government industrial policy'.

11 NAZ RC, L. C21.6.9R, B141849, Commerce and Industry, 1963-1972, ARnI: ARnI Presidential Address, March 1966.

12 Ibid, ARnI: Debates at the 10th Annual Congress, 1967.

13 NAZ RC, L. C21.6.9R, B141849, Commerce and Industry, 1963-1972, ARnI, Ministry of Commerce and Industry Memo on the Use of Import Control as an Instrument of Industrial Policy, 7 March 1966.

industry subject to the discipline of external competition within defined limits.'[14] Besides, administratively they were simpler and cheaper in terms of personnel and money, both for the government and the importers. With the declaration of UDI and the attendant sanctions, however, circumstances necessitated the 'imposition of *balance of payment import controls* to supplement and complement the customs tariff, meeting the *special short term problems of the present time* [my emphasis].'[15]

Two crucial observations are discernible from the quotation. First, for the government, import controls were a temporary measure that could be removed when normal trade relations returned (after a possible political settlement) and the balance of payments was secured. Second, their primary role was to address the balance of payments. Nonetheless, they had the consequential effect of providing an additional share of the local market for domestic industries that suffered a net loss of export markets. Import controls also encouraged new or expanded industrial capacity to produce goods whose supply they curtailed, thereby freeing up scarce foreign exchange for essential imports. This marked the beginning of the domestic expansion that became synonymous with secondary industry during UDI.

While the ARnI appreciated the primary logic behind import controls as well as the protective role offered to local industry, their operative life span dissatisfied them. Explaining its concerns, the ARnI remarked that it 'found it difficult to understand the apparent desire of the government to abandon import control with the least possible delay and to rely upon tariff protection as the general rule.'[16] Citing the example of South Africa, which retained both tools, industry further found it 'incomprehensible that a dual system of this kind should be good for South Africa but bad for Rhodesia.' For the ARnI, import controls were a much more precise, expeditious, and predictable instrument than tariffs for both protecting and attracting new industries. Thus, as long as they were judiciously and selectively applied, import controls needed to be a permanent feature of industrial policy.[17] The ARnI representatives argued before the Ministry of Commerce and Industry's Advisory Committee in 1966 that 'import controls should not be withdrawn immediately [even if] the balance of payments position is secured,' lest it cause dismay and despondency among Rhodesian industry.[18] In addition, removing them would act as

14 *Ibid.*

15 *Ibid.*

16 NAZ RC, L. C21.6.9R, B141849, Commerce and Industry, 1963–1972, ARnI: ARnI, Memorandum on the Use of Import Controls as an Instrument of Industrial Policy, June 1966.

17 *Ibid.*

18 *Ibid.*, Summary of Evidence Submitted to the Advisory Committee on Commerce and Industry on the State of Manufacturing Industry in General by Representatives of the ARnI, 30 August 1966.

a deterrent to the attraction of new industrial undertakings. Clearly, industrialists desired the retention of import controls as the best way of attracting and protecting secondary industry.

The government acknowledged that import control was the most effective way of maintaining and stimulating the balance of payments. 'However', it insisted, 'the retention of import control in the long term would not be in the interest of industry or the nation.'[19] It reiterated its earlier position that the government's long-term policy was to look to the customs tariff for the protection of industry. The government further believed that the healthy development of local industry could also take place with some reasonable degree of competition with imports. Competition would ensure 'greater efficiency in industry, competitive prices, maintenance of standards and quality, up-to-date designs and innovations to match external achievements, the timely adoption of technological developments and greater variety for the consuming public', it reasoned.[20] Nevertheless, the government promised to intensify its support, with priority given to growth industries, import-substituting industries, those producing the basic materials for other industries, and those with good export prospects. To this end, assistance by the government included protection by means of import control for selected industries for a specified period, greater use of the customs tariff, and increased funding through the IDC.[21] While the ARnI welcomed the government's promises, this was not the end of the matter. The ARnI generally remained unsatisfied with the government's intervention in the economy, yet it insisted on the retention of import controls at every opportunity.

Meanwhile, to improve relations and better manage industrial development, the ARnI and the Ministry of Commerce and Industry formed a consultative committee, which met regularly. This represented a consolidation of societal corporatism between the government and industrialists. In one of the meetings, they agreed to create a machinery for closer consultation on matters affecting the prospects of the development of the manufacturing industry. In compliance, the ARnI reorganised its structures to align with the ministry's setup. It established six subcommittees, namely the Finance Committee, Economic Affairs Committee, Labour Committee, Export Advisory Committee, Legislation and Taxation Committee, and Transport Committee. It was through these subcommittees that the ARnI would achieve closer collaboration between government and industry, both during the abnormal trading conditions of the UDI and in the future. Even as the ARnI pressed for consultation, it accepted that ultimately the decisions rested with the government, but requested that it

19 NAZ RC, L. C21.6.9R, B141849, Commerce and Industry, 1963–1972, ARnI: ARnI, Tenth Annual Congress, 6 April 1967.

20 *Ibid.*

21 *Ibid.*

be given the opportunity of expressing an opinion on important matters before the government reached its decision, as it was industry that had to act upon it. Furthermore, the early dissemination of government intentions among industrialists would help to minimise any adverse reaction on implementation.

M. Cawood, the Secretary of Commerce and Industry, welcomed arrangements that brought the ministry and the private sectors of both commerce and industry closer together. He believed that consultations helped to avoid misunderstandings and that the ministry, therefore, would 'cooperate to its maximum ability, although there was a limit to the extent which government could go in [that] direction.'[22] Despite these seemingly amicable overtures, by the end of 1967 industry had raised concerns over the lack of two-way discussion in the consultative committees. The ARnI enumerated the cases for which it had not been consulted. For instance, on consultation over import control application, the ARnI's Chegwidden complained that the ministry tended 'to widen or reduce the scope of the Open General Licence without preference to ARnI and then expected ARnI to make consequent adjustments to its import quota arrangement.'[23] Unsympathetically, Cawood replied that 'if ARnI had consulted the Ministry, the answers to their grievances could have been given,' and that the ministry would 'only consult ARnI if it felt that such advice was needed.'[24] The secretary's response revealed the disdain that lingered in the government's perception of industrialists, despite their new-found significance to the economy.

Meanwhile, the Industrial Development Corporation (IDC) criticised the import control system (ICS). Through the ICS, the government allocated the total amount of foreign currency to be spent on imports. This amount was then divided among individual firms by means of a series of committees which were each representative of individual sectors of the economy. This was intended to keep total external spending within prescribed limits with minimal disruption to individual firms. For the IDC, the system was not 'designed to ensure the fullest possible measure of substitution for imported products, and in consequence the maintenance of a high level of domestic industrial production.'[25] The reasons for this weakness were two-fold. First, the officials responsible for administering the system of import control were not in sufficiently close contact with industry to effectively assess its requirements and more, particularly its ability to produce goods to replace imports. The second weakness lay in the system of allocation used by industry and commerce to make currency

22 *Ibid.*

23 *Ibid.*, Meeting between the ARnI Consultative Committee and Ministry of Commerce and Industry, 5 December 1967.

24 *Ibid.*

25 NAZ RC, L. C21.6.9R, B141849, Commerce and Industry, 1963–1972, ARnI: The Industrial Development Corporation of Southern Rhodesia Limited on Import Control, 16 March 1966.

available to specific firms for specific classes of imports. For instance, an allocation for a group of clothing manufacturers also competed with a global allocation for imports of individual clothing manufacturers. Ultimately, this affected the ability of firms to produce.

In light of these criticisms, intensive economic coordination and priority planning became imperative. Consequently, the Cabinet reinvigorated coordination by establishing the Ministerial Economic Coordination Committee (MECC) in 1967. Tinashe Nyamunda has provided a detailed analysis of the functions of the MECC.[26] Chaired by the Ministry of Finance, the MECC comprised strategic ministries, namely those of Agriculture, Commerce and Industry, Internal Affairs, Mines and Lands, and Transport and Power. Nyamunda concluded that 'the [MECC's] protective approach to the Rhodesian economy required very astute, collaborative, informed and inventive management strategies ... which insured the stability of the Rhodesian pound and the Rhodesian dollar (after decimalisation in 1970) for the better part of the UDI period'.[27] These ministries were responsible for coordinating economic planning in order of priority and recommending to the Cabinet for approval the projects that should receive government financial support.

At the same time, the government also commissioned Professor J. L. Sadie of the University of Stellenbosch in South Africa to offer advice on planning for the economic development of Rhodesia.[28] This commissioned review of the existing economic planning machinery was redundant, as the MECC was already doing this. Sadie examined the 'characteristics of the Rhodesian economy and broad lines of policy suggested by them; priorities in a programme of development and administrative machinery for economic development'.[29] In respect of the characteristics of the economy, Sadie noted that Rhodesia was endowed with natural resources, namely rich soils, a pleasant climate, diversity of mineral deposits, and human resources, all of which were necessary for economic development. He recommended that 'the goal [was] optimum economic development – that is, the maximum rate of growth in

26 For a detailed analysis, see Nyamunda, 'Financing rebellion', especially from p. 122 onwards. See also T. Nyamunda, 'How racist Rhodesia did it and "independent" Zimbabwe is getting it wrong: comparing currency and finance under sanctions', in *Developing Economics: A Critical Perspective on Development Economics*, https://developingeconomics.org/2017/03/06/how-racist-rhodesia-did-it-and-independent-zimbabwe-is-getting-it-wrong-comparing-currency-and-finance-under-sanctions/, Accessed 8 April 2018, 3:37pm.

27 Nyamunda, 'How racist Rhodesia did it and "independent" Zimbabwe is getting it wrong'.

28 J. L. Sadie, *Report on Planning for the Economic Development of Rhodesia* (Salisbury: Government Printers, 1967) [henceforth, Sadie Report].

29 Sadie Report, 12.

employment accompanied by structural changes, consistent with maximum productivity per factor of production.'[30]

Sadie concluded that optimum economic growth could be achieved along the following broad lines of policy on:

> Water conservation, the productive use of all land capable of economic exploitation, intensive geological surveys of all areas not yet fully explored, research and application of developments in technology, family planning, European immigration, developing the labour skills required by a growing economy, transformation of the subsistence sector, introduction of import substitution as a growth factor in addition foreign to trade, unflagging attention to product promotion in foreign markets and agreements with trading partners.[31]

Sadie also suggested an organisational apparatus to handle indicative planning. He further qualified that this recommendation was not criticism of the existing machinery, but was meant to emphasise the need for dynamic and effective economic leadership at government level for the 'pursuit of the maximum effort on the part of the administration as well as the private sector, and to mirror the government's determination to succeed.'[32] Such administrative machinery was to comprise an independent economic adviser to the prime minister. This suggestion never saw the light of day, as the MECC rejected it.[33]

The ARnI strongly criticised the Sadie recommendations and produced a nineteen-page position paper showing some of the shortcomings of the Sadie Report in assisting the Rhodesian government to plan its economic development. According to the ARnI Economic Affairs Committee, the Sadie Report regurgitated what had already been observed before by others regarding the necessity of developing certain sectors of the Rhodesian economy. It further remarked that Professor Sadie directed himself towards what he termed 'the broader issues in priorities,' but

> the final result of such consideration is simply the listing of various criteria ... for assessing which aspects of development may be more desirable than others. This might be said to be akin to showing an unskilled labourer the tools and then expecting him to be able to get on with whatever job crops up, whereas what he needs is to be shown the job and then told what tools he will need to do it.[34]

30 *Ibid.*, 12.
31 *Ibid.*, 13–14.
32 Sadie Report, 37.
33 Smith Papers, [R]hodes [U]niversity [C]ory [L]ibrary, (Unprocessed), Box 2.027(A), Ministerial Economic Coordinating Committee, Minutes of a meeting held on 30 May 1968.
34 NAZ RC, L. C21.6.9R, B141849, Commerce and Industry, 1963–1972, ARnI: ARNI, Economic Affairs Committee: Some Comments on the Report by J. L. Sadie on

Explaining its understanding of a proper economic plan, the committee said 'the essential feature of any economic plan is the determination of a clear order of priorities to which scarce resources are to be allocated to yield the maximum development. Judged by this yardstick, Professor Sadie's Report must be considered a complete failure.'[35] Even after allowing for probable oversights, the committee generally found the report inadmissible.

The looseness of Sadie's advice and recommendations is further laid bare in the following criticism of his broad lines of policy. He drew attention to the ratio of Africans to Europeans and to the fact that without European immigration, this ratio would increase from 19:1 to 29:1 over the next twenty years, because the natural rate of increase of the former outpaced that of the latter.[36] This, he argued, would have serious economic consequences for the Africans, because the Europeans exuded 'the spirit of enterprise which is *fons et erigo* [the source and origin] of economic advancement and the generation of employment opportunities'.[37] He, therefore, proposed that in the interest of the Rhodesian economy and the generality of the country's African inhabitants, the threat of the numerical imbalance should be corrected by introducing family planning to control Africans and increasing European immigration. Although the idea of White immigration and Black fertility control was couched in economic terms, it had the ultimate goal of ensuring political survival and the brutal entrenchment of White supremacy.[38]

An underlying point from this analysis demonstrates how race politics played out in Rhodesia. If Sadie's argument meant anything at all in economic terms, it was an attempt to determine, in a developing economy, a relationship between its requirements of skilled labour, understood as European, Asian and Coloured labour, and unskilled labour, taken to be African labour. But one would be entitled to assume that one of the marks of a developing economy would be that a demand for skilled relative to unskilled labour would rise as development progressed. Moreover, by equating the possession of skills to skin pigmentation, Sadie assumed that there were no skilled African employees, which was not factual. More importantly, he also assumed that Black people were unable or reluctant to acquire skills. He was wrong. This was bigotry of the highest order from Sadie, and amounted to racism. This was not surprising, however, for ultra-racism was the foundation of the Rhodesian Front regime,

---

Planning for the Economic Development of Rhodesia, January 1968.

35 *Ibid.*

36 *Ibid.*

37 Sadie Report, 2.

38 For a detailed discussion on this, see M. O. West, 'Nationalism, race, and gender: the politics of family planning in Zimbabwe, 1957–1990', *Social Science and Medicine*, 7, 3 (1994), 456–59; J. Brownell, *The Collapse of Rhodesia: Population Demographics and the Politics of Race* (London: I. B. Tauris Publishers, 2011), 25–42.

hence their appointment of Sadie, who was a Neo-Malthusian demographer and came from an even more racist society, as well as being resident at the Afrikaner Stellenbosch University, where he played a central role in the debate over racial population politics.[39]

Sadie also commented on ISI. He remarked that import substitution had not been a major incentive or goal in industrial development, as was evidenced by the high percentage of locally produced manufacturers that were exported.[40] Though this was true, two points need to be made here. First, since the end of 1965, ISI had by default become inevitable and was one of the criteria employed by the Ministry of Commerce and Industry in assessing the desirability of the new industrial projects submitted to it for approval. Secondly, the high percentage of manufactured goods exported in 1965 was probably indicative of the fact that both Zambia and Malawi, which took the bulk of Rhodesia's manufactured exports, temporarily remained captive markets after the break-up of the common market of the federal era. The point here is that it was not obvious that the high percentage of manufactured products exported in 1965 was concrete evidence of the low degree of import substitution. If anything, it could be argued that high exports showed that ISI had actually expanded domestic production.

As ARnI took issue with Sadie's report, ACCOR also criticised industrialists. Organised commerce had qualms with the potential impact of ISI on its interests. In his address to the ACCOR congress in 1967, Professor L. H. Samuels described ISI as 'an objective of development policy for its own sake instead of a means for ensuring an efficient allocation of development resources'.[41] While it acknowledged the likely benefits, commerce worried that ISI was 'unlikely to improve the foreign exchange position', yet that was the 'basic justification for its implementation'.[42] It also took the view that import substitution was unsound in theory and did not deliver the goods. It argued that the policy created a foreign exchange drain at a time when the distributive sector was already decimated by cuts in import allocations.[43] Cuts in foreign exchange and a lack of import allocations resulted in shortages and a lack of choice. In addition, as manufacturing expanded, there emerged a practice of direct selling by manufacturers which reduced the dependence of some retailers on the wholesaler. Thus, commerce complained that when goods were imported, it was usually a function of the wholesaler, but now 'the purchase direct from

39 See B. Brown, 'Facing the "black peril": the politics of population control in South Africa', *Journal of Southern African Studies*, 13, 3 (1987), 256–73.

40 Sadie Report, 2.

41 As cited in J. M. Britten, 'The effects of industrialization on the distributive trade and the consumer', *Rhodesian Journal of Economics*, 3, 2 (1969), 21–28; see also the rest of that journal issue.

42 Britten, 'The effects of industrialization on the distributive trade and the consumer'.

43 *Ibid.*

manufacturer has become easier and this is of course encouraged by the manufacturer ... the trend continues to be towards increased direct selling and it is unlikely that with the weapons at the manufacturer's command,' the wholesaler will be able, or will attempt, to reverse the trend.[44]

ACCOR also used the veil of consumer interests to criticise both the government and industry. In particular, it felt that the government privileged industry by giving it a monopoly over the local market. It thus asserted that 'the most important single point over which government and commerce disagree[d] [was] on the importance of the consumer'.[45] Commerce maintained that 'the consumer [was] king, but Government in its own wisdom [was] prepared to sacrifice the consumer on the altar of a supposedly increased growth rate with import substitution as the sacrificial sword'.[46] In this regard, it felt that the government was slow to safeguard the consumer in cases where policy decisions for import substitution were taken.[47] The criticisms were not surprising because, for a long time, commerce had held prejudices regarding local industry. For instance, in 1966 commerce had said it wanted import control changes and that there were grave anomalies between the allocation systems operated by ACCOR and the ARnI.[48] More bluntly, it charged that 'some parts of the manufacturing sector apparently enjoy[ed] greater allocations than are necessary. The government must ensure a more equitable balance between manufacturing and commerce'.[49] These conflicting interests between commerce and industry had persisted since the 1940s, when industrial development had become the third pillar of the economy.

Consequently, ACCOR insisted that a watchdog organisation was necessary to protect consumers' interests. While ACCOR's concern for consumer interests may have been genuine, it is more plausible that its concern was driven by its dislike of the ISI, and the preferences and privileges that industry received from the government. Nonetheless, it was indeed true that there was a real concern with the pricing and quality of local products. The government, commerce, and the public generally raised complaints on numerous occasions about the lack of both quality and variety in Rhodesian products. As ACCOR had hinted in 1969, it appeared that the Standards Association of Central Africa, the body tasked with ensuring quality, was being virtually by-passed and that, perhaps, the government intentionally disregarded its obligation to act as a watchdog.[50]

44 *Ibid.*
45 *Ibid.*
46 *Ibid.*
47 *Ibid.*
48 *Rhodesia Herald*, 7 September 1966.
49 *Ibid.*
50 Britten, 'The effects of industrialization on the distributive trade and the consumer'.

The complaints resulted in a meeting between the ARnI and representatives of official bodies within the private sector to discuss quality control in industry in 1970. The organisations present at the meeting were the Rhodesian Institute of Management, the Buy Home Products Campaign, the Standards Association of Central Africa, and ACCOR.[51] The meeting stressed the need to improve the standard of quality control in industry to ensure a competitive product when import controls were lifted. The question was how to achieve this. The natural starting point was to ascertain where the fault was in the enforcement and implementation of quality control. It was observed that the small manufacturers were the most notorious, because they did not 'know how to institute quality control on their products and they were generally struggling to establish themselves and did not, as a result, have the time or money to orientate their production to emphasise the quality control aspects'. [52] The meeting also observed that many of the defective products supplied in the market were not being replaced or fixed.

To deal with this, there was 'a need for a machinery with power of wielding a "big stick"'.[53] A number of suggestions emerged that included the granting of tax concessions and incentives to those firms that could achieve a certain quality of production. Citing the example of South Africa, where the import of a minimum of 15% of any item was allowed to act as a check on the quality and price of local products, the meeting suggested that 'a similar approach could be used in Rhodesia with the threat of increasing the imports to say 20% if the quality of the local products did not prove satisfactory'.[54] Others, like George Hindley of the Buy Home Products Campaign, suggested that 'each firm should name a Quality Controller, who would be charged with the responsibility of ensuring an acceptable quality to that firm's product. This person could be called upon to answer complaints relating to the product.'[55] In addition, firms in the same industry could pool their resources for testing their products. He gave the example of firms in Britain that pooled resources for advertising, marketing, testing, development, and quality improvement. Moreover, when approving a new project, the Minister of Commerce and Industry 'should make it a prerequisite for a standards mark to be obtained either prior to full-scale production or in the shortest possible time thereafter'.[56]

As if the poor quality of the goods was not bad enough, they were also highly priced. Evidence of profiteering led to renewed pressure on the government to impose price controls. Profiteering aside, in the early years of the UDI

51 NAZ RC, L. C21.6.9R, B141849, Commerce and Industry, 1963–1972, ARnI: Meeting with Representatives of Official Bodies within the Private Sector, 17 February 1970.

52 *Ibid.*

53 *Ibid.*

54 *Ibid.*

55 *Ibid.*

56 *Ibid.*

price hikes were also caused by shortages of goods as the economy adjusted to sanctions. Due to these exigencies, industrialists and some retailers manipulated prices. Commerce did not like price controls. It gave a qualified criticism of the intention to introduce price control. The ACCOR secretary thus said that

> organised commerce always has been, and still is, strongly against price control. The small number of manufacturers and retailers who stoop to such unorthodox methods of retailing, for instance, the sale of seconds or damaged goods at normal prices, upsets the confidence of the public, and they are entitled to call for some added safeguards. The solution, I need to reiterate, is competition allied to a sense of responsibility, which will no doubt arise when the industry has become more mature.[57]

Similarly, Noel Bruce, the Governor of the Reserve Bank, bemoaned the price controls. He suggested that 'recommended retail prices be shown by manufacturers on their packaging as a guide to their ultimate customers', adding that he did 'not necessarily advocate a system of fixed retail prices but one which can at least give a shopper a better measure of protection'.[58] He was, however, quick to qualify that the government did not, in principle, support trade practices that tended to be restrictive or limit free enterprise and market conditions. Industry and commerce continued to protest against price controls and made it very plain that the measures taken were impracticable and, therefore, unacceptable. Other challenges also blighted the manufacturing sector, requiring the state's assistance, as the next section shows.

Industrial Problems and Prospects

Between 1966 and 1972, secondary industry endured other challenges that often led to incessant engagements with the government. The major challenges facing industry, in the Rhodesian context, were familiar. These included access to foreign exchange, shortages of skilled manpower and housing, inadequate transport facilities, and decentralisation. The following paragraphs thus focus on the interaction between the government and industry over these matters. The top priority area in which industrialists needed assistance was currency allocations. While indeed industrial development had been immensely stimulated and encouraged by measures to preserve the country's scarce foreign exchange and by import substitution, the real opportunities for industry's continued expansion through ISI were not limitless and could diminish. Furthermore, the significant reduction in industry's foreign exchange allocation

57 Britten, 'The effects of industrialization on the distributive trade and the consumer'.

58 NAZ RC, L. C21.6.9R, B141849, Commerce and Industry, 1963–1972, ARnI: Ministry of Commerce and Industry on Resale Price Maintenance, 17 May 1968.

made it less possible to continue rapid industrial expansion through ISI alone. Import substitution is limited in scope and is only sustainable if accompanied by an expansion of the internal market. In light of this, the ARnI pleaded for a higher proportion of the foreign exchange available to industry to enable local production to expand.[59]

Industry's expectation was that the additional foreign exchange required for the maintenance and expansion of industrial output should be provided by reducing allocations to other sectors of the economy. In that regard, it argued that

> during the current quota period, the allocation to industry was the lowest since November 1965. Yet this allocation has to provide for the import inputs into a constantly expanding sector of the economy. In addition, about 1,000 new industrial projects have been approved since November 1965. All this would naturally seem to imply that industry's total allocation should be increasing and not decreasing.[60]

More bluntly, the ARnI's president said 'all industry asks for is to be given sufficient foreign exchange to enable it to achieve that volume of production necessary to satisfy both export and home demand', and besides, 'foreign exchange is the one tool of our trade which we cannot substitute'.[61]

One of the causes of the hard currency shortage was the decline in exports and fast-growing internal economy, which still needed imports in some sectors. To deal with the matter, the Minister of Commerce and Industry set up a National Priorities Committee (NPC) in January 1970.[62] Representatives from the ARnI, ACCOR, the RNFU, and the Chamber of Mines, together with government officials, constituted the NPC, under the chairmanship of the Secretary for Commerce and Industry, J. E. Baker. The NPC, through a joint allocation sub-committee, dealt with applications for supplementary currency allocations by industry and commerce.[63] Working in consultation with industry and commerce, the NPC called upon the ARnI to examine its own particular subsectors 'in order to advise the Committee of any economies or savings of foreign exchange which they felt they could achieve of their own accord'.[64] Similarly, ACCOR was requested to report on importations under each tariff item. All these reports were of great assistance to the NPC, but 'understandably they did not go far enough to meet the very stringent restrictions

59 *Ibid.*, ARnI, Background Paper on Matters for Discussion with the Minister of Finance, 10 February 1969.

60 *Ibid.*, Treasury Meeting with ARnI, 10 February 1969.

61 *Ibid.*, ARnI, Address by W. R. Perry at the Twelfth Annual General Meeting and Congress of the Association, 10 April 1969.

62 ARNI, *Annual Report*, 1970.

63 *Ibid.*

64 *Ibid.*

dictated by the extremely limited amount of foreign exchange available.'[65] All less essential manufacturing production and merchant imports were categorised and given less priority in currency allocation. Because these categories covered the great majority of industrial enterprises, the impact of the currency cuts was severe.

Despite this priority allocation, foreign exchange shortages still persisted. The Minister of Finance, John Wrathall, announced the adoption of further stringent measures in allocating foreign currency for imports.[66] Echoing the prime minister's warning that 'the country's development was outstripping its foreign exchange resources', Wrathall stated that timely action was necessary in a situation of impending strain. He further said that the tightening up would affect allocations both for new projects, whether agricultural, building, commercial, industrial, mining, or public sector, and for normal importations. Allocations for new projects were made only if they had substantial advantages for the country and especially for the balance of payments within a short period. Of course, this had been a standard practice since 1965. Even so, industry and commerce were guaranteed their allocations.[67]

Industry shared the concern regarding the strain the development of the country had on foreign exchange. Consequently, ARnI believed it 'necessary to take some steps to dampen down domestic demand until foreign exchange allocations can be significantly increased.'[68] One way of achieving this was to curb building activity, especially the construction of large buildings with a high import content, and slow down the rapidly expanding construction of private dwellings. Coupled with that, 'immigration could be slowed to ensure that only those immigrants are accepted who would make an immediate and positive contribution to the expansion of resources and not simply add to demand pressures.'[69] Foreign currency curbs continued and even threatened the survival of some firms. For instance, Rhodesian furniture manufacturers protested about the lack of foreign exchange allocations. One local furniture manufacturer complained that his allocation had been cut by $1,000.[70] Although the amount appeared small, it could import quite a large amount of small items needed in the final product. The ARnI also acknowledged that there were firms having trouble with their allocations.[71]

65 *Ibid.*
66 *The Financial Gazette*, 2 October 1970.
67 *Ibid.*
68 *Ibid.*, 6 November 1970.
69 *Ibid.*
70 *Ibid.*, 22 January 1971.
71 *Ibid.*

To deal with the foreign exchange shortages, business engaged in No-Currency-Involved (NCI) deals.[72] NCI was a method of importing goods into Rhodesia without any foreign exchange being paid out of the country. The system operated in two ways. In one method, a Rhodesian businessperson gathered information on foreign exchange about to enter into the country, possibly through an immigrant. The businessperson then engaged with the potential immigrant while still in his or her home country and bought the currency. The payment for the currency was done in Rhodesian dollars at a premium. The businessperson then used the foreign currency bought while still in a foreign bank to make his purchases and pay for imports. This circumvented foreign exchange controls but had the effect of actually attracting the imports into the country without putting pressure on the reserves held by the state. The immigrant sold his or her currency before reaching Rhodesia. They would then receive the currency once in the country. NCI deals were subject to abuse. For instance, the premium payable for buying the foreign exchange was not fixed by the Reserve Bank or treasury officials. Often it resulted in the emergence of 'middlemen' connected to potential immigrants, who then speculated with official foreign exchange rates.[73]

In the other method, Rhodesian industrialists imported industrial machinery from South Africa and paid through equity interests. Sadly, many South African industrialists were dishonest. Some sent in obsolete machines that were already written off, and gained equity ownership in a Rhodesian firm on the cheap. This created a long-term problem because Rhodesian industrialists expanded on the basis of obsolete equipment that soon needed replacement. Yet in some cases they continued paying dividends to a South African industrialist who provided a written-off machine. The Rhodesian treasury intervened to stop the system. Thus, restrictions on NCI deals combined with restraints on foreign currency allocations led to increasing shortages of imported material, many of which were needed in industrial production.

Bulawayo was the hardest hit by these reductions. A report in *The Financial Gazette* of 29 January 1971 showed that in Bulawayo,

> chain groups [were] closing down stores, developers [were] fighting shy of further investment and finance houses [were] reported to be concerned by the general lack of interest. In January alone, Cash Wholesalers announced plans to close 5 stores, Furniture and Electrical Mart to close 6, the 2 newly opened Pick n Pay supermarkets folded and Foodtown has shut down.[74]

72 The following explanation on NCIs relies on H. R. Strack, *Sanctions: The Case of Rhodesia* (New York: Syracuse University Press, 1978), 106–07.

73 Strack, *Sanctions*, 106–07.

74 *The Financial Gazette*, 29 January 1971.

Despite this obvious crisis, there was no movement in foreign currency allocations. Speaking in parliament, Jack Mussett, the Minister of Commerce and Industry, stated that the 'present system of allocating foreign exchange will be continued as no equitable alternative has been found', but efforts to find one were continuing.[75] With currency allocations declining, so did imports. Newspapers reported widely on the crisis.[76] Retailers, through ACCOR, appealed to the government for increased foreign currency allocations but met with no success. Discontent over currency allocations persisted.

The manufacturing sector also faced associated problems of a shortage of both skilled manpower and housing facilities. The shortage of a skilled workforce was directly attributable to the emigration that resulted from the imposition of sanctions and the departure of individuals who found the UDI detestable. Paradoxically, it also arose from the immediate requirements of a resurgent UDI economy. The resurgent economy then increased the demand for housing, leading to shortages in the main centres. This was more pronounced in Bulawayo. The ARnI approached the Ministry of Local Government and Housing to persuade it to encourage local authorities to recognise modern developments in factory-built houses by relaxing the regulations governing the areas in which they could be erected. Factory-built houses were pitched as the answer to Rhodesia's immediate needs. The ARnI felt that 'industrial expansion would be inhibited if there was insufficient accommodation for skilled immigrants' and that 'this urgent requirement would lag alarmingly if it was dependent entirely upon the inevitably slow resuscitation of the brick-making industry and the recoupment of previous emigration losses amongst building artisans'.[77] To its credit, the ministry reacted quickly and appointed a special National Housing Advisory Committee. This committee was representative of private enterprise, including the ARnI. Consequently, the ARnI was convinced that if the committee's advice was heeded, housing shortages would be expeditiously overcome without 'the irksome inhibitions of restrictive legislation that has plagued the same issue in the past'.[78]

Housing shortages were particularly acute for African labour. Noticing this mounting challenge, the government placed the responsibility of providing housing for African workers on industrialists and employers. In 1970, the Ministry of Local Government introduced a capital levy to raise funds for African worker housing projects. With the support of the Confederation of Rhodesian Employers, the ARnI objected to the levy on the grounds that the proposed capital levy would be selective and discriminatory, as it was to be

75 *Ibid.*, 18 June 1971.

76 See, for instance, *The Financial Gazette*, 2 July 1971.

77 NAZ RC, L. C21.6.9R, B141849, Commerce and Industry, 1963–1972, ARnI: ARnI, *Annual Report of the Management Committee for the Presidential Year 1967/68.*

78 *Ibid.*

imposed on employers of African labour in prescribed areas.[79] The ARnI's objections should be considered in the context of the many other impositions which commerce and industry already bore. 'In the first place', elucidated ARnI,

> the private sector is now so circumscribed with regulations and controls ... the activities of nearly every business enterprise are today restricted either directly or indirectly by the foreign currency situation and the Exchange Control Regulations. On top of this, the recently imposed 10% income tax surcharge has now been incorporated in to the tax structure, thereby raising company tax from 40% to 44%. Added to this were further restrictions arising from price control regulations.[80]

All these obligations circumscribed the extent to which the manufacturing sector could expand.

Transport challenges, especially shortages of railway facilities, also proved a huge setback. While the local market was hard hit, the effects were equally felt on a much wider scale, as ARnI received complaints regarding delays in the delivery of export orders.[81] This was despite the government and Rhodesia Railways explaining that priority was given to the railage of goods destined for export markets. Even then, the ARnI enumerated a number of instances in which manufacturers were short-changed by the railways. For instance, one manufacturer who, after extensive and costly promotion, enjoyed a growing external market for his product, was embarrassed by delays of up to a month between the date of dispatch and arrival.[82] The inability of the railways to haul the goods to the seaports of Mozambique and South Africa had an adverse effect on the country's exports. As one government official noted, 'the railways are holding up the export effort more than are the sanctions'.[83] Moreover, a paradox emerged: 'the foreign currency needed for capital equipment was generated by exports, but the ability to export was being hampered by railway congestion; and the congestion existed because of the need for replacement and additions of capital equipment'.[84] The delays in exporting were also aggravated by the introduction of a five-day week for civil servants. Customs offices operated on Saturdays only at the borders and not at the internal centres. This meant no service on weekends, adding to the delays.[85]

79 ARnI, Annual Report, 1970.

80 *Ibid.*

81 NAZ MS 1198 AEA4/2/2, Shortage of Railway Facilities, ARnI Memorandum on the Shortage of Railway Facilities, 30 June 1970.

82 *Ibid.*

83 Quoted in Strack, *Sanctions: The Case of Rhodesia*, 88.

84 *Ibid.*

85 NAZ MS 1198 AEA4/2/2, Shortage of Railway Facilities, ARnI Memorandum on the Shortage of Railway Facilities, 30 June 1970.

In 1971, stakeholders in Umtali demanded a review of the railway charges. A report jointly compiled by the Umtali town council, the Chamber of Commerce, and the Manicaland Chamber of Industries complained that 'railway charges [are] unfair to Umtali' and 'are retarding industrial development in Manicaland'.[86] Explaining the effect of the lopsided railway tariffs, the report's authors pointed out that 'it is cheaper for manufacturers to rail raw materials from Umtali to factories in Salisbury and Bulawayo for processing than it is to establish factories in Manicaland and rail out the finished product'.[87] This was particularly true of timber. 'Why should raw timber grown in the region be railed to another centre instead of being processed in Umtali and then railed out?' asked the report's authors.[88] For them, the answer lay in the discriminatory railways rates, which militated against the establishment of industries in Umtali. Emphasising this point, it highlighted, 'we believe that the rating system of the Railways has a big effect on the dispersal of industry in Rhodesia to the detriment of the smaller centres'.[89]

It was the railways' established practice to allow raw materials consigned to Rhodesian industry to qualify for lower rates, while higher rates applied to the goods manufactured from those raw materials. This encouraged industrialists to transport the raw materials they required to the centres where there were active markets and process the raw materials there. The skewed pricing later pushed the Manicaland Chamber of Industries to agitate for decentralisation of industries. The alternative for players in the region was road transport. Again, the government circumscribed this. Operating road transport services was expensive because of many levies and surcharges imposed on road transporters in order to protect the monopoly of Rhodesia Railways, which also ran road motor services. To deal with these transport challenges, bigger firms in Manicaland operated their own transport fleets, which proved efficient. However, while the large firms found an answer to this problem, the smaller industrialists could not afford the capital outlay involved. Consequently, the stakeholders appealed to government, stating that road transport 'must be competitive'.[90] Despite these representations, the situation did not improve.

As the Umtali municipality highlighted, skewed railway tariffs were biased against towns with smaller-scale industrial development. As the drive for ISI intensified, so did the problem of over-concentration and centralisation in the two major cities, Salisbury and Bulawayo. The trend triggered complaints and demands from other cities, towns, and industrialists for decentralisation of development. However, these calls were not new. During the CAF, decentralisation was so topical that in 1956 the federal government appointed the

86 *The Financial Gazette*, 26 March 1971.
87 *Ibid.*
88 *Ibid.*
89 *Ibid.*
90 *The Financial Gazette*, 26 March 1971.

Committee on Decentralisation.[91] The matter re-emerged in 1969 when the Midlands Chamber of Industries enquired as to what the government's policy regarding decentralisation of industry was.[92] The MP for Gwelo Rural, Clark, also asked the question in parliament, to which the Minister of Commerce and Industry replied that

> Government does not believe it is right to direct industry in the matter of siting. Government creates the climate to encourage development of industry in Rhodesia, but the actual siting must be the prerogative of the industrialist. If we force an industrialist to go to a particular town, then we, Government must accept responsibility for that direction if the industry fails and therefore although we accept Government policy is decentralisation, we cannot direct it. That is not policy.[93]

The minister reiterated his response in a letter to the ARnI on 1 October 1969. Importantly, this letter makes clear that the government still believed in its declared policy of minimum interference in the private sector and maintaining a free-enterprise system in Rhodesia.

Decentralisation attracted comments from concerned quarters. An editorial in *The Financial Gazette* of 16 September 1970 suggested that 'positive action was needed to curb big brother's growth.'[94] Justifying decentralisation, the editorial highlighted that

> the urgency about implementing a decentralisation policy in Rhodesia does not stem simply from the fact that growth of Salisbury and to a lesser extent Bulawayo has so overshadowed the development of the country's other urban centres. Instead, it arises partly from the fact that unless positive action is taken in due time, the trend towards agglomeration will get progressively worse in these two centres especially in Salisbury, but even more so from the close interrelation that exists between decentralisation and Tribal Trust Land development.[95]

The Tribal Trust Land Development Corporation (TILCOR) policy was to establish 'border industries' or satellite industrial areas. For instance, TILCOR chose Seke, close to Salisbury, and Thabazinduna, close to Bulawayo, as suitable

91 See NAZ F292/16/14, Decentralisation of Industries, 1 August 1957.

92 NAZ RC, L. C21.6.9R, B141849, Commerce and Industry, 1963–1972, ARnI: Letter by Midlands Chamber of Industries to the Minister of Commerce and Industry, 3 September 1969.

93 As quoted in *ibid.*, Letter by ARnI CEO, J. C. Graylin, to Midlands Chamber of Industries, 8 September 1969.

94 *The Financial Gazette*, 16 September 1970.

95 *Ibid.*

for satellite industrial development.[96] But this raised yet more questions about whether this was the most desirable type of decentralisation.

For one, decentralising to *Seke* was the least attractive option because it did not necessarily ease congestion in Salisbury. It could lead to a situation whereby Black African workers would live in Salisbury (as, presumably, would the White supervisors and executives) and commute to the border area. Indeed, this did become the trend, even in post-colonial Zimbabwe. At another level, there was the political argument that it was in the long-term interests of the country's White population to take the jobs to the people, than create 'border industries.' This would also be a better way to develop the African areas than turning to peasant agriculture. These factors thus needed adequate attention from the central government, industrialists, and TILCOR.

Meanwhile, smaller towns pushed for intensified decentralisation of industries. 'Give us more industries,' cried town councils and leaders of commerce and industry in the various towns across the country.[97] They put up a strong case to justify their demand. Just as was raised in *The Financial Gazette* editorial, the galloping growth of industry in Salisbury and Bulawayo was a worrying issue. Using population statistics, smaller towns showed that in 1956, 57% of Rhodesia's White population was centred in Salisbury and Bulawayo. By 1970, 64% of the total White population was concentrated in the two cities. Between 1965 and 1970, 76% of all new immigrants headed for either Salisbury or Bulawayo, and these two centres accounted for 87% of all new building development.[98] The total population figures gave credence to the demands of the smaller towns. In 1956 out of a total of 180,000 Whites in Rhodesia, there were 61,850 in Salisbury and 40,940 in Bulawayo, and by 1970 Salisbury claimed 102,900 Whites and Bulawayo 51,800 out of a total of 239,000.[99] Surely, this justified a new approach from the government to balance the country's economic growth.

However, this was not a call for direct intervention from government. The hope was merely that controlled development in Salisbury and Bulawayo would allow the smaller centres to grow in proportion to the major centres. To achieve proportional development, government could begin by 'encouraging manufacturers to set up factories at the source of their supplies of raw materials rather than transporting these to Salisbury and Bulawayo from outlying areas, then sending the finished product out again.'[100] 'Incentives like tax relief on capital expenditure, income tax allowances and an overhauling of transport tariffs,

96 *Ibid.*

97 *The Financial Gazette*, 19 March 1971.

98 *Ibid.*; similar statistics were confirmed by the government on 23 April 1971 when it used them as part of its justification in appointing a Select Committee on Decentralisation.

99 *The Financial Gazette*, 19 March 1971.

100 *Ibid.*

particularly by rail, would make firms more willing to move out', suggested the councils.[101] These suggestions resonated strongly with suggestions proffered in the report by the Umtali players earlier, when they raised concerns about the skewed transport tariffs.

Because of persistent demands by small towns, the government appointed a Select Committee on Decentralisation in April 1971. The terms of reference of the committee were 'to investigate ways and means of reducing the concentration of commerce, industry and population in and around the two cities to ensure a more equitable expansion of the country's economy in the future'.[102] Expressing concern with the lopsided growth of industries, the government took verbatim the justifications presented by smaller towns and regional Chamber of Industries as the reason for appointing the select committee. In a way, this was a victory for councils and business. Table 5.1 shows the distribution of industry that justified the necessity for decentralisation.

As the government appointed the committee, commentators predicted and warned of strong opposition and competition between industrialists and town councils in Salisbury and Bulawayo on one hand and the smaller towns on the other. A commentary in *The Financial Gazette* editorial of 23 April 1971 noted that

> [The] most conflicting views to be put to the Select Committee of Decentralisation to date come from local authorities who stand to gain or lose the most if the government carries out a dispersal programme. In one camp are Salisbury and Bulawayo City Councils who will be [trying hard] to ensure the growth of their areas is not curtailed. In the opposing camps are the councils of Umtali, Fort Victoria and the Midlands triplets – Gwelo, Que Que and Gatooma – who have for years enviously eyed the rapid growth of the twins. The small centres have put a strong case for a bigger share of the country's expansion which in some cases has by-passed them altogether.[103]

Indeed, Salisbury and Bulawayo opposed decentralisation. First, they expressed that 'any decentralisation programme initiated by the government will produce undue interference in private enterprise to the detriment of the national economy as a whole'.[104] But this was not a convincing argument, since at the time the government had already been very interventionist in the economy since 1965. Second, the two councils contended that 'any curbs placed on the expansion of their city areas will harm them while producing little or no benefits to the smaller centres' and further that 'concentrations of commerce, industry and population in the two centres will help the rest of the

101 *Ibid.*; and also a report in *The Financial Gazette*, 7 April 1971 entitled 'Tax holiday for firms willing to move out'.

102 *The Financial Gazette*, 23 April 1971.

103 *The Financial Gazette*, 23 April 1971.

104 *Ibid.*

Table 5.1. Distribution of industrial activity by area, 1963 and 1972.

	1963				1972			
Area	**Net output $'000**	**% of total**	**Average no. employed**	**% of total**	**Net output $'000**	**% of total**	**Average no. employed**	**% of total**
Bulawayo	38,466	30.8	27,107	35.0	96,599	27.9	43,493	32.1
Fort Victoria	632	0.5	5,272	0.7	1,882	0.5	1,034	0.8
Gatooma	2,436	1.9	437	3.1	8,459	2.4	4,533	3.3
Gwelo	2,744	3.0	3,277	4.2	13,716	4.0	6,043	4.5
Que Que	6,862	5.5	4,054	5.2	26,980	7.8	6,390	4.7
Salisbury	63,530	50.9	32,751	42.3	166,755	48.1	59,750	44.0
Umtali	3,518	2.9	2,636	3.4	11,301	3.3	5,350	3.9
All other areas	5,704	4.5	4,663	6.1	20,684	6.0	9,093	6.7
Total	123,892	100.0	80,197	100.0	346,376	100.0	135,686	100.0

Source: The *Census of Industrial Production*, 1972/1973.

country by providing a healthy, growing central market'.[105] To an extent, this was a reasonable argument, at least industrially, given that market size is a crucial factor in the siting of an industry.

Although broadly, leading businesspersons advocated some form of incentive to encourage regional development, they were cautious. They presented a logical but seemingly self-defeating argument. Business had a general feeling that

> it [was] far too early yet for the government to consider direct action to encourage the development of the regions at the expense of the two central industrial and commercial complexes. Agriculture and mining [were] still the country's main prop with manufacturing and commerce only taking a secondary role. It [was] a natural process, therefore, that the country's manufacturing industries should group together around the centres of their mainly home-markets.[106]

Another leading business executive also pointed out:

> Most firms are still in their infancy, producing consumer goods for consumption. To move them out to the regions, hundreds of miles from their main markets can only increase their costs, which eventually will have to be met by the consumer in higher prices. In the end no-one benefits. If the government is intent on decentralisation, then it must make the regions more attractive to industrialists than Salisbury and Bulawayo are.[107]

Amid the conversation, industrialists suggested alternatives to decentralisation and discussed the practicalities of these. Appearing before the Select Committee on Decentralisation, the ARnI proposed the establishment of a 'separate and distinct agency' with the specific responsibility of promoting 'regional' economic development through what it called the 'growth point' approach.[108] The agency would carry the 'overall responsibility of coordinating various regional policies to ensure that not only did they promote growth in the development areas but that they also did not conflict with national economic policy'.[109] It would therefore work in collaboration with and under the oversight of the Ministry of Commerce and Industry. Underpinning this approach was the desire to avoid the dissipation of the limited resources available, especially finance capital.

Laying out the *modus operandi* of its proposed plan, the ARnI recommended that no more than one – or at the most two – areas for regional development be designated at any one time. These would be areas where maximum

105 *Ibid.*
106 *Ibid.*
107 *Ibid.*
108 *Ibid.*, 11 June 1971.
109 *Ibid.*

assistance to encourage industry to locate itself would be given for a minimum time period of at least five years, after which the results would be reviewed. The agency would designate regional development areas which had not fully participated in economic growth to the same degree as the two main urban areas of Bulawayo and Salisbury, but which were nevertheless sufficiently advanced economically to present promising prospects for rapid future development.[110] Thus all assistance given by the agency or coordinated through its activities would be concentrated where it could be most effective. In this way, a growth point or growth area approach would be followed, rather than an attempt to promote the development of a number of areas or centres simultaneously. The areas so designated would be ones likely to attract immigrants and industrialists. It identified Gwelo and Umtali as the two centres most suitable to pilot the growth point development. The Umtali municipality fully supported the ARnI's suggestions. The Mayor of Umtali, John Kircos, said there was no doubt that Umtali was ideally situated for the establishment of certain industries. 'Our industrial area,' he explained, 'has all the facilities required by prospective industrialists.'[111] What is observable is that, despite some differences on the operative details, in principle the state, organised industry, and local councils all agreed on the need for decentralisation.

Business, Economy, and Politics

Despite the challenges enumerated in the preceding paragraphs, the Rhodesian economy broadly enjoyed a sustained growth up until late 1974, aided by the economic planning and closer coordination between the government and industry. This momentum of the Rhodesian economy slackened. A number of internal and global dynamics, which started in 1973 but whose effects only became apparent between 1974 and 1976, account for the economic stagnation. Signs of stagnation started with the reintroduction of price controls in 1974 and their review in 1975 with the cooperation of the ARnI. However, price controls were acceptable at the time because they 'seemed to be a lesser evil than the dangers of unrestrained inflation,' explained the ARnI.[112] Meanwhile, between 1973 and 1976, the Organisation of the Petroleum Exporting Countries (OPEC) reduced its production and manipulated prices, which had the effect of trebling the value of Rhodesia's oil imports during the same period.[113] The hiking of the oil prices triggered a world economic recession. Consequently, industrial production in the industrialised Western countries declined, leading to a depressed world market and demand for primary commodities. This caused a

110 *Ibid.*
111 *Ibid.*, 18 June 1971.
112 *The Financial Gazette*, 12 March 1976; and ARnI, Annual Report, 1976.
113 Strack, *Sanctions: The Case of Rhodesia*, 88.

deterioration in the prices of Rhodesia's enduring exports. At the same time, the industrialised Western countries suffered inflation that in turn caused an increase in the cost of Rhodesian imports. All of this significantly strained Rhodesia's balance of payments.

Meanwhile, the Portuguese withdrawal from Mozambique in 1975 aggravated problems for Rhodesia: Portugal's presence in Mozambique had proved a lifeline for Rhodesia.[114] As Portugal left, 'the operational efficiency dropped at Beira and Lourenco Marques'.[115] At the same time, the new Black Mozambican government, sympathetic to African nationalists, closed the country's border with Rhodesia, cutting off the country from the Beira trade route. South African railway lines and ports became the only available trade routes for Rhodesia, inducing Rhodesian and even South African businesspersons to rely on this route. The result was severe congestion on the railway and ports in South Africa, causing continuous delays in the transportation of goods and increased shipping and freight costs, all of which further eroded Rhodesia's balance of payments.

To contain the situation, the government intensified control measures to conserve foreign exchange. The controls attracted the ARnI's criticism,[116] but its complaints did not go unchallenged. An anonymous letter sent to the *Property and Finance* (P&F) newspaper in 1975 justified these controls and urged support for the government. The letter commented:

> Every possible assistance and support must therefore be given to the government. The voicing of grievances, about import restrictions, to colleagues, friends and neighbours white-ants our stability. Personal ambition and business dreams must of necessity take a back seat. That we cannot all make comfortable profits and set up chains of new businesses is to be expected in times like the present.[117]

Necessary as they were, control measures restricted the raw material imports crucial for Rhodesian manufacturers to sustain production. Meanwhile, the armed struggle intensified, triggering a budget provision increment of '40% for the Ministry of Defence and 23% for police'.[118] Critical foreign exchange was committed to military expenditure, thus contributing to the dwindling domestic allocations to industry and commerce. Moreover, the expanding

114 For more on this see, Nyamunda, 'In defence of white rule in Southern Africa: Portuguese–Rhodesian economic relations to 1974', *South African Historical Journal* (2019), https://doi.org/10.1080/02582473.2019.1610902.

115 *Ibid.*, 89.

116 See, for example, NAZ RC, L. C21.6.9R, B141849, Commerce and Industry, 1963–1972, ARnI: Review of Policies and Administrative Procedures; ARnI, Annual Report, 1970; *The Financial Gazette*, 23 July 1976; and ARnI, Annual Report, 1976.

117 P&F, April 1975.

118 Strack, *Sanctions: The Case of Rhodesia*, 89.

conflict caused instability and insecurities that dampened tourism, a significant foreign exchange earner, resulting in sharp declines in hard currency earnings in 1976. Without adequate foreign exchange, in 1975 the volume of manufacturing production declined for the first time since 1966.

Meanwhile, between 1974 and 1976, small businesses that were given a voice through an anti big business publication, P&F, heavily criticised the impact of the currency allocation system and the economic planning on them and the economy. In September 1974, the paper celebrated the appointment of a commission to inquire into currency allocations. Since UDI, currency allocations had operated on the principle of past performance (that is, the extent of use of foreign currency before UDI). P&F criticised the system as 'a millstone inhibiting free competition and new blood in commerce and industry.'[119] In 1975 it brought forward a similar criticism, accusing the government of sacrificing small businesses by not supporting them financially, despite contributing hugely to the economic development of Southern Rhodesia.[120]

P&F favoured traditional importers based on past performance; many of these importers were agents of British suppliers who, having been protected by imperial preference, enjoyed the lion's share of the local market. One of the results was that agents of foreign manufacturers (German, French, Italian, and Japanese), often supplying equivalent products of better quality at a lower price, were prevented from establishing themselves as capable suppliers. P&F's posture on this matter should, however, be understood in the context that the paper had become anti-British and anti big business since UDI, hence the seemingly condescending view on imperial preference, British goods, and 'big boys.'[121] Of the 'big boys,' Anglo American Corporation and Lonrho were always the main targets, as they exhibited monopolistic tendencies.

More tellingly, P&F alleged that these big businesses gained the great share of currency allocations at the expense of smaller firms and also that they used foreign currency clandestinely and sometimes in cahoots with the government. The latter, said P&F, explained why the 'Government does nothing, even though one of the principles of the Rhodesian Front is anti-monopoly.'[122] In 1976, in reference to Anglo, the paper accused 'some importers and manufacturers [of] exploiting the public to a shameful degree ... yet for reasons that are known to some, no decisive action has been taken against them. The dismantling of some monopolies is urgent.'[123] Referring once again to the collusion between government and big business, the paper said 'millions in foreign exchange are

119 P&F, September 1974.

120 *Ibid.*, April 1975.

121 For a detailed discussion of P&F's stance, see A. Cohen and R. Pilossof, 'Big business and white insecurities at the end of empire in Southern Africa, c. 1961–1977,' *Journal of Imperial and Commonwealth History*, 45, 5 (2017), 777–99.

122 P&F, April 1975.

123 *Ibid.*, February 1976.

leaving the country illegally', yet 'only the small fry are prosecuted. The acute are thus asking: "Is it perhaps a matter of who you know – and who at the top you, in turn, can oblige?"'[124] Because of this, it suggested that the government should investigate financial links between politicians and private interests.

While indeed the marginalisation of small industrialists was a concern, the role of big business in keeping the economy going when sanctions and the war were biting deep should be acknowledged.[125] It was in the interest of Rhodesia that big business was given a free role, as the following case of Anglo demonstrates. With its octopus-like tentacles wrapped around the Rhodesian economy, Anglo played a key role in supplying oil into the country. Prior to Mozambican independence in 1975, the bulk of Rhodesia's fuel supplies were sent from South Africa via Mozambique. While the Rhodesian state, through its company, GENTA, had supplied the country with oil, big business took over from 1974 when fuel companies expressed reservations in dealing with GENTA. An intermediary company called Freight World Services – owned by the Anglo American Cooperation – became an active player.[126] Usually hiding behind the name 'Minerals Exploration Ltd', Freight Services acted as the intermediary company for Mobil and Shell/British Petroleum's fuel supplies to Rhodesia. Shell and BP supplied Rhodesia with R150 million worth of oil. For instance, eighty-three fuel-filled railway wagons went up the line on 23 October 1974, and the fuel in every one of them belonged to Freight Services. The company bought and sold oil products valued at tens of millions of dollars each year for Mobil; it arranged printing of bogus invoice forms for these companies and handled their money. Clearly, big business was a lifeline for

124 *Ibid.*, August 1976.

125 See I. Phimister and V. M. Gwande, 'Secondary industry and settler colonialism: Southern Rhodesia before and after UDI', *African Economic History*, 45, 2 (2017), 85–112, at pp. 101–02. See also NAZ S3285/9/40, Minister of Commerce & Industry Speeches: Minister's Address to the Institute of Directors, 17 March 1971. For an alternative view on the role of big business during decolonisation, see variously S. Stockwell, *The Business of Decolonization: British Business Strategies in the Gold Coast* (Oxford: Oxford University Press, 2000); N. White, 'The business and politics of decolonization: the British experience in the twentieth century', *Economic History Review*, 53, 3 (2000), 544–64; L. J. Butler, 'Business and British decolonization: Sir Ronald Prain, the mining industry and the Central African Federation', *Journal of Imperial and Commonwealth History*, 35, 3 (2007), 459–84; and Cohen, 'Business and decolonization in Central Africa reconsidered', *Journal of Imperial and Commonwealth History*, 36 (2008), 641–58.

126 The following account relies on the investigative work of the two British researchers Martin Bailey and Bernard Rivers, who produced a report on the Rhodesia Oil Conspiracy in 1976. http://schuitemaberend.blogspot.com/2012/01/howrhodesiagotitsoil.html, Accessed 10 May 2022, 8:31pm.

the Rhodesian economy, as it kept the country supplied with fuel, although the supplies were not adequate, as evidenced by the introduction of fuel rationing.[127]

As fuel rationing hit hard, the problem of labour shortages continued to plague industrialists. The government and industrialists had tried to deal with the shortages through an immigration drive.[128] However, housing shortages restricted immigration, especially of skilled immigrants. In 1976, the Minister of Commerce and Industry admitted that Rhodesia had a skilled manpower shortage, and that it had reached the stage where the government was pondering instituting an inquiry into the situation.[129] Military call-ups compounded labour scarcity. As the war against African liberation fighters intensified, call-ups of personnel for military service increased; industrialists were concerned at the cost of these call-ups to industry. The cost was two-fold. First, the military call-ups took away skilled personnel, thereby depriving industries of the expertise required to keep production going. Second, an employee conscripted for military call-up remained entitled to his salary from the primary employer. Consequently, employers had to budget for 'make-up pay' to cater for the employees recruited for military service.[130]

Make-up pay for military call-ups became a thorny issue for industry. The Salisbury Chamber of Industries (SCI) believed that industry employers should not be prejudiced against employees because of military call-up.[131] However, the Chamber was increasingly concerned with its impact. Some employers were able to meet the demands of the make-up pay, while others could not, especially smaller firms. For many employers who had continued to pay wages to employees during periods of call-ups, the financial burden became unbearable. This problem was aggravated by the fact that companies engaged temporary assistance to fill the gaps. Furthermore, the Chamber believed that any additional financial burden resulting from military call-up 'should not be borne by our territorial servicemen or by individual employers but should be spread over the community as a whole'.[132] The matter created another challenge for industrialists. The ARnI feared that 'the differences in the attitudes adopted by various employers not only [created] strained industrial relations on the home front, but [could] adversely affect the morale of territorial forces in the operational areas'.[133]

127 See L. Maphosa, 'Fuel policy in Rhodesia during economic sanctions, 1965–1979' (MA, University of Zimbabwe, 2015).

128 NAZ RC, L. C21.6.9R, B141849, Commerce and Industry, 1963–1972, ARnI: ARnI, *Annual Report of the Management Committee for the Presidential Year 1967/68.*

129 *The Financial Gazette*, 9 April 1976.

130 *Ibid.*; see also ARNI, Annual Report, 1976.

131 *The Financial Gazette*, 9 April 1976.

132 *Ibid.*

133 *Ibid.*

To remedy this, industrialists appealed for the government to 'increase the rates of pay and allowances within the territorial forces to realistic levels'.[134] But that depended upon the cooperation of the whole sector: 'there would be little merit in urging government to introduce increases in military pay if some employers continued to pay full wages and to allow their employees to keep the whole of their military pay'.[135] It was necessary for those employers who paid their employees during periods of call-up to adopt a uniform policy which would limit 'payment in each case to not more than the employee's civilian wages less whatever the employee received by way of basic military pay and allowances including the service allowance, marriage allowance and children allowance'.[136] Alongside this, industrialists asked for tax relief to employers who paid make-up pay. No one was supposed to be worse off financially because of call-up.

Reeling under the pressure of economic stagnation, criticism from small business, and political instability and other related problems, the Smith government reluctantly engaged in a series of negotiations with both Britain and the African nationalists in search of political settlement. For a long time, Rhodesian organised business had shied away from expressing an opinion, save for its pleas to the government to end the political crisis. As Rowe noted,

> after UDI, opposition to government was stifled. Because outspoken opponents of the regime would be unlikely to receive government favours, fears about economic survival also led many businessmen to suppress their criticisms of the government ... people were so interested in making their own businesses work ... [besides] the government retaliated harshly against any who sought to mobilise political opposition against the regime.[137]

But from around 1976, the private sector entered the political arena. There were two factors in this. The first came about at the instigation of the Private Sector Coordinating Committee (PSCC) formed in 1974, comprising the leaders of ACCOR, the ARnI, the RTA, the RNFU, and the Chamber of Mines. The difficulties that the country and the economy were experiencing inspired considerable cohesion among the economic interest groups. Consequently, a single voice on national issues emerged in the private sector. The second factor was the Geneva initiative. With the prospect of African politicians becoming more involved in government than ever before, the private sector thought it prudent to put their case to those involved in the initiative.

Explaining why it was now drawn into politics, the ARnI's president, Les Gallon, said:

134 *Ibid.*
135 *Ibid.*
136 *Ibid.*
137 Rowe, *Manipulating the Market*, 109–13.

Figure 5.1. Business's call for harmony, 1977 (Source: *The Financial Gazette*, 7 September 1977). *Left*: Two clasped hands symbolising harmony and understanding between all races. The message at the bottom reads, 'Let us turn our backs on prejudice and make a real effort to understand one another.' *Right, left to right (from top)*: The Presidents of Chamber of Mines, RNFU, ACCOR, RTA, and ARnI, accompanied by the message, 'We, in our capacities as Presidents of the five leading private sector associations, are dedicated to the promotion of harmony between Rhodesians. We would ask you all to support us.'

> the point has been well made on a number of occasions recently that the dividing line between politics and economics is by no means precisely defined. On this basis, there are occasions when, of necessity, we must involve ourselves in political matters. This is certainly the case when political decisions may have a dramatic effect on the future viability of industry in this country.[138]

Even as it offered its perspectives, the private sector emphasised its apolitical standpoint. Gallon thus explained that,

> both at Geneva and at subsequent meetings connected with the Geneva Conference, ARnI and the PSCC have confined themselves to briefing the parties on the economic structure of this country and the possible effect on the structure of whatever political decisions may be made.[139]

However, as Rory Pilossof showed with White farmers, the discourse of apoliticism was unsustainable.[140] The nexus between the economy and politics is too strong to be separable. Gallon further cautioned the ARnI's members that 'when acting or speaking on behalf of ARnI, [they] must always bear in mind that they are representing a large group of people with widely differing political beliefs and must, therefore, be on their guard against giving any impression of political partisanship.'[141]

Additionally, business called for harmony between races. The PSCC publicised its call to harmony, as seen in Figure 5.1 opposite.

Partnership between races was also encouraged, with a view to enhancing economic cooperation and fostering development for the 'benefit of all.' Of course, this was a self-serving mantra. Business was set on securing its interests in the likelihood of an African majority rule. Speaking at the SCI's AGM, the Chamber's president, John Shand, said

> emigration is rapidly producing a hard core of Rhodesian whites, free from bigotry and cooperative within reason. What is urgently required is a responsible black community with enough realism to gauge the limits of white co-operation. An economic alliance between the two, backed by mutual respect, would result in the widespread enjoyment of the bounteous resources that lie at doorstep of all Rhodesians – black and white.[142]

138 *The Financial Gazette*, 4 February 1977.

139 *Ibid.*

140 See R. Pilossof, 'Remaining apolitical in a political crisis: exploring interest group politics,' *Journal of Developing Societies*, 26, 1 (2010), 71–97; and R. Pilossof, *The Unbearable Whiteness of Being: Farmers' Voices from Zimbabwe* (Harare: Weaver Press, 2012), 67–116.

141 *The Financial Gazette*, 4 February 1977.

142 *Ibid.*

Of course, Shand was overplaying the benevolence of the Rhodesian Whites and subtly bigoted about Africans, but the general underlying point was sensible, if qualified.

Some African nationalists in principle agreed to the call for harmony but demanded that certain conditionalities should be met. One of the conditions, according to James Chikerema of the Front for the Liberation of Zimbabwe (FROLIZI), was 'the scrapping of the controversial Land Tenure Act as a pre-requisite for the re-awakening of Rhodesian industry after majority rule'.[143] Just like its predecessor – the Land Apportion Act (1930) – the Land Tenure Act of 1969, amended in 1977, racially divided land ownership and inhibited African permanency in urban areas. The act's provision was one of the major causes of the armed conflict that was raging in the country. Its repeal, therefore, would entail cessation of hostilities and the right of Black Africans to participate fully in the urban economy, with the consequential benefit to secondary industries. Chikerema also assured that the economy would 'continue to run along free-enterprise lines and at the same time, the nationalist government would do everything within its power to retain the skills, know-how and industrial abilities of the country's white community'.[144] It is significant to note that of the nationalists that responded to this plea, the two major African nationalist parties, the Zimbabwe African National Union (ZANU) and the Zimbabwe African People's Union (ZAPU), completely ignored these efforts. The business community did not approach them because it perceived ZANU and ZAPU as extremists and communists.

Following Shand's suggestion, the business community and the African nationalists that were considered moderate reconstituted the Rhodesian Promotion Council.[145] It now comprised the RNFU, ARnI, and ACCOR, as well as the 'desirable' African nationalists and other private businesspersons, the mining industry, and financial houses. Writing on the initiative, *The Financial Gazette* reported that

> Rhodesia is undertaking the biggest black–white get-together of industrial, economic, financial, business and agricultural experts ever held in an African country on the eve of a settlement situation. The move is, basically, aimed at side-stepping most of the pitfalls common to independent African countries which, once fallen into, lead to rapid deterioration of the economy, an exodus of whites – particularly farmers – and then massive dependence on expensive imported expatriates and cash injections from Western and Communist countries.[146]

143 *Ibid.*, 23 September 1977.

144 *Ibid.*

145 *The Financial Gazette*, 21 October 1977.

146 *Ibid.* They had learnt from the experiences of Zambia, Uganda, and Mozambique, which saw an exodus of business, skilled manpower, and economic decline after independence.

The Reverend Ndabaningi Sithole of ZANU also welcomed the idea. He said his movement was 100% behind the industrial/farming détente undertaking.[147] Meanwhile, Bishop Muzorewa's United African National Council (UANC) allayed the fears that majority rule would result in wholesale nationalisation.[148]

By 1979, there was a significant shift in the business community's attitude towards the formerly excluded African nationalists. 'With the handwriting on the wall,' wrote Henry Wiseman and Alastair Taylor,

> Members of the Rhodesian Promotion Council, who earlier in February had sought a coalition that would freeze out or diminish the role of Mugabe and ZANU PF in the new government, now made overtures of accommodation. Meetings were hastily arranged between Mugabe and key figures in the cabinet, Rhodesian forces, intelligence and treasury.[149]

What is noticeable from this discussion is that, indeed, business in general, and the ARnI in particular, conceded the inevitability of majority rule and the return to normality. In order to benefit from the impending new environment, it needed to realign itself, hence the engagement with African nationalists, and at the same time advocate policy restructuring.

Also optimistic about the possibility of a political settlement that could potentially herald the lifting of sanctions, the ARnI steadily pushed for industrial policies aimed at preparing industry for a return to normal trading conditions. The policies it advocated were, however, not new. It had clamoured for the same policies throughout the period under study. Accordingly, the association pushed that 'customs duties at levels sufficient to protect local manufacturers against foreign products should be introduced before the existing import controls are phased out or withdrawn, following upon the lifting of economic sanctions.'[150] In 1979, it still insisted on industrial protection in order to promote technological development and ensure quality production.

Problems still persisted. Reflecting on the economy, the ARnI's president commented that

> the national economy continued throughout the year under review to be disrupted not only by the *work force demands of the security forces* [my emphasis] but also by an alarming increase in the *rate of emigration*. While the economy has so far been able to withstand this dual burden, the limit is rapidly being reached.[151]

147 *Ibid.*
148 *The Financial Gazette*, 9 December 1977.
149 H. Wiseman and A. M. Taylor, *From Rhodesia to Zimbabwe: The Politics of Transition* (New York: Pergamon Press, 1981), 41–42.
150 ARnI, Annual Report, 1978.
151 *Ibid.*, 1979.

What certainly became clear was the need for a political solution; this eventually happened in December 1979 with the Lancaster House Agreement that ushered in a new Black government.

Manufacturing Growth under Sanctions

Economic policies and government–business relations certainly shaped the nature and structure of the manufacturing sector that emerged during the UDI. It is to this aspect that this section now turns. Inevitably, the manufacturing sector that emerged during this period was akin to ISI, stimulated by sanctions, import control, and foreign currency saving. ISI was, however, incidental to the primary objective of hedging foreign currency reserves. While ISI sustained industrial growth, it was the high domestic demand that provided much growth impetus to the manufacturing sector. Sanctions and the foreign currency allocation system affected imports and export growth. Rhodesia looked to her own industries, thus triggering a massive demand in locally produced goods. Table 5.2 below shows the sources of industrial growth between 1965 and 1979.

Table 5.2. Rhodesia, sources of industrial growth, 1965–1979 (%).

SUBSECTORS	Export expansion	Import substitution	Demand expansion
Beer, wine and spirits	-2.8	1.2	101.6
Fertilisers	-1.5	23.4	78.1
Rubber products	1.2	19.6	79.2
Plastic products	0.0	51.4	48.6
Ferro alloys & iron products	35.9	14.3	49.8
Textiles	4.7	26.8	68.5
Clothing and footwear	7.3	8.0	84.7
Paper, printing, and publishing	-1.4	19.6	81.8
Non-metallic mineral products	-0.5	3.6	96.9
Wood and furniture	4.4	14.9	80.8

Source: World Bank, Report No. 6349-ZIM, *Zimbabwe: An Industrial Sector Memorandum* (22 May 1987), Appendix.

Despite the foreign exchange restraints on imported materials, the performance of the manufacturing sector was nevertheless satisfactory. Table 5.3 shows changes in the manufacturing subsectors. Strack observed that 'the range of output expanded from 602 products in 1963 to 1059 in 1966 to 3837 in

Table 5.3. Rhodesia, subsectorial change and structure of production, 1967–1979 (% of Total Gross Output).

SUBSECTORS	1967	1975	1979
Foodstuffs	24.6	19.7	23.5
Drink and tobacco	9.4	7.0	7.5
Textiles and ginning	9.2	10.4	11.2
Clothing and footwear	8.5	6.8	6.1
Wood and furniture	3.7	2.8	3.1
Paper, printing, and publishing	5.8	5.7	4.7
Chemicals and petroleum	13.3	14.0	13.3
Non-metallic mineral products	3.1	3.7	2.6
Metals and products	14.5	22.1	21.5
Electrical machinery	4.1	3.0	2.7
Transport equipment	2.8	3.9	2.7
Other	1.0	1.0	1.2

Source: World Bank, Report No. 6349-ZIM, *Zimbabwe: An Industrial Sector Memorandum* (22 May 1987), Appendix.

1970. However, 65% of these products in 1970 were monopoly products which probably would not be able to survive a return to competitive conditions.'[152]

Production also tended to be concentrated in the hands of a few big firms, as Table 5.4 shows. By 1972, 98 (representing 7.6% of the total firms) firms with a gross output of $2,000,000 and over, out of a sectorial total of 1,285 firms, accounted for $520,663,000 worth (60.4%) of all industrial production.[153]

Between 1974 and 1978, manufacturing production declined by 27%, capacity utilisation fell by 38%, and there was net loss of 50,000 urban private jobs, mainly in 'manufacturing and construction.'[154] Nevertheless, industry held its own. Presenting his 1979 report, the ARnI's President Hillis said 'manufactured products now account for between 25% and 30% of the country's export receipts and virtually all consumer goods, as well as a growing proportion of intermediate and capital goods are now supplied from local manufacture.'[155] While this was generally satisfying for industrialists, they still bemoaned it

152 Strack, *Sanctions: The Case of Rhodesia*, 90.

153 D. G. Clarke, 'The political economy of discrimination and underdevelopment in Rhodesia with Special reference to African Workers, 1940–1973' (PhD, University of St Andrews, 1975), 192.

154 Quoted in Bond, *Uneven Zimbabwe*, 125.

155 *Ibid.*; ARnI, Annual Report, 1979.

Table 5.4. Operations of manufacturers by size of gross output, 1972.

Gross output	No. of units	%	Gross output ($'000)	%
Up to $10,000	55	4.3		0.0
$10,001–$20,000	58	4.5	841	0.1
$20,001–$30,000	67	5.2	1.662	0.2
$30,001– $40,000	76	5.9	1,713	0.3
$40,001–$50,000	56	4.4	2,532	0.3
$50,001–$100,000	234	18.2	17,666	2.1
$100,001–$150,000	116	9.0	14,594	1.7
$150,001–$200,000	129	10.0	25,625	3.0
$200,001–$500,000	180	14.0	63,062	7.3
$500,001–$1,000,000	132	10.3	92,429	10.7
$1,000,000–$2,000,000	84	6.6	119,501	13.9
Over $2,000,000	98	7.6	520,663	60.4
Total	1,285	100.0	860,586	100.0

Source: *The Census of In-dustrial Production*, 1972/1973.

as paradoxical that in a country that officially espoused the free-enterprise concept, entrepreneurs 'operated under conditions of greater state control than probably anywhere else outside the communist bloc'.[156] Although the restrictions and regulations of the time were acceptable for the overall 'national good', the ARnI remained determined to guard against any apathetic acquiescence to erosion of the free-enterprise principle. Exuding optimism, the ARnI expected 'old and new export markets to become available, domestic and foreign investment to rise, import allocations for raw materials, spare parts and new machinery to be substantially increased and the pace of overall economic advance to quicken' and ultimately a new era of growth and development for secondary industry.[157] Of course, all this depended on the achievement of a political solution that would lead to the cessation of hostilities and the lifting of sanctions. Overall, the fact that industry maintained its viability, despite the depressed conditions, is a tribute to the determination, versatility, and hard work of the industrial sector.

156 *Ibid.*
157 *Ibid.*

Conclusion

This chapter discerned a self-serving decision by business to cooperate and collaborate with the government – in a manner that Skålnes refers to as societal corporatism – to reduce the severity of sanctions and protect its business interests. Neither can the economic planning and government intervention during the era be seen as economic nationalism. As demonstrated in the chapter, there was actually consultation between government and industry: for instance, it was the ARnI and ACCOR that administered currency allocations, and they all sat in various government committees to plan for the economy. Collaboration was not limited to relations with the government, but also extended to African nationalists in anticipation of a political settlement. Admittedly, there were instances of confrontation and disgruntlement from industry. However, this did not subsist throughout the era.

It is also of note that the period of UDI was also a time in which the government favoured industrial development and gave it considerable support. This was of course in the government's own political interests – to defeat the severity of sanctions following political rebellion. As the government sought to save its foreign currency reserves, it incidentally adopted ISI, but this was never intended. Industrialists took the opportunities offered by the closed economy and the government's overreliance on them to expand secondary industry. But the limits of ISI (a limited internal market and the elasticity of diversification and innovation) circumscribed the extent of the expansion. Other challenges, such as foreign currency shortages, skilled labour shortages exacerbated by military call-ups and emigration, and transport shortages, all combined to slacken industrial growth. Against all these vicissitudes, industry held its own, as the statistics given in the chapter showed.

Conclusion

Colonial Zimbabwe's Industrialisation in Retrospect

This book has offered an alternative historical account of colonial Zimbabwe's industrial policy formulation and implementation which places industrialists, through their successive representative organisations, at the centre of the country's industrial development. Local nascent industrialists and other local capital interests challenged the metropolitan 'tradition', which did not favour industrial development in colonies. That Southern Rhodesia was a settler colony with relative independence from metropolitan control helped, as it was able to formulate its own economic policies that were contrary to the British manufacturers and exports. However, the settler colonial state in Southern Rhodesia did not willingly introduce its economic policies. In many cases, this happened at the behest of the various economic interest groups. Manufacturing development was a case in point. With minimal government direction, and aided only by the smallest degree of protection afforded through the customs tariff, selectively granted only after careful consideration of various factors, industrialists risked their money and laid a sound base for the sector and the diversification of the economy evident in Southern Rhodesia by 1965. Although the government attitude changed between 1966 and 1979, its pro-industrialisation stance was not of its own volition. Industrialists and the state, each determined to protect their own interests, worked closely to sustain the economy under the weight of economic sanctions, international ostracisation, and the escalating armed liberation struggle.

The book has built on the observation – which scholars of Zimbabwean industrialisation have surprisingly ignored or overlooked – that the manufacturing sector in Rhodesia generally suffered from 'the lack of state support … right up to the Federal period, through UDI and sanction', a reality conceded in 1971 by the government, through the Minister of Commerce and Industry,

Jack Mussett.[1] According to Mussett, whose view is reinforced in this study, economic growth

> was achieved by private enterprise and certainly in so far as manufacturing industry was concerned, with very little encouragement from government, for it was only towards the end of the Federal era that the Federal Government instituted a policy of assisting and protecting local industry through the Customs Tariff.[2]

But even the claim by Mussett that the government introduced tariff protection towards the end of the Federation is contestable. For example, the Phillips Report of 1962 discussed in Chapter 5 showed that the government still believed that the manufacturing sector was dependent on agriculture and mining for its growth. It would thus be inaccurate to claim that there was a government policy to protect local industries through customs tariffs when the priority was still on the primary exporting industries.

If anything, the central theme threaded throughout the chapters of the book is that any government industrial policy interventions that can be discerned in colonial Zimbabwe did not come easily. These were a result of the active lobbying by organised secondary industry through incessant complaints, petitions, and proposals to the state demanding an active and favourable industrial policy. In all these attempts, the industrialists were either completely dismissed or only listened to when the state realised it was in its political, social, and economic interests to introduce a particular policy that supported local industries. Moreover, organised secondary industry faced stiff opposition from other organised economic interests like commerce, miners, and farmers. Even in the face of such antagonism, however, organised secondary industry relentlessly fought for a progressive industrial policy. The relationship between the state, industrialists, and other economic interest groups was fluid, uneven, and dynamic, and depended on the context. By paying attention to the voices of industrialists, this instalment is an addition to the limited historiography of Zimbabwean industrialisation, economy and business, with implications for the country's interest group politics.

Privileging the role of private enterprise, as represented by organised secondary industry, in the industrial development of Southern Rhodesia has offered an alternative to the narrative of industrialisation in colonial Zimbabwe

1 A. S. Mlambo, E. S. Pangeti, and I. Phimister, *Zimbabwe: A History of Manufacturing, 1890-1995* (Harare: University of Zimbabwe Publications, 2000), 124; and also J. A. C. Girdlestone, 'Manufacturing and construction', in G. M. E. Leistner (ed.), *Rhodesia: Economic Structure and Change* (Pretoria: African Institute of South Africa, 1976), 120–35, at pp. 122–24, which made a similar observation.

2 NAZ S3285/9/40, Minister of Commerce & Industry Speeches: Minister's Address to the Institute of Directors, 17 March 1971.

which emphasises state actions.[3] Although it is acknowledged that the government was involved in the planning and establishment of major industries of national importance such as iron and steel and the textile industries, privileging its role in the development of secondary industry in colonial Zimbabwe leaves us with an incomplete story. The great expansion and diversification of secondary industries which took place, this study has argued, was in large part a result of incessant lobbying by private entrepreneurs. They achieved this through their representative organisations: Salisbury and Bulawayo Manufacturers' Association (*c.*1920), Salisbury and Bulawayo Chambers of Industries (*c.*1930s), Association of Chambers of Industries of Rhodesia (ACIR: 1941–1949), the FRI (1949–1957), ARNI (1957–1964), and the ARnI (1964–1979).

Right from Rhodesia's establishment as a colony in 1890, successive administrations believed that the country was destined to remain essentially a producer and exporter of primary products. Consequently, for these governments, fostering secondary industries by measures such as the granting of tariff protection or the imposition of import controls posed a risk of raising local prices and costs of production, with the effect of undermining the competitiveness of the agricultural and mining industries in their export markets by raising their prices. This was likely to attract retaliation from other countries against the country's primary exports. The government regarded this as sound economic logic.[4] Following this rationale, the government exercised considerable caution in fostering secondary industries lest it jeopardise what they assumed to be the main drivers of growth in the economy.

Changing economic and political conditions sometimes engendered closer cooperation between business and government. The Second World War and UDI years are cases in point. The notion of societal cooperation was best demonstrated during these periods. By emphasising cooperation between business and the state, the book has challenged some long-standing assertions from scholars that the business community was muzzled during UDI. Explaining business quiescence, Rowe, for example, pointed out that the government retaliated harshly against anyone who mobilised political opposition against the regime. Further, it changed the institutional structure of the colony's market in a way that increased the economic dependency of business on the government, and finally, it took advantage of the differential effect of sanctions on different sectors of the business community to prevent business from speaking with one voice. Rowe claimed 'the RF was highly distrustful of the business community. It suspected that business might not only lobby against it politically, but use

3 E. S. Pangeti, 'The state and manufacturing industry: a study of the state as regulator and entrepreneur in Zimbabwe' (PhD, University of Zimbabwe, 1996).

4 See C. H. Thompson and H. W. Woodruff, *Economic Development in Rhodesia and Nyasaland* (London: Dennis Dobson Ltd, 1953).

its powers over investment, employment, and finance to impose significant penalties on the government for provoking sanctions.'[5]

The Rhodesian Front's distrust and suspicion of the business community may have been well founded, but there is a paradox to this government attitude. When sanctions were imposed on Rhodesia, the government depended on the same business for its survival. The UDI state specifically and deliberately supported industrialists, as it saw these as the lifeline for the economy and for creating employment. By its own admission, 'the extraordinary expansion of manufacturing industry in Rhodesia … [was] one of the main reasons for [the country's] success in achieving, *despite all opposition* (my emphasis), a rate of economic growth that is the envy of the many developed, let alone undeveloped countries'.[6] As *Property and Finance* (P&F) reported in April 1975, there was collusion between government and conglomerates. The admission by the government and reports by P&F were not unfounded. They reveal the existence of collaboration (though this may have been clandestine) between the state and business. Judged against these realities, the characterisation that the business community, including industrialists, was muzzled, is unsustainable.

The government also altered the institutional structure of markets through import control and foreign currency allocation. Rowe explains that this was used by the government to dampen collective political opposition through either withholding a currency allocation or an import licence from an individual firm, or rewarding compliant political behaviour. 'The government used its discretion in awarding allocations to build networks of political support among the business community. In particular, the government targeted the industrial sector because of this sector's now critical role in maintaining employment and replacing goods lost to sanctions.'[7] By contrast, this study demonstrated that as far as currency allocations and import control were concerned, the private sector was consulted from the outset. In fact, the Association of Rhodesian Industries (ARnI) and the Associated Chambers of Commerce of Rhodesia (ACCOR) were the principal agents in the administration of import control and currency allocation. The Ministry of Commerce and Industry split the treasury's allocation of foreign exchange into the broad categories of special requirements, ARnI allocations, and ACCOR allocations, and the detailed apportionment of these shares to individual firms was done by ACCOR and the ARnI in accordance with agreed guidelines. This is evidence of close

5 D. M. Rowe, *Manipulating the Market: Understanding Economic Sanctions, Institutional Change and the Political Unity of White Rhodesia* (Chicago: Chicago University Press, 2001), 113.

6 NAZ S3285/9/40, Minister of Commerce & Industry Speeches: Minister's Address to Midlands Chamber of Industries, 25 February 1971; and also I. Phimister and V. M. Gwande, 'Secondary industry and settler colonialism: Southern Rhodesia before and after UDI', *African Economic History*, 45, 2 (2017), 85–112.

7 Rowe, *Manipulating the Market*, 117.

collaboration between government and business during UDI, not business acquiescing to the dictates of government. Societal corporatism was at work.

The government felt that the detailed distribution of import allocations could best be done by businessmen who knew every facet of the trade or industry, so they made the decision to leave currency allocation to commerce and industry. Here one need not see manipulation but cooperation and collaboration between the government and business. If anything, government was finally acting in a manner that industrialists had long clamoured for. Besides, failing to foster industrial development during those times was a gamble which the government could not afford, vis-à-vis sanctions. In the circumstances, the government had limited options, if any, but to assist. So it was not out of any tactical plan to control business but a pragmatic existential strategy to keep the industrial sector going in light of its now crucial role.

Rowe further argues:

> by seeding serious conflicts between firms over the distribution of foreign exchange, the government also impeded their ability to act collectively on larger issues. Thus, the very structure of the foreign exchange system created a pattern of incentives that divided firms and raised the level of mistrust between them, weakening their ability to pursue a collective policy of opposition.[8]

Although foreign currency allocations created tensions between industry and commerce, as commerce claimed that government favoured industry, it was not a deliberate plan to play divide and rule between the sectors, thereby thwarting collective political opposition. It was inevitable during the sanctions, as the government sought to conserve foreign currency. In so doing, domestic expansion became the preferred policy, and this favoured local industrialists. Logically, they received favourable allocations in order to import critical capital goods and the raw materials necessary for industrial expansion. This sharply contrasts with previous years, when the government policy of limited interference favoured commerce.

Since the focus was now on expanding and diversifying the local economy, huge currency allocations for inessential imports were no longer necessary, as they eroded limited foreign exchange reserves. The government prioritised the capitalisation of local industry to enable it to increase chances of exports that could gain more foreign exchange. Rowe overlooked this when emphasising the divide-and-rule tactics. Instead of manipulation, this study therefore suggested that the relationship between the state, industrialists, and other economic interest groups following the Unilateral Declaration of Independence (UDI) can be described, in Skålnes's terms, as societal corporatism. Government intervention in the economy was inevitable under the circumstances.

8 *Ibid.*, 120.

The study has also cast doubt on the characterisation of Southern Rhodesia's industrialisation as import substitution industrialisation (ISI). Even the Sadie Report made this observation: 'Import substitution has, up to 1965 at least, not been the major incentive or goal in industrial development.'[9] This book has demonstrated that even during the UDI, ISI was not a deliberate government industrial policy. Like in the case of British India during the Great Depression of the 1930s, ISI in Rhodesia occurred by default. As attested to by Shigeru Akita,

> the Government of India introduced emergency measures like surcharges and increased tariff rates to tackle the fiscal problems. These policies, in turn, unintentionally accelerated the growth of Indian cotton industries, and the same tendency could be found in the case of Indian iron and steel, and the development of the Tata Iron and Steel Works.[10]

In the case of Rhodesia, it was by default because of the interruptions in international trade caused by the war and sanctions. War and sanctions cut off imports, forcing the country to rely on local industries. Freed from international competition, local factories maximised and filled in the vacuum. It is to this extent that some scholars refer to the industrial development of that era as ISI, but to say that ISI was the case in Rhodesia may have been an overstatement; rather, ISI was met by the barrier of its own limitations.[11] The characterisation of Rhodesia's industrial growth as an ISI falls short in that the phenomenon only explains developments in a particular period, for example the Second World War and UDI, but not the whole story of how colonial Zimbabwe industrialised. As this study has demonstrated, industrialisation in Southern Rhodesia can be accounted for by examining the role of organised secondary industry.

During UDI, ISI was also incidental because it was a by-product of the state's desire to conserve foreign exchange. It is the sequencing that one should pay closer attention to on this matter. The government's primary goal was to preserve its foreign exchange reserves and maintain a favourable balance of payments. To achieve that, it needed to cut back on imports and expand on exports. Consequently, the government turned to the local manufacturing sector, encouraging it to diversify in order to satisfy domestic demand and widen exportable finished goods. Moreover, the continued threat by the government that it would remove import control once a political settlement was reached shows that the government was not prepared to adopt import substitution as its industrial policy. This sharply contrasts with the experiences

9 Sadie Report, 8.

10 S. Akita, 'British economic interests and international order of Asia in the 1930s', in S. Akita and N. J. White (eds), *The International Order of Asia in the 1930s and 1950s* (Farnham: Ashgate Publishing Company, 2010), 17–48, at p. 43.

11 Phimister and Gwande, 'Secondary industry and settler colonialism', 85.

of ISI in some Latin American countries (Brazil, Chile, and Argentina) and several newly independent African countries, which adopted it as a deliberate developmental policy.[12]

What has also become apparent from this analysis is that the major point of contention between the state, industry, and other economic interest groups was protection. The discussion about protection opens a long-standing debate on the best way for developing countries to achieve economic development. The experiences of Zimbabwe and the East African Community (EAC) referred to in the book's introduction clearly demonstrate how contested this policy has always been. Does free-market enterprise or state-protected development provide developing countries with the best opportunities to develop?[13] Southern Rhodesia's industrialisation was continuously dogged by this debate. As Bozzoli observed with reference to South Africa, industrialists complained that the country's industries were 'backward' due to 'the hesitating and uncertain policy pursued in regard to protection by public opinion and by successive governments. The want of a firm, settled policy is one of the principal causes of the backward state of most of our industries ... let the country commit itself definitely to [protection] policy, and our industries will at once make large strides in development.'[14]

In Southern Rhodesia, the state, miners, farmers, and commerce were heavily reliant on the export market and international trade for survival. Therefore, they argued that adopting a protectionist policy would prejudice them in a number of ways. First, they would suffer retaliation from other countries. Second, protecting local industry would increase the cost of production for the primary exporting industries, and the unintended effect of this would be a decline in international trade as both exports and imports

12 O. Hirschman, 'The political economy of import-substituting industrialization in Latin America,' *Quarterly Journal of Economics*, 82, 1 (1968), 1–32; W. Baer, 'Import substitution and industrialization in Latin America: experiences and interpretations,' *Latin American Research Review*, 7, 1 (1972), 95–122; See R. Prebisch, *The Economic Development of Latin America and Its Principal Problems* (New York: United Nations, 1950); P. A. Baran, *The Political Economy of Growth* (New York: Monthly Review Press, 1957); A. G. Frank, *Latin America: Underdevelopment or Revolution: Essays on the Development of Underdevelopment and the Immediate Enemy* (New York: Monthly Review Press, 1969); A. P. F. Mendes, M. A. Bertella, and R. F. A. P. Teixeira, 'Industrialization in sub-Saharan Africa and import substitution policy,' *Brazilian Journal of Political Economy*, 34, 1 (134), 120–38; and R. C. Riddell (ed.), *Manufacturing Africa: Performance and Prospects of Seven Countries in Sub-Saharan Africa* (London: James Currey, 1990).

13 P. G. Sampath, 'Industrial development for Africa: trade and technology and the role of the state,' *African Journal of Science, Technology, Innovation and Development*, 6, 5 (2014), 439–53.

14 B. Bozzoli, *The Political Nature of a Ruling Class: Capital and Ideology in South Africa 1890–1933* (London: Routledge and Keagan Paul, 1981), 112.

became uncompetitive on the international and local markets, respectively. The ultimate consequence would then be a loss of revenue for the government and a slackening of the country's economic growth and development.

Rhodesia also shied away from using import control as an instrument of government policy designed to stimulate industrial development, despite industrialists pressing for it relentlessly. The responsible ministers usually counter-argued that the General Agreement on Trade and Tariffs (GATT) ruled out the use of import control for promoting industrialisation. Instead, they proposed that industrial development would be better encouraged through a judicious customs tariff. This view prevailed until the government introduced intensive import controls during UDI. Even then, this introduction opened a debate on the operative longevity of these controls. Industrialists wanted import control retained as a means of fostering industrial development, while both commerce and importers, in particular, desired the removal of the import controls as soon as possible and the tariff restored as the main government stimulant for industrial development. As a result, industry was never wholly protected. In this regard, the book supports the conclusion reached by Mlambo and Phimister in their study on the origins and development of the textile industry in Southern Rhodesia.[15] They concluded that the sector was partly protected. This study has demonstrated that not only the textile sector but the whole of secondary industry was, in part, protected.

Prominent in the debate about protection was the idea of interest group politics or intergroup conflicts. Mussett, the Minister of Commerce and Industry during UDI, was aware of their existence and acknowledged the inevitability of the struggles. Addressing industrialists in 1971, he conceded that 'a fast developing economy such as ours is ... full of apparent conflicts, jostling and splashing, but all going in the same direction and getting bigger all the time.'[16] Bozzoli made similar observations in her analysis of the rise of a national bourgeoisie in South Africa.[17] Unlike Rhodesian manufacturing interests, South African manufacturing capital had the advantage of having an organic intellectual, W. J. Laite, in its ranks, who provided the sector with organisational and ideological capabilities when needed for the furtherance of its interests in the face of opposition from the state and other classes. Because of the absence of a Rhodesian Laite, secondary industry in Southern Rhodesia took longer to establish and galvanise. The country's industrial development received much criticism from other interest groups, who alleged that manufacturing development was 'an exotic plant, artificially matured in the hot house atmosphere of sanctions and import controls that will wither away at

15 A. S. Mlambo and I. Phimister, 'Partly protected: origins and growth of colonial Zimbabwe's textile industry, 1890–1965', *Historia*, 52, 2 (2006), 145–75.

16 NAZ S3285/9/40, Minister of Commerce & Industry Speeches: Minister's Address to Midlands Chamber of Industries, 25 February 1971.

17 Bozzoli, *The Political Nature of a Ruling Class*, 104–41.

the first cold blast of competitive air from the outside world'.[18] In addition, the government and the ministry were blamed for approving new industrial projects injudiciously and diverting scarce foreign exchange into keeping production going in the industrial sector to the detriment of other sectors and of the availability of consumer goods.

However, for the first time since the 1930s, in the 1970s the government defended industrial development. The government explained that a thriving industrial sector generated widespread economic benefits; even where their raw materials were imported, their transformation into finished goods utilised local resources such as other materials and labour, supported service industries, created a demand for goods and services of all kinds, and, in general, supported a far higher level of economic activity than the bare importation and distribution of goods would have.[19] Manufacturing provided an important core of stable employment and activity, little affected by the vagaries of weather or fluctuating market prices. For these reasons, the manufacturing sector deserved preferential treatment. Noting the state's position during UDI does not undermine the overall argument that private enterprise drove the industrialisation of colonial Zimbabwe between 1890 and 1979; it merely acknowledges the occasionally positive attitude of the state towards industrial development. Otherwise the contention remains that it was industrialists, with uneven and irregular state support, who laid the base for a solid secondary industrial sector.

As Southern Rhodesia industrialised, this had implications on its major trading partners, especially South Africa, Zambia, and Malawi. For a long time, the Union of South Africa looked north to Southern Rhodesia for its market for manufactured goods. Similarly, Southern Rhodesia turned to Zambia and Malawi for its industrial exports. The result was a series of trade agreements among these countries which formed the basis of their trading relations. For the Union of South Africa and Southern Rhodesia, the trading relations turned out to be based on cooperation and competition. Each saw the other as a threat to their manufacturing interests and yet they could not avoid working together to advance their economies and strengthen White solidarity in Southern Africa. Zambia and Malawi were captive markets for Southern Rhodesia's industrial products. This was particularly entrenched during the federal period. The 1955 trade agreement among the three countries gave Southern Rhodesia exclusive access to the Zambian and Malawian markets, as evidenced by the fact that about four-fifths of the manufactured imports of these two countries came from Southern Rhodesia. At the same time, the dominance of Southern Rhodesia's manufacturing economy over its two northern neighbours meant

18 NAZ S3285/9/40, Minister of Commerce & Industry Speeches: Minister's Address to Midlands Chamber of Industries, 25 February 1971.

19 *Ibid.*

their industrial growth was stifled: both Zambia and Malawi had negligible manufacturing sectors as a result of Southern Rhodesia's overbearing shadow. The situation only changed when the Federation collapsed in 1963 and the two countries became independent in 1964. Although the instrument of trade agreements was employed to manage regional trading relations, often the negotiated agreements favoured two powerful southern neighbours, South Africa and Southern Rhodesia, over Zambia and Malawi.

Zimbabwe's Manufacturing Sector Post-1979

By 1980, when Zimbabwe gained its independence from Britain, it was the second most industrialised country in sub-Saharan Africa, only inferior to South Africa. The preceding discussion in this book has demonstrated how that status came to be, but it is also necessary to highlight how the manufacturing sector has fared since the end of colonial rule by drawing out the major factors that shaped its trajectory and performance. This examination will focus on how state–industry relations played out under a new political and economic environment, which policies guided industrialisation, and the impact of what has now become known as the 'Zimbabwean crisis'.

The trajectory, prospects, and performance of the manufacturing sector in the post-colonial years have been recounted in the existing scholarship, with two major perspectives standing out. There is consensus that during the first ten years of majority rule, the economy in general and the manufacturing sector in particular held its own, experiencing expansion between 1980 and 1982, maintaining stability in the middle years, and eventually showing signs of stagnation in the twilight of that decade.[20] After 1990, the manufacturing sector declined considerably under the weight of the Economic Structural Adjustment Programme (ESAP) adopted by the government between 1991 and 1995, and other constraints, as will be discussed subsequently.[21] Arguably,

20 For the state of the economy during this period, see I. Mandaza (ed.), *Zimbabwe: The Political Economy of Transition, 1980–1986* (Dakar, Senegal: CODESRIA, 1986). The perspectives on the manufacturing sector are discussed in D. B. Ndlela, 'Problems of industrialisation: structural and policy issues', in Mandaza, *The Political Economy of Transition*, 141–64; A. S. Mlambo, 'Manufacturing in Zimbabwe, 1980–1990', in A. S. Mlambo, E. S. Pangeti, and I. Phimister, *Zimbabwe: A History of Manufacturing, 1890–1995* (Harare: University of Zimbabwe Publications, 2000), 80–109; C. Stoneman, 'The industrialisation of Zimbabwe: past, present and future', *Afrika Focus*, 6, 3–4, DOI: https://doi.org/10.21825/af.v6i3-4.6126; Riddell, 'Industrialisation in sub-Saharan Africa: country case study – Zimbabwe', Working Paper 25, Overseas Development Institute (1990).

21 A. S. Mlambo, 'From an industrial powerhouse to a nation of vendors: over two decades of economic decline and deindustrialization in Zimbabwe 1990–2015', *Journal of Developing Societies*, 33, 1 (2017), 99–125.

this period marked the beginning of the deindustrialisation that has become synonymous with post-colonial Zimbabwe to date.

Much as the manufacturing sector performed appreciably well in the 1980s, it still manifested the relics of its colonial structure. Though relatively developed and diversified, the sector, like the colonial economy as a whole, reflected the legacy of settler colonialism characterised by racial exclusion and inequality. Black exclusion and marginalisation from the economy had been legislated under a plethora of laws, chief among these being the Land Apportionment Act of 1930. This act, the Magna Carta of settler colonial rule, ensured that Blacks 'could not legally own land in parts of the country which were designated "white areas", which also happened to include all urban and mining centres and areas where commercial agriculture was possible.'[22] Under its provisions, Black Africans were elbowed out of any significant involvement in the economy except as unskilled or semi-skilled cheap labour and petty business owners. 'Black entrepreneurs were in practice barred from establishing manufacturing enterprises outside the informal sector and because of both racial residential discrimination and harsh laws restricting the movement of blacks in urban areas, the small scale informal manufacturing sector in Zimbabwe has been far less developed than in many other African countries', explains Riddell.[23]

The colonial economy broadly, and the manufacturing sector in particular, benefitted a small White section of the population. As Riddell explained,

> neither decisions related to the establishment of the country's manufacturing base nor to its expansion owe very much to the indigenous black people of the country. Manufacturing has always been largely owned, managed and operated by skilled personnel from either the settler white community or else owned by foreign capital interests which made use of these settler skills.[24]

On account of this exclusion, Africans could not enter into any meaningful business enterprises, particularly in the manufacturing sector, whose capital outlay was huge. Resorting to financial and banking institutions was out of the question for them because they were considered a high risk, and in any case, they lacked collateral. Consequently, Black business operators were concentrated in commerce and transport businesses located in the African reserves and townships.[25] These factors account for the absence of Black entrepreneurs in the manufacturing sector at the dawn of majority rule.

22 *Ibid.*, 101.

23 Riddell, 'Industrialisation in sub-Saharan Africa: country case study', 7.

24 *Ibid.*, 6.

25 For a discussion on African businesses during this period, see T. Chambwe, 'A history of African entrepreneurship in Southern Rhodesia, 1944–1979' (PhD, University of the Free State, 2020).

This structure, *ipso facto*, invited the state to intervene, seeking to realign the ownership of the means of production and facilitate the participation in the economy of the previously marginalised and disadvantaged Black majority. Some initiatives were highly noticeable in this regard. The new government invested massively in social development, especially in the expansion of education and health services and pro-worker legislations.[26] Even as these efforts were made, the structure and ownership of the economy broadly, and the manufacturing sector in particular, remained unaltered as White private and foreign capital still dominated. According to Ndlela, during this period about '65 to 75% of the country's capital assets [were] held by foreigners.'[27] 'With foreign companies responsible for the ownership of some 48% of the total assets of the manufacturing sector', remarked Riddell, 'they accounted for about 80% of the total capital of private manufacturing companies.'[28] The ownership pattern reflected more of 'continuity than change' in spite of the political shift in the country. That trend was equally applicable to government industrial policy, to which the next paragraphs turn.

The colonial manufacturing industrial architecture remained largely unchanged in the post-colonial years. For instance, the post-colonial state inherited the UDI-era interventionism. According to Stoneman, 'in the years after 1980, the state slowly developed a somewhat greater role in industry, with the IDC both taking over a number of ailing companies, and becoming involved in a wider range of investments, sometimes of a majority nature.'[29] Policy instruments such as price, quantitative import, and foreign exchange controls remained firmly rooted. While these had worked well under the environment of sanctions and hostility, their utility under an open economy became questionable. As the World Bank noted, 'The system of allocating foreign exchange to individual firms on the basis of historical patterns has introduced an element of rigidity into the industrial and commercial structure.'[30] While these dirigiste policies can be criticised for creating inefficiencies, they should also be understood within the broader Marxist–socialist aspirations of the new government: 'the new state's desire for control over the mainly White or foreign owners of industry, its desire not to risk de-industrialisation by removing protection, and a stated desire to plan the economy.'[31]

26 See the discussions under 'The Labour Movement' and 'Social Development' in Mandaza, *The Political Economy of Transition*, from page 243 onwards.

27 D. B. Ndlela, 'Manufacturing industry: a critical review', *Social Change and Development*, 5 (1983), 4–5.

28 Riddell, 'Industrialisation in sub-Saharan Africa: country case study', 7.

29 Stoneman, 'The industrialisation of Zimbabwe: past, present and future', 248.

30 World Bank, Report No. 5458-ZIM, *Zimbabwe Country Economic Memorandum Performance, Policies and Prospects* (28 October 1985), 52.

31 Stoneman, 'The industrialisation of Zimbabwe: past, present and future', 249.

The government's industrial policy operated under three broad development plans: *Growth with Equity* (1981), the *Transitional National Development Plan* (1983–1986), and the *First Five Year National Development Plan* (1986–1990). The first two spelled out the broad economic policy, geared towards economic growth, full employment, and price stability, among other policy goals. They also showed the government's commitment to improving efficiency, viability, and competitiveness in the industrial sector.[32] To achieve that, the government committed to foster the expansion of the sector to meet the growing local and international demand, increase its export earning capacity, and promote ISI. Under the First Five Year National Development Plan, the manufacturing sector was recognised as the key factor in 'changing the structure of the Zimbabwean economy and ... achieving rapid and sustained overall economic growth and development'.[33] The government would act largely as a regulator and emphasised the use of local products in production. Despite pronouncing all these broad policy guidelines, Stoneman and Ndlela contend that the new government did not have an official policy as regards the manufacturing sector. For Ndlela, an explicit industrial policy and strategy was absent and the state was less specific on what it sought to achieve.[34] According to Stoneman, 'despite the fanfares associated with [the *Development Plans*], no coherent industrialisation plan was included, and no instruments or institutions for such a plan were processed'.[35]

The 1990s

The 1990s opened with the Zimbabwean government's adoption of the World Bank- sponsored ESAP. Scholars have examined the impact of the ESAP on Zimbabwe's economy and the manufacturing sector in particular.[36] The manufacturing sector suffered the most. With its package entailing trade liberalisation, devaluation, and removal of subsidies, the ESAP exposed the local

32 Mlambo, 'Manufacturing in Zimbabwe, 1980–1990', 82.

33 As cited in *ibid.*, 83.

34 Ndlela, 'Problems of industrialisation', 156.

35 Stoneman, 'The industrialisation of Zimbabwe: past, present and future', 249.

36 A. S. Mlambo, *The Economic Structural Adjustment Programme: The Case of Zimbabwe, 1990–1995* (Harare: University of Zimbabwe Publishers, 1997); A. S. Mlambo, 'The manufacturing sector under ESAP, 1990–1995', in Mlambo, *Zimbabwe: A History of Manufacturing*, 110–23; A. M. Chakaodza, *Structural Adjustment in Zimbabwe and Zambia: Restructive or Destructive?* (Harare: Third World Publishers, 1993); J. T. Chipika *et al.*, *Effects of Structural Adjustment in Southern Africa: The Case of Zimbabwe's Manufacturing Sector during Phase 1 of ESAP: 1991–1995* (Harare: SAPES, 2000); and J. W. Gunning and R. Oostendorp (eds), *Industrial Change in Africa: Zimbabwean Firms under Structural Adjustment* (New York: Palgrave, 2002).

manufacturing sector to full-blast competition from imports. The years of state and natural protectionism were gone. According to Mlambo,

> the manufacturing sector struggled, leading to some companies either downsizing or closing down. Particularly hard hit was the textile industry, which found itself having to compete with cheaper imports at a time when the economic climate was not particularly conducive. As companies under stress were forced to retrench some of their staff, with 25,000 employees reportedly retrenched by 1992, the shrinking domestic market translated into weakening consumer demand, which further put a strain on the companies that remained operative.[37]

While the adoption of liberalisation proved deleterious to the manufacturing sector, it also brought forth a paradox. Given the likely impact of liberalisation, one hoped industrialists would be the loudest in resisting it. Yet, as Skålnes showed, the Confederation of Zimbabwe Industries (CZI) was instrumental in the adoption of the ESAP.[38] What motivated the CZI to shift tact and support liberalisation was its resentment towards many controls, especially stricter price controls, extended price freezes, and restrictions to retrench workers. Additionally, the interest group was worried about 'the unavailability of foreign exchange except on the black market ... the [low] level of net investment in the economy ... [and] equipment [becoming] ever more obsolete'.[39] As debates at their 1987 and 1988 congresses, as well as their consultations through the CZI Industrial Review Committee, revealed, 'industrialists wanted to work in an open environment, and take the consequences, even if it meant restructuring and closing down some operations'.[40] This was clear embracement of liberalisation, and partly on this basis, the Zimbabwean government agreed to the World Bank's sponsored adjustment programmes.

What was also apparent in the adoption of ESAP was the strong presence of societal corporatism. As the CZI lobbied, Skålnes explains, 'it had the support of other white-dominated productive sectors'.[41] And, indeed, the Zimbabwe Association of Business Organisations, the umbrella body of most private sector organisations in the country, had expressed support when it 'submitted a letter to government calling for a phased programme of trade liberalisation coupled with relaxation of controls on prices, wages, investment and hiring and firing, as well as supportive policies of public expenditure reductions and the like'.[42] For a moment, the role of interest groups (in this case the CZI)

37 Mlambo, 'From an industrial powerhouse to a nation of vendors', 104–05.

38 Skålnes, 'The state, interest groups and structural adjustment in Zimbabwe', *Journal of Development Studies*, 29, 3 (1993), 401–28.

39 *Ibid.*, 415.

40 *Ibid.*, 418–19.

41 *Ibid.*, 419.

42 *Ibid.*, 417.

in influencing economic reform and policy was renewed as they pushed for structural adjustment.

Alongside the adoption and implementation of liberalisation, another debate emerged. As alluded to earlier, during the first decade of independence, the remnants of the UDI economy, particularly the ownership and structure of the economy, which remained predominantly White, were visible. The status quo triggered some attempt at Africanisation of the economy under the guise of what was termed 'affirmative action or economic indigenisation' in the opening years of the 1990s, and reached its pinnacle with the enactment of the Economic Indigenisation and Empowerment Act of 2007, whose impact shall be discussed later.[43] The idea of Africanisation or economic indigenisation was not new, however; this had been attempted elsewhere across the continent with mixed results.[44]

The slow pace of transformation, coupled with the adversarial effects of the ESAP, triggered calls for economic indigenisation. This culminated in the establishment of the Indigenous Business Development Centre in 1991, which pressed for more Black participation and control of the Zimbabwean economy.[45] More pressure groups emerged in the mid-1990s, which insisted on Black economic empowerment. The pressure groups included the Indigenous Business Women's Organisation (IBWO), Affirmative Action Group (AAG), Zimbabwe Bank Workers' Union, Boka Group and the University of Zimbabwe Sangano Munhumutapa, which later coalesced to form the United Indigenous Pressure Group (UIPG).[46] Even as these groups intensified calls for indigenisation, the structure of the economy remained largely unchanged.

Meanwhile, there was a leadership change at the CZI. In 1992, Eugene Matikiti, Chief Executive Officer of the Zimbabwe Grain Bag, a subsidiary of Tregers Zimbabwe, was elected the first Black president of the CZI. Realising the lack of representation and participation of Blacks in industry, in November 1995, CZI and the US Agency for International Development (USAID) launched a business linkage project under the name Zimbabwe Enterprise Development Programme (ZEDP). USAID extended a grant to CZI of approximately USD 280,000 to fund ZEDP for a three-year period. This project 'was designed to

43 For early attempts at indigenisation, see B. Raftopoulos and S. Moyo, *The Politics of Indigenisation in Zimbabwe* (Harare: Institute of Development Studies, University of Zimbabwe, 1995); see also Government of Zimbabwe, *The Indigenisation and Economic Empowerment Act* (Harare: Government Printers, 2007).

44 See A. Adedeji (ed.), *Indigenisation of African Economies* (London: African Publishing Company, 1981).

45 Raftopoulos and Moyo, *The Politics of Indigenisation in Zimbabwe*, 19.

46 M. M. Madimutsa, 'Affirmative action: the theory and practice', *Zimbabwe News*, 27, 11 (1995), 7. See also M. Ndakaripa, 'State, civil society and the politics of economic indigenisation in Zimbabwe, 1980 to 2016' (PhD, University of the Free State, 2017).

encourage manufacturers to subcontract their non-core activities to small- and medium-sized enterprises (SMEs)'.[47] The linkages were seen as a form of indigenisation of the manufacturing sector. The success or otherwise of this initiative was not fully evaluated. What was clear, however, was the mistrust between the White-controlled industry and the Black-controlled government, as well as industrialists' resistance to the changing elements of their businesses. Noteworthy also is that CZI took the initiative to open up avenues for Black entrepreneurs to enter the manufacturing sector. The strong effects of the ESAP, combined with other factors, as will be discussed shortly, however, adversely affected any progress made by the ZEDP.

Withering Industry, 2000 to Date

Other ad hoc government decisions, in particular the payment of compensation to liberation war veterans in 1997 and the deployment of the Zimbabwean army in the war in the Democratic Republic of Congo from 1998 to 2002, compounded the situation. Following on the heels of these controversial decisions was the government's implementation of a rather chaotic fast-track land reform programme in 2000. Scholars concur that the land reform programme exacerbated the economic decline and marked the beginning of what is now commonly referred to as the Zimbabwean crisis.[48] In relation to the manufacturing sector, the fast-track land reform disrupted agriculture, which for a long time had been both a supplier of raw materials and a consumer of finished products to industry. In addition, the chaotic redistribution attracted 'international condemnation, ostracism, and sanctions by some Western countries ... which ... made the country less attractive to investors'.[49] As Mlambo has

47 D. C. Mead and P. Kunjeku, *Business Linkages and Enterprise Development in Zimbabwe*, GEMINI Technical Report No. 55, 1993.

48 See A. Hammar, B. Raftopoulos, and S. Jensen (eds), *Zimbabwe's Unfinished Business: Rethinking Land, Nation and State in the Context of the Crisis* (Harare: Weaver Press, 2003); C. Richardson, *The Collapse of Zimbabwe in the Wake of the 2000–2003 Land Reforms* (Lampeter: Edward Mellen, 2004); and L. M. Sachikonye, 'From "growth with equity" to "fast-track" reform: Zimbabwe's land question', *Review of African Political Economy*, 30, 96 (2003), 227–40. J. L. Jones, '"Nothing is straight in Zimbabwe": the rise of the Kukiya-kiya economy 2000–2008', *Journal of Southern African Studies*, 36, 2 (2010), 285–99; I. Phimister, '"Rambai Makashinga (continue to endure)": Zimbabwe's unending crisis', *South African Historical Journal*, 54, 1 (2005), 112–26; B. Raftopoulos, 'The crisis in Zimbabwe 1998–2008', in B. Raftopoulos and A. S. Mlambo (eds), *Becoming Zimbabwe: A History from the Pre-colonial Period to 2008*, 201–32; P. Bond and M. Manyanya, *Zimbabwe's Plunge: Exhausted Nationalism, Neoliberalism and the Search for Social Justice* (Harare: Weaver Press, 2003).

49 Mlambo, 'From an industrial powerhouse to a nation of vendors', 113.

shown, from then on Zimbabwe has been characterised by deindustrialisation, with the exception of Zimbabwe's compromise Government of National Unity (GNU), comprised of the Zimbabwe African National Union-Patriotic Front (ZANU-PF) and the Movement for Democratic Change (MDC), between 2009 and 2013.[50]

Between 2000 and 2008, the manufacturing volume fell to 33%, while its capacity utilisation reached a meagre 10% in 2008. The policy environment, characterised by acute shortage of foreign exchange, hyperinflation which peaked at 87.5 sextillion % in 2008, and populist decisions by the government, through the National Incomes and Price Commission, to freeze price hikes, contributed to the stagnation in the manufacturing sector and the broader economy.[51] Even the 2004–2010 Industrial Development Policy could not see the light of the day because of the economic environment. The Ministry of Industry and Commerce best evaluated the situation, pointing out that it

> was further compounded by the drying up of lines of credit … due to the impact of sanctions. Industry … was operating at low capacity utilisation across the board which reached record lows of 5% on average in 2008 … the country suffered an exodus of qualified and technical personnel … raw material shortages owing to low agricultural productivity and foreign currency shortages … situation was made worse by the poor performance of and delivery by, utilities such as telecommunications, water, electricity and rail transport. The sum total of these woes has been the informalisation of the economy.[52]

As David Coltart observed, Zimbabwe was 'in more danger than ever of becoming a failed state'.[53]

The country enjoyed some reprieve between 2009 and 2013. The short-lived economic recovery and stability of the GNU owed much to two key policy decisions: the abandonment of the Zimbabwean currency and its substitution with a multi-currency regime dominated by the US dollar. Under the GNU, manufacturing 'grew by 10 percent in 2009, with capacity utilization rising from 10 percent at the beginning of the year to about 32.3 percent' in 2010.[54] Even with this temporary stability, the sector was still blighted by a number of challenges, chief among these being infrastructure decay, liquidity crunch, competition from imports, low product demand, lack of working

50 *Ibid.*, 106.

51 V. M. Gwande, '"By whatever means necessary!": surviving in post-2000 Zimbabwe', *African Historical Review*, 49, 1 (2017), 91–103.

52 Republic of Zimbabwe, Industrial Development Policy, 2012–2016 (Ministry of Industry and Commerce, 2012).

53 D. Coltart, *The Struggle Continues: 50 Years of Tyranny in Zimbabwe* (Johannesburg: Jacana Media, 2016), 485.

54 As cited in Mlambo, 'From an industrial powerhouse to a nation of vendors', 108.

capital, machine breakdown, high cost of production and utilities, all of which conspired to proscribe the rate at which manufacturing grew. On the backdrop of these factors, the CZI warned that 'the manufacturing sector was in crisis ... was undergoing "serious de-industrialisation which has reached 'catastrophic levels'" ... with 4,610 companies having closed since 2011, resulting in the loss of 55,000 jobs.'[55] Indeed, much as there was stability, the economy remained in the doldrums.

At the same time, the government of Zimbabwe enacted the Indigenisation and Economic Empowerment Act in 2007 and began implementing it with vigour in 2010. The act entailed the cessation of 51% of ownership by foreign businesses with a threshold of US $500 000 to local indigenous Zimbabweans.[56] The law sent a very wrong message to potential investors. According to Mlambo,

> the legislation discouraged potential investors and made those already involved in the country's economy to adopt a wait-and-see attitude regarding the implications of the policy on their investments in the country ... conflicting public statements by government leaders [on what the policy really meant], only made the situation worse as it suggested policy inconsistency and lack of clarity which made would-be investors even more hesitant.'[57]

The net effect of this policy was to deepen the economic crisis.

Another notable development during the GNU was the government's announcement regarding its Industrial Development Policy (2012–2016).[58] The overall objective of this was to raise the manufacturing sector's contribution to GDP from 15% to 30% and its contribution to exports from 26% to 50% by 2015. In addition, the government hoped to 're-equip and replace obsolete machinery and new technologies for import substitution and enhanced value addition.'[59] To achieve these objectives, a number of strategies were suggested. These included industrial financing through lines of credit, a revolving fund for distressed strategic companies, review of import tariffs, and strengthening existing research institutions 'to coordinate the crucial role of modernizing industry's plant and equipment and to improve on its systems and quality of products in line with international best practice.'[60] The twin strategies of import substitution and tariff review were followed through, as the government considered these crucial in offering 'protection for our industry to counter the

55 *Ibid.*
56 Government of Zimbabwe, *The Indigenisation and Economic Empowerment Act*, 2007.
57 Mlambo, 'From an industrial powerhouse to a nation of vendors,' 113.
58 Republic of Zimbabwe, Industrial Development Policy, 2012–2016 (Ministry of Industry and Commerce: 2012).
59 *Ibid.*
60 *Ibid.*

surge in the disruptive imports of cheap and "dumped" goods which can easily be produced locally'. It was on this premise that the government introduced Statutory Instrument 64 of 2016 (SI 64/2016), to boost domestic industrial production by protecting local industries from unfair competition from foreign firms.[61]

Although the implementation of SI 64 resulted in an increase in average manufacturing sector capacity utilisation from 34.3% in 2015 to 47.4% in 2016, that trajectory was undercut by other policy decisions.[62] The introduction of SI 64/2016 also marked the beginning of a flurry of statutory instruments which resulted in the overregulation of the economy, especially the currency. In addition, the numerous regulations amounted to policy inconsistencies which dampened business sector and investor confidence. From a multi-currency regime during the GNU, in 2016 the re-elected ZANU-PF government and the Reserve Bank of Zimbabwe introduced a pseudo-currency, the Bond Note, allegedly to incentivise exporters.[63] The Bond Note was pegged at par with the US dollar. This surrogate currency was introduced against the backdrop of a liquidity crunch that emanated from a lack of fresh capital injection. The pseudo-currency bred high levels of speculation. Instead of easing cash shortages, it triggered the disappearance of US dollars from circulation. This gave rise to the trading of the USD on the black market. An almost identical situation occurred during UDI, as is discussed in Chapter 5. Gresham's law or monetary principle, which states that bad money drives out good money, soon kicked in.[64] The shortage of foreign exchange, coupled with speculation and inflation, increased the cost of doing business for manufacturing industries. Moreover, cash shortages meant consumers had no spending power, thus reducing demand for the available industrial products.

Following the introduction of the Bond Note, the government also enacted two more currency regulations which further dampened business confidence and muddied the policy environment. Under Statutory Instrument 33 of 2019 or Presidential Powers (Temporary Measures) (Amendment of Reserve Bank of Zimbabwe Act and Issue of Real Time Gross Settlement Electronic Dollars (RTGS Dollars) Regulations (2019)), the government announced yet another currency. Essentially, the RTGS dollar was an electronic currency version of the Bond Note declared as legal tender. In terms of the SI 33/2019, 'all assets and liabilities that were … valued and expressed in United States dollars shall

61 B. Sibanda, *Zimbabwe's Statutory Instrument (SI) 64 of 2016 on Control of Goods on the Open General Import License: The Gains and Pains* (Harare: Parliament of Zimbabwe, 2017).

62 CZI, *Manufacturing Sector Survey*, 2016.

63 https://www.rbz.co.zw/documents/publications/press/press-statement-on-the-introduction-of-bond-notes.pdf, Accessed 28 November 2021, 11:40pm.

64 A. C. Sparavigna, 'Some notes on the Gresham's law of money circulation', *International Journal of Science*, 3, 2 (2014), 80–91.

… be deemed to be valued in RTGS dollars at a rate of one-to-one to the United States dollar'.[65] The artificially pegged value of these currencies quickly depreciated, as the transacting public and business did not regard them as 'real money'. Business actually rejected them as a medium of exchange, creating a transacting crisis. In response to this currency crisis, the government introduced yet another regulation: Statutory Instrument 142 of 2019 or Reserve Bank of Zimbabwe (Legal Tender) Regulations, 2019 which outlawed the use of the 'British pound, United States dollar, South African rand, Botswana pula and any other foreign currency whatsoever [as] legal tender alongside the Zimbabwe dollar in any transactions in Zimbabwe'.[66] The reintroduced Zimbabwe dollar became the sole legal tender.

For the CZI, these policy reversals introduced uncertainty to the market. In particular, the inconsistency stemmed from the fact that as authorities announced de-dollarisation, re-dollarisation was simultaneously taking root, as evidenced by free circulation of multi-currency in the economy as well as the government demanding certain taxes and fees in foreign currency.[67] The introduction of a local currency and a forex interbank market where foreign currency can be traded failed to improve forex liquidity. Overregulation and overcontrol has left manufacturing firms laden with too much bureaucracy before they can access foreign currency. 'Currently, the manufacturing sector is being affected by acute foreign currency shortages needed for importing raw materials', the CZI bemoaned.[68] Two practices have emerged from this policy environment. First, manufacturing firms have resorted to a parallel market to source foreign currency, often at a high premium, leading to companies pegging their prices beyond market affordability. Second, the continued devaluation of the RTGS dollar forces manufacturing companies to sell goods at a loss or to set their goods' prices at fluctuating foreign exchange rates. According to the CZI, 'this results in some companies scaling down, or closing some of their production lines'.[69] The net effect of all this is that the manufacturing sector continues to decline.

Even as this policy environment persists, the government has still adopted the Zimbabwe National Industrial Development Policy (ZNIDP) (2019–2023). The broad principles underpinning the new industrial policy are 'value

65 Government of Zimbabwe, *Statutory Instrument 33 of 2019: Presidential Powers (Temporary Measures) (Amendment of Reserve Bank of Zimbabwe Act and Issue of Real Time Gross Settlement Electronic Dollars (RTGS Dollars)) Regulations* (2019).

66 Government of Zimbabwe, *Statutory Instrument 142 of 2019: Reserve Bank of Zimbabwe (Legal Tender) Regulations* (2019).

67 G. Shumba, 'Industry agonises over de-dollarisation', *Business Weekly* (Zimbabwe), 7 August 2020.

68 https://www.panapress.com/Zimbabwe-adopts-National-industr-a_630592424-lang2-free_news.html, Accessed 28 November 2021, 10:48pm.

69 *Ibid.*

addition and beneficiation; export-led industrialisation; promotion of sustainable industrial development; gender mainstreaming and modernisation as well as upgrading of industrial equipment and machinery'.[70] The key targets of the policy are to realise 'a manufacturing sector annual growth rate of at least two percent per annum; a 30 percent contribution to the national gross domestic savings; a manufacturing value added growth of 16 percent per year; a merchandise export growth rate of 10 percent per year; and increased employment in the manufacturing sector to 20 percent by 2023'.[71] To achieve these goals, the government committed to financing industrial development; embracing the fourth industrial revolution; establishing industrial clusters; pursuing the concept of Special Economic Zones; providing fiscal incentives for the manufacturing sector; and providing industrial skills training.

The irony seems to be lost on the government. As it makes these pledges, it acknowledges that the manufacturing sector is weighed down by a shortage of foreign currency, yet, it makes no plans for how it will address this constraint. Whether the targets of this industrial policy will be achieved remains to be seen, but as things stand, the CZI bemoans that the manufacturing sector still faces the high cost and shortage of raw materials; foreign currency shortages; antiquated machinery and breakdowns; high cost of doing business; and drawbacks from the current macro-economic environment. This suggests that the fortunes of the sector remain stunted, and puts the attainment of the government's key targets in doubt.

Concluding Remarks

From the foregoing, there are striking observations worth noting and emphasising. First, it is clear that the state continued to be interventionist for its own reasons. By playing the role of an investor and centrally planning the economy, the state crowded out and muzzled industrialists. The once vociferous industrial lobby group, now organising under the title of the CZI, became muted, with very little throughput into policy. The near silence of the CZI can be accounted for in the following two ways. At one level, state interventions were in some way beneficial to industry by providing protection and also guaranteeing foreign exchange allocations to established firms. At another, confronting the state would likely invite retribution, especially given that the CZI largely comprised White capital. They feared that the state may threaten nationalisation or Africanisation should they be seen as boisterous and too challenging (in spite of racial reconciliation). Politically, the ZANU-PF government pursued a one-party state agenda, thus restricting the space for autonomy or the role of interest

70 https://www.panapress.com/Zimbabwe-adopts-National-industr-a_630592424-lang2-free_news.html, Accessed 28 November 2021, 10:48pm.

71 *Ibid.*

groups in influencing public policy. The CZI temporarily found its voice in the 1990s, leading debate in the idea of liberalisation of the economy, particularly when foreign currency allocations and pro-labour policies started impacting on their factory operations. However, the government of Zimbabwe's descent into political authoritarianism and anti-neoliberal imperialist rhetoric since the beginning of the twenty-first century has precluded effective, if any, representation of business interest groups in policy formulation. The omnipresence of the state in the economic sphere has been disastrous, as manifested in the enduring Zimbabwean crisis and the sharp deindustrialisation. Alongside this, political pressure by business civil organisations has disappeared.

The history presented here has sought to direct the attention away from the omnipotence of the state towards the power of active and organised interest groups who go toe to toe with the government in pursuit of their interests. Some of the challenges and constraints facing African economies are a result of the overreliance of business and societies on the state. The lesson to draw from this study is that the state does not always *mero motu* develop policies that favour various economic sectors and their progress. Another important takeaway might be that active and skilled citizenry and organised interest groups are probably a country's greatest asset. This is particularly crucial in light of the many pitfalls that post-colonial African economies have seen. Many post-colonial states have put effort into initiating capital formation and assisting a number of economic sectors. However, the absence or lack of organised, active, and committed economic interest groups to implement and give life to the various state economic policies has hampered progress. The many African economies are going to require a committed private sector, willing to support the state endeavours. This is especially imperative if the African Continental Free Trade Area (AfCFTA) is going to succeed. Lastly, it is hoped that this book will inspire more research to inform how best Africa on a broader scale can achieve meaningful industrialisation despite the constraints posed by globalisation, the many world trade organisations of which it is a member, and the agreements that it is party to and thus obligated to abide by.

Bibliography

Primary Sources

Archives

NASA HEN Vol. No. 3896 Ref. 710, Trade Relations between the Union of South Africa and Southern Rhodesia, 1950.

NASA HEN Vol. No. 3896 Ref. 710, Trade Relations.

NASA HEN Vol. No. 3902 Ref. 710/1, Meeting of the Sub-Committee on Policy held 21 January 1947.

NASA HEN Vol. No. 3910 Ref. 710/1, Trade with Southern Rhodesia, 1951.

NASA-P HEN Vol. No. 3907 Ref. 710/1, Vol. 16, Memorandum on the Effects of the Customs Union (Interim) Agreement between the Union of South Africa and Southern Rhodesia on the Textile Industry of the Union of South Africa, 8 July 1953.

NASA, BTS, Box 72, 1/58/7 Vol. 1, Native Policy in Central African Federation, 1952–1955.

NAZ F184/B/218/01, Federal Information Department: Policy in regard to US Investors, 1954–1956.

NAZ F187/E/598/02, Committee of Enquiry into the Manufacturing Industry, 1958–1966.

NAZ F292/1/16/3, Secondary Industry in Southern Rhodesia, May 1953.

NAZ F292/14/9/1, Federation of Rhodesian Industries, General: 1954–1963.

NAZ F292/14/9/1, Industrial Policy Part 2, 1955–1962.

NAZ F292/16/2, Memorandum for Cabinet on Industrial Development by the Minister of Commerce and Industry, 26 August 1955.

NAZ F292/16/3, Industrial Policy 1953–1963.

NAZ F292/16/3, Secondary Industry in Southern Rhodesia, May 1953.

NAZ F292/16/10, Industrial Incentives and Structure for Industrial Development, 1956.

NAZ F292/16/14, Decentralisation of Industries.

NAZ F344/39/5/1/50, Federation of Rhodesian Industries, 1950–1953.

NAZ LE3/1/1, Letter from E. C. Baxter to the Treasurer, 11 February 1929.

NAZ H.Mss LE 3/1/1, Customs Agreement between Southern Rhodesia and the Union of South Africa, 1931.

NAZ MS 1198 AEA4/2/2, Shortage of Railway Facilities.
NAZ MS 1198 AEA/7/2, Tariff Protection, 1960–1972.
NAZ MS 1198 AEA2/2, Currency Control Regulations, 1958–1977.
NAZ MS 1198 EA/4, Memo by P. C. Aldridge to the Office of the Rhodesian Prime Minister, 25 March 1963.
NAZ MS 1198 EA4/1/1, Import Control Policy, 1965.
NAZ MS 1198 E.A.4/4 Protection of Industry, Resolution by the Salisbury Chamber of Industries, 1962.
NAZ MS 1198 EA6, Overseas Investments, 1957–1962.
NAZ MS 1198, ARnI, Correspondence, 1957–1976.
NAZ MS 1198 AEA.5, Association of Rhodesian Industries: Industrial Development, 1958–1968.
NAZ MS 1198, Industrial Development Fund.
NAZ MS 1199 AEA18/14, South Africa, 1953–1961.
NAZ MS 1199/18/4, ARNI, Trade Agreement with South Africa.
NAZ MS 1200 A.50, Unemployment Conference, 1961.
NAZ MS 1201/A.44/1, ARNI Reports, 1959–1960, Committee on Policy – Underdeveloped Countries, 1959.
NAZ MS 1201/EA1, Minutes of a Meeting between the Minister of Commerce and Industry and Reps of the ARNI held on 17 April 1958.
NAZ [R]ecords [C]entre, [L]ocation. C21.6.9R, [B]ox 141849, Commerce and Industry, 1963–1972, ARnI.
NAZ S104, Industrial Development Advisory Committee, 1940–1945.
NAZ S106, Industrial Development Advisory Committee: Reports, 1942–1945.
NAZ S110, Southern Rhodesia, Development Coordinating Commission, First Interim Report to the Prime Minister of Southern Rhodesia, March 1948.
NAZ S1246/5/30, Memorandum by the Manager of Neill's Bacon Factory, 21 December 1933.
NAZ S1906/1, Evidence to the Howman Commission, 1943.
NAZ S2225/4, H. C. B. Mynors' Report on the Question of a Central Bank, 1949.
NAZ S2538/180/57, Investment of Foreign Capital in Southern Rhodesia and the Colonies, 1950.
NAZ S3269/34/30, Industrial Booklet, 1955–1964.
NAZ S3285/9/40, Minister of Commerce & Industry Speeches, dates?.
NAZ S482/101/42, Secondary Industries: 1942–1949.
NAZ S482/134/48, Government's Policy towards Assisting Development of Industries in Southern Rhodesia, 1949.
NAZ S482/152/42, Industrial Development in Southern Rhodesia, 1942.
NAZ S482/181/42, Industrial Development Advisory Committee, Minutes, Memoranda, Reports, 1942–1946.
NAZ S482/458/39, Manufacturing Companies in Southern Rhodesia.
NAZ S482/459/39, Trade of Southern Rhodesia, undated.
NAZ S679/14/4, Salisbury Chamber of Industries: Memorandum on Customs Agreement between Southern Rhodesia and the Union of South Africa as Concerns Secondary Industries in Southern Rhodesia, 1933.
NAZ S679/15/2, Letter by Bulawayo Chamber of Commerce to the Secretary of Tariff Commission, 16 December 1929.
NAZ S679/15/2, Treasurer's Memorandum to the Prime Minister, 11 January 1928.

NAZ S679/15/4, Memorandum prepared by the Salisbury Chamber of Industries on the Customs Agreement at present existing between the Union of South Africa and Southern Rhodesia; Reasons for Requesting Cancellation, no date.
NAZ S679/15/8, Association of Chambers of Commerce of Southern Rhodesia: Memorandum on Customs Agreement with the Union of South Africa, 1933.
NAZ S679/116/22, Report of the Economic Development Committee, 1939.
NAZ S915/304/174/1, Riscom, Memoranda and Reports, 1940–1942.
NAZ S915/40, Excess Profit Tax, 1944–1946.
NAZ S916/20, Protection of Rhodesian Industry, Customs Duties and Rebates, 1945.
NAZ S918/3, Commerce and Industry Department, Policy and Development: 1944–1945.
NAZ S932/14, Industrial Development in Southern Rhodesia, Memoranda, 1942–1950.
NAZ S932/14/1, National Industries.
NAZ S932/25b, Press Cuttings, 1939–1948.
Rhodes University, Smith Papers (Unprocessed), Box 2.027(A), Ministerial Economic Coordinating Committee.

Official Publications

ACCORN, *Minutes and Proceedings of the Annual Congress*, 1961.
——— *Programme and Agenda*, 1963.
ARNI, *Annual Congress*, 1958.
Annual Report, 1970–1979.
——— *Blueprint of an Industrial Policy*, 1961.
——— *Record of Proceedings of Sixth Annual Congress*, 1962.
——— *Report for the Presidential Year*, 1962/1963.
——— *Review of the Presidential Year*, 1959–1962.
——— *Register of Manufacturers*, 1964–1967.
Associated Chambers of Commerce, *Annual Congress*, 1941.
Association of Chambers of Industries of Rhodesia, *Report of Proceedings of the Annual Congresses [Nos 1–5]*, 1942–1946.
Central Statistics Office, *Report on the Results of the National Income and Balance of Payments Questionnaire Sent to Companies Operating in Malawi, Rhodesia and Zambia in 1963* (Salisbury: Government Printers, 1964).
Confederation of Zimbabwe Industries (CZI), *Manufacturing Sector Survey*, 2016.
Economic Survey of Rhodesia, 1969–1972.
Federal Government Notice No. 493, 22 October 1954.
Federation of Rhodesia and Nyasaland, *Census of Industrial Production, 1957–1958*.
——— *Economic Report*, 1955.
——— *Federal Assembly Report of the Select Committee on Decentralisation*, 6 August 1957.
______ *Monthly Digest of Statistics*, June 1954.
Federation of Rhodesian Industries, *Annual Congresses*, 1953–1957.
Government of Southern Rhodesia, *Census of Industrial Production, 1938–1962*.
——— *Industrial Development Act* (Salisbury: Government Printers, 1959).

——— *Report on Industrial Relations in Southern Rhodesia* (Salisbury: Government Printers, 1930).

——— *Report of the Advisory Committee on the Development of the Economic Resources of Southern Rhodesia, with Special Reference to African Agriculture* (Salisbury: Government Publishers, 1962).

——— *Report of the Commission of Enquiry into the Protection of Secondary Industry in Southern Rhodesia* (Salisbury: Government Printer, 1946).

——— *Report of the Commission of Inquiry into the Operations of RISCOM* (Salisbury: Government Printers, 1954).

——— *Report of the Committee of Inquiry into the Economic Position of the Agricultural Industry of Southern Rhodesia* (Salisbury: Government Printers, 1934).

Government of Zimbabwe, *The Indigenisation and Economic Empowerment Act* (Harare: Government Printers, 2007).

——— *Statutory Instrument 33 of 2019: Presidential Powers (Temporary Measures) (Amendment of Reserve Bank of Zimbabwe Act and Issue of Real Time Gross Settlement Electronic Dollars (RTGS Dollars)) Regulations* (2019).

——— *Statutory Instrument 142 of 2019: Reserve Bank of Zimbabwe (Legal Tender) Regulations*, (2019).

Industrial Rhodesia: A Record of Industrial Development in Southern Rhodesia (Salisbury: Rhodesian Publications, 1945).

Industries of the Federation: A Study in Progress (Salisbury: Industrial Press, 1954).

Mead, D. C., and Kunjeku, P., *Business Linkages and Enterprise Development in Zimbabwe*, GEMINI Technical Report No. 55 (1993).

Official Catalogue and Guide to the Central Africa Rhodes Centenary Exhibition (Bulawayo, 1953).

Rhodesia Government Notice No. 721A, Control of Goods (Import) Regulations, 1965.

Sadie, J. L., *Report on Planning for the Economic Development of Rhodesia* (Salisbury: Government Printers, 1967).

Sibanda, B. *Zimbabwe's Statutory Instrument (SI) 64 of 2016 on Control of Goods on the Open General Import License: The Gains and Pains* (Harare: Parliament of Zimbabwe, 2017).

Southern Rhodesian Legislative Assembly Debates, 1930–1960.

Union of South Africa, *Government Gazette, Notice No. 4059, Customs Union (Interim) Agreement between the Governments of the Union of South Africa and Southern Rhodesia*, 18 November 1948.

United Nations (UN), *Community Development and National Development: Report by an ad hoc Group of Experts appointed by the Secretary-General* (New York: Department of Economic and Social Affairs, 1963).

United Nations Economic Commission for Africa (UNECA), *African Alternative Framework to Structural Adjustment Programmes for Socio-Economic Recovery and Transformation* (Addis Ababa: UNECA, 1989).

United Nations Economic Commission for Africa (UNECA), Organization for African Unity (OAU) and United Nations Industrial Development Organization (UNIDO), *A Programme for the Industrial Development Decade for Africa* (New York: United Nations, 1982).

World Bank, *Accelerated Development in Sub-Saharan Africa: An Agenda for Action* (Washington, DC: World Bank, 1981).

——— *Financing Adjustment with Growth in Sub-Saharan Africa 1986–90* (Washington, DC: World Bank, 1986).
——— *Zimbabwe: A Strategy for Sustained Growth* (Washington, DC: International Bank for Reconstruction and Development, 1987).
——— *Zimbabwe: An Industrial Sector Memorandum* (Washington, DC: International Bank for Reconstruction and Development, 1987).
——— *Zimbabwe Country Economic Memorandum Performance, Policies and Prospects*, Report No. 5458-ZIM (28 October 1985).
——— *Sub-Saharan Africa: From Crisis to Sustainable Growth* (Washington, DC: World Bank, 1989).
——— *The Economy and Development Plans of Southern Rhodesia* (Washington, DC: International Bank for Reconstruction and Development, 1952).
World Bank and United Nations Development Programme, *Africa's Adjustment and Growth in the 1980s* (Washington, DC: World Bank, 1989).

Secondary Sources

Newspapers and Periodicals

Bulawayo Chronicle.
Business Weekly.
Cape Times.
Property and Finance.
Rand Daily Mail.
Rhodesia Herald.
Rhodesian Recorder.
The Financial Gazette.
The Star.
The Sunday Mail.

Journal Articles and Book Chapters

Akita, S., 'British economic interests and international order of Asia in the 1930s', in S. Akita and N. J. White (eds), *The International Order of Asia in the 1930s and 1950s* (Farnham: Ashgate Publishing Company, 2010), 17–48.
Alam, M. S., 'Colonialism and Imperialism: Empirical Results', https://mpra.ub.uni-muenchen.de/37866/, Munich Personal RePEc Archive Paper No. 37866, Posted 7 Apr 2012, 12:32pm.
Arrighi, G., 'The political economy of Rhodesia', *New Left Review*, 39 (1966), 35–65.
Baer, W., 'Import substitution and industrialization in Latin America: experiences and interpretations', *Latin American Research Review*, 7, 1 (1972), 95–122.
Baldwin, R. E., 'The changing nature of U.S. trade policy since World War II', in R. E. Baldwin and A. O. Krueger (eds), *The Structure and Evolution of Recent U.S. Trade Policy* (Chicago: University of Chicago Press, 1984), 5–32.
Britten, J. M., 'The effects of industrialization on the distributive trade and the consumer', *Rhodesian Journal of Economics*, 3, 2 (1969), 21–28.

Brown, B., 'Facing the "black peril": The politics of population control in South Africa', *Journal of Southern African Studies*, 13, 3 (1987), 256–73.

Buehler, A. G., 'The taxation of corporate excess profits in peace and war times', https://scholarship.law.duke.edu/cgi/viewcontent.cgi?article=2017&context=lcp, Accessed 6 August 2018.

Burdette, M. M., 'Industrial development in Zambia, Zimbabwe and Malawi: the primacy of politics', in Z. A. Konczack *et al.* (eds), *Studies in the Economic History of Southern Africa: The Frontline States, Volume 1* (London: Frank Cass and Co. Ltd., 1990), 75–126.

Butler, L. J., 'Industrialisation in Late Colonial Africa: aBritish perspective', *Itinerario*, 23 (1999).

——— 'Business and British Decolonization: Sir Ronald Prain, the Mining Industry and the Central African Federation', *Journal of Imperial and Commonwealth History*, 35, 3 (2007), 459–84.

Chang, H., and A. Andreoni, 'Industrial policy in the 21st century', *Development and Change*, 51, 2 (2020), 324–51.

Coggins, R., 'Wilson and Rhodesia: UDI and British policy towards Africa', *Contemporary British History*, 20, 3 (2006), 363–81.

Cohen, A., 'Business and decolonization in Central Africa reconsidered', *Journal of Imperial and Commonwealth History*, 36 (2008), 641–58.

Cohen, A., and Pilossof, R., 'Big business and White insecurities at the end of empire in Southern Africa, c.1961–1977', *Journal of Imperial and Commonwealth History*, 45, 5 (2017), 777–99.

Cole, R., 'The tariff policy of Rhodesia, 1899–1963', *Rhodesian Journal of Economics*, 2, 2 (1968), 28–48.

Coltart, D., *The Struggle Continues: 50 Years of Tyranny in Zimbabwe* (Johannesburg: Jacana Media, 2016).

Daimon, A., '"Ringleaders and troublemakers": Malawian (Nyasa) migrants and transnational labour movements in Southern Africa, c.1910–1960', *Labour History*, 58, 5 (2017), 656–75.

Dilley, A., 'Un-imagining markets: Chambers of Commerce, globalisation and the political economy of the commonwealth of nations, 1945–1975', in D. Thackeray, A. Thompson, and R. Toye (eds), *Imagining Britain's Economic Future, c.1800–1975: Trade, Consumerism, and Global Markets* (Cham: Palgrave Macmillan, 2018), 253–77.

Eichengreen, B., and D. Irwin, 'The slide to protectionism in the Great Depression: who succumbed and why?', *Journal of Economic History*, 70, 4 (2010), 875–77.

Girdlestone, J. A. C., 'Manufacturing and construction', G. M. E. Leistner (ed.), *Rhodesia: Economic Structure and Change* (Pretoria: African Institute of South Africa, 1976), 120–35.

Gordon, A., 'Review of Riddell (ed.), *Manufacturing Africa*', *Journal of Modern African Studies*, 29 (1991), XXX–XXX.

Gwande, V. M., '"By whatever means necessary!": surviving in post-2000 Zimbabwe', *African Historical Review*, 49, 1 (2017), 91–103.

——— 'Federation, factories, and foreign capital: economic growth in Southern Rhodesia, 1953–1956', *International Journal of African Historical Studies*, 52, 2 (2019), 231–53.

Groves, Z., 'Urban migrants and religious networks: Malawians in colonial Salisbury, 1920 to 1970', *Journal of Southern African Studies*, 38, 3 (2012), 491–511.
Harris, P., 'Industrial workers in Rhodesia, 1946–1972: working class elites or lumpenproletariat?' *Journal of Southern African Studies*, 1, 2 (1975), 139–61.
Hazlewood, A., 'The economics of federation and dissolution in Central Africa', in A. Hazlewood (ed.), *African Integration and Disintegration: Case Studies in Economic and Political Union* (Oxford University Press: London, 1967), 185–250.
Hirschman, O., 'The political economy of import-substituting industrialization in Latin America', *Quarterly Journal of Economics*, 82, 1 (1968), 1–32.
Hulec, O., 'Some aspects of the 1930s depression in Rhodesia', *Journal of Modern African Studies*, 7, 1 (1969), 95–105.
Hyam, R., 'The geopolitical origins of the Central African Federation: Britain, Rhodesia and South Africa, 1948–1953', *The Historical Journal*, 30, 1 (1987), 145–72.
Jesudason, J. V., 'Statist democracy and the limits to civil society in Malaysia', *Journal of Commonwealth and Comparative Politics*, 33, 3 (1995), 335–56.
Jones, J. L., '"Nothing is straight in Zimbabwe": the rise of the Kukiya-kiya economy 2000–2008', *Journal of Southern African Studies*, 36, 2 (2010), 285–99.
Madimu, T., 'Responsible Government and miner–farmer relations in Southern Rhodesia, 1923–1945', *South African Historical Journal*, 68, 3 (2016), 366–89.
Madimutsa, M. M., 'Affirmative action: the theory and practice', *Zimbabwe News*, 27, 11 (1995).
Mendes, A. P. F., Bertella, M. A., and Teixeira, R. F. A. P., 'Industrialization in sub-Saharan Africa and import substitution policy', *Brazilian Journal of Political Economy*, 34, 1 (2014), 120–38.
Mlambo, A. S., 'From an industrial powerhouse to a nation of vendors: over two decades of economic decline and deindustrialization in Zimbabwe 1990–2015', *Journal of Developing Societies*, 33, 1 (2017), 99–125.
——— 'From the Second World War to UDI, 1940–1965', in B. Raftopoulos and A. S. Mlambo (eds), *Becoming Zimbabwe: A History from the Pre-colonial Period to 2008* (Harare: Weaver Press, 2009), 75–114.
——— '"Honoured more in the breach than in the observance": economic sanctions on Rhodesia and international response, 1965 to 1979', *South African Historical Journal*, 71, 3 (2019), 371–93.
Mlambo, A. S., and Phimister, I., 'Partly protected: origins and growth of colonial Zimbabwe's textile industry, 1890–1965', *Historia*, 52, 2 (2006), 145–75.
Mlombo, A., 'Settler colonialism and trade in the periphery: customs relations between Southern Rhodesia and South Africa, 1924–1935', *African Economic History*, 47, 1 (2019), 92–115.
Mseba, A., 'Money and autonomy in a settler colony: the politics of monetary regulation in colonial Zimbabwe, 1930s–1965' in C. Yin Hsu *et al.* (eds), *The Cultural History of Money and Credit: A Global Perspective* (London: Lexington Books, 2016), 133–48.
Murphy, P., '"Government by blackmail": the origins of the Central African Federation reconsidered', in M. Lynn (ed.), *The British Empire in the 1950s: Retreat or Revival?* (London: Palgrave Macmillan, 2005), 53–76.

Ndlela, D. B., 'Problems of industrialisation: structural and policy issues', in I. Mandaza (ed.), *Zimbabwe: The Political Economy of Transition, 1980–1986* (Dakar, Senegal: CODESRIA, 1986), 141–64.

Nyambara, P., 'The politics of locating the third spinning mill in Southern Rhodesia, 1951–1953', *Historia*, 59, 2 (2014), 46–68.

Nyamunda, T., 'How racist Rhodesia did it and "independent" Zimbabwe is getting it wrong: comparing currency and finance under sanctions', in *Developing Economics: A Critical Perspective on Development Economics*, https://developingeconomics.org/2017/03/06/how-racist-rhodesia-did-it-and-independent-zimbabwe-is-getting-it-wrong-comparing-currency-and-finance-under-sanctions/wrong-comparing-currency-and-finance-under-sanctions/, Accessed 8 April 2018.

——— 'In defence of white rule in Southern Africa: Portuguese–Rhodesian economic relations to 1974', *South African Historical Journal* (2019), https://doi.org/10.1080/02582473.2019.1610902.

Palmer, G. F. D., 'A note on the trade agreement between the Union and the Federation of Rhodesia', *South African Journal of Economics*, 23, 3 (1955), 203–12.

Passmore, Gloria C., 'Historical rationale of the policy of community development in the African rural areas', *Zambezia*, II, i (1971).

Phimister, I. R, 'Accommodating imperialism: the compromise of the settler state in Southern Rhodesia, 1923–1929', *Journal of African History*, 25, 3 (1984), 279–94.

——— '"Rambai Makashinga (continue to endure)": Zimbabwe's unending crisis', *South African Historical Journal*, 54, 1 (2005), 112–26.

——— 'Rethinking the reserves: Southern Rhodesia's Land Husbandry Act reviewed', *Journal of Southern African Studies*, 19, 2 (1993), 225–39.

———'Rhodes, Rhodesia and the Rand', *Journal of Southern African Studies*, 1, 1 (1974), 77–84.

———'Secondary industrialisation in Southern Africa: The 1948 Customs Agreement between Southern Rhodesia and South Africa', *Journal of Southern African Studies*, 17, 3 (1991), 430–42.

Phimister, I., and Gwande, V. M., 'Secondary industry and settler colonialism: Southern Rhodesia before and after UDI', *African Economic History*, 45, 2 (2017), 85–112.

Phimister, I., and Raftopoulos, B., '"Kana sora ratswa ngaritswe": African nationalists and Black workers – the 1948 general strike in colonial Zimbabwe', *Journal of Historical Sociology*, 13, 3 (2000), 289–324.

Pilossof, R., 'Remaining apolitical in a political crisis: exploring interest group politics', *Journal of Developing Societies*, 26, 1 (2010), 71–97.

Raftopoulos, B., 'The crisis in Zimbabwe 1998–2008', in B. Raftopoulos and A. S. Mlambo (eds), *Becoming Zimbabwe: A History from the Pre-colonial Period to 2008* (Harare: Weaver Press, 2009), 201–32.

Rennie, G., 'Federation: an appraisal', *Investment: British Investment and Industry in Central Africa, Quarterly Review* (1960).

Rhodesian Journal of Economics, Special Issue on Rhodesian Industry, 3, 2 (1969).

Riddell, R. C., 'Zimbabwe', in R. C. Riddell (ed.), *Manufacturing Africa: Performance and Prospects of Seven Countries in sub-Saharan Africa* (London: James Currey, 1990), 337–411.

——— 'A forgotten dimension? The manufacturing sector in African Development', *Development Policy Review*, 8 (1990), 5–27.

Sachikonye, L. M., 'From "growth with equity" to "fast-track" reform: Zimbabwe's land question', *Review of African Political Economy*, 30, 96 (2003), 227–40.

Sampath, P. G., 'Industrial development for Africa: trade and technology and the role of the state', *African Journal of Science, Technology, Innovation and Development*, 6, 5 (2014), 439–53.

Shaw, J. S., 'Public choice theory', *The Concise Encyclopedia of Economics*, http://www.econlib.org/library/Enc1/PublicChoiceTheory.html, Accessed 30 July 2018.

Skålnes, T., 'The state, interest groups and structural adjustment in Zimbabwe', *Journal of Development Studies*, 29, 3 (1993), 401–28.

Sparavigna, A. C., 'Some notes on the Gresham's law of money circulation', *International Journal of Science*, 3, 2 (2014), 80–91.

Stoneman, C., 'Foreign capital and the prospects for Zimbabwe', *World Development*, 4, 1 (1976), 25–58.

——— 'Foreign capital and the reconstruction of Zimbabwe', *Review of African Political Economy*, 5, 11 (1978), 62–83.

——— 'Industrialisation in Zimbabwe: past, present and future', *Afrika Focus*, 6, 3–4 (1990), 245–82.

West, M. O., 'Nationalism, race, and gender: the politics of family planning in Zimbabwe, 1957–1990', *Social Science and Medicine*, 7, 3 (1994), 456–59.

White, N., 'The business and politics of decolonization: the British experience in the twentieth century', *Economic History Review* 53, 3 (2000), 544–64.

Wield, D., 'Manufacturing', in C. Stoneman (ed.), *Zimbabwe's Inheritance* (New York: St Martin's Press, 1981), 151–70.

Wolff, E, A., 'The global politics of African industrial policy: the case of the used clothing ban in Kenya, Uganda and Rwanda', *Review of International Political Economy*, (2020), https://doi.org/10.1080/09692290.2020.1751240.

Zinyama, L., 'Prospects and problems of industrial decentralization in Zimbabwe', in G. Williams and A. Wood (eds), *Geographical Perspectives on Development in Southern Africa* (Australia: Commonwealth Geographical Bureau, 1986), 122–36.

Books

Adedeji, A. (ed.), *Indigenisation of African Economies* (London: African Publishing Company, 1981).

African Development Bank, *Industrialise Africa: Strategies, Policies, Institutions and Financing* (African Development Bank Group, 2017), http://bit.ly/2AfU14P, Accessed 10 November 2020, 1:07pm.

Alexander, J., *The Unsettled Land: State Making & the Politics of Land in Zimbabwe, 1893–2003* (Oxford: James Currey, 2006).

Arrighi, G., *The Political Economy of Rhodesia* (The Hague: Mouton, 1967).

Baran, P. A., *The Political Economy of Growth* (New York: Monthly Review Press, 1957).

Bond, P., *Uneven Zimbabwe: A Study of Finance, Development and Underdevelopment* (Trenton, NJ: Africa World Press, 1998).

Bond, P., and Manyanya, M., *Zimbabwe's Plunge: Exhausted Nationalism, Neoliberalism and the Search for Social Justice* (Harare: Weaver Press, 2003).

Bowman, L., *Politics in Rhodesia: White Power in an African State* (Cambridge, MA: Harvard University Press, 1973).

Bozzoli, B., *The Political Nature of a Ruling Class: Capital and Ideology in South Africa 1890–1933* (London: Routledge and Keagan Paul, 1981).

Brownell, J., *The Collapse of Rhodesia: Population Demographics and the Politics of Race* (London: I. B. Tauris Publishers, 2011), 25–42.

Cain, P. J., and Hopkins, A. G., *British Imperialism, 1688–2000* (London: Longman, 2001).

Chakaodza, A. M., *Structural Adjustment in Zimbabwe and Zambia: Restructive or Destructive?* (Harare: Third World Publishers, 1993).

Chipika, J. T., *et al.*, *Effects of Structural Adjustment in Southern Africa: The Case of Zimbabwe's Manufacturing Sector during Phase 1 of ESAP: 1991–1995* (Harare: SAPES, 2000).

Clarke, D. G., *Foreign Companies and International Investment in Zimbabwe* (Gwelo: Mambo Press, 1980).

Clements, F., *Rhodesia: The Road to Collision* (London: Pall Mall Press, 1969).

Cohen, A., *The Politics and Economics of Decolonization in Africa: The Failed Experiment of the Central African Federation* (London: I. B. Tauris Publishers, 2017).

Croxton, A. H., *Railways of Rhodesia: The Story of the Beira, Mashonaland and Rhodesia Railways* (Newton Abbot: David & Charles, 1973).

Feinstein, C. H., *An Economic History of South Africa: Conquest, Discrimination and Development* (Cambridge: Cambridge University Press, 2005).

Frank, A. G., *Latin America: Underdevelopment or Revolution: Essays on the Development of Underdevelopment and the Immediate Enemy* (New York: Monthly Review Press, 1969).

Gann, L. H., *A History of Southern Rhodesia: Early Days to 1934* (London: Chatto and Windus, 1965).

Gann, L. H., and Gelfand, M., *Huggins of Rhodesia: The Man and His Country* (London: George Allen and Unwin, 1964).

Gargett, E., *The Administration of Transition: African Urban Settlement in Rhodesia* (Gwelo: Mambo Press, 1977).

Gramsci, A., *Selections from Prison Notebooks* (London: Lawrence and Wisehart, 1971).

Gray, R., *Two Nations: Aspects of the Development of Race Relations in Rhodesia and Nyasaland* (Oxford: Oxford University Press, 1960).

Groves, Z., *Malawian Migration to Zimbabwe, 1900–1965: Tracing Machona* (Cham: Palgrave Macmillan, 2020).

Gunning, J. W., and Oostendorp, R. (eds), *Industrial Change in Africa: Zimbabwean Firms under Structural Adjustment* (New York: Palgrave, 2002).

Hailey, W., *An African Survey: A Study of Problems Arising in Africa South of the Sahara* (London: Oxford University Press, 1938).

Hammar, A., Raftopoulos, B., and Jensen, S. (eds), *Zimbabwe's Unfinished Business: Rethinking Land, Nation and State in the Context of the Crisis* (Harare: Weaver Press, 2003).

Handford, J. A., *Portrait of an Economy: Rhodesia under Sanctions* (Salisbury: Mercury Press, 1976).

Herbst, J., *State Politics in Zimbabwe* (Berkeley: University of California Press, 1990).

Johnson, D., *World War II and the Scramble for Labour in Colonial Zimbabwe, 1939–1948* (Harare: University of Zimbabwe Publications, 2000).

Jones, H. S., and Muller, A., *The South African Economy, 1910–90* (London: Palgrave Macmillan, 1992).

Kanduza, A. M., *The Political Economy of Underdevelopment in Northern Rhodesia, 1918–1960: A Case Study of Customs Tariff and Railway Freight Policies* (Lanham: University Press of America, 1986).

Leys, C., *European Politics in Southern Rhodesia* (Oxford: Clarendon Press, 1959).

Leys, C., and Pratt, C. (eds), *A New Deal in Central Africa* (London: Heinemann, 1960).

Lunn, J., *Capital and Labour on the Rhodesian Railway System, 1888–1947* (Oxford: Macmillan Press, 1997).

Mandaza, I. (ed.), *Zimbabwe: The Political Economy of Transition, 1980–1986* (Dakar, Senegal: CODESRIA, 1986).

Mlambo, A. S., *A History of Zimbabwe* (Cambridge: Cambridge University Press, 2014).

——— *The Economic Structural Adjustment Programme: The Case of Zimbabwe, 1990–1995* (Harare: University of Zimbabwe Publishers, 1997).

Mlambo, A. S., Pangeti, E. S., and Phimister, I., *Zimbabwe: A History of Manufacturing, 1890–1995* (Harare: University of Zimbabwe Publications, 2000).

Mlombo, A., *Southern Rhodesia–South Africa Relations, 1923–1953: Political, Social and Economic Ties* (Cham: Palgrave Macmillan, 2020).

Mosley, P., *The Settler Economies: Studies in the Economic History of Kenya and Southern Rhodesia 1900–1963* (Cambridge: Cambridge University Press, 1983).

Murray, D. J., *The Governmental System in Southern Rhodesia* (Oxford: Clarendon Press, 1970).

Palley, C., *The Constitutional History and Law of Southern Rhodesia 1888–1965 with Special Reference to Imperial Control* (Oxford: Clarendon Press, 1966).

Palmer, R., *Land and Racial Domination in Rhodesia* (London: Heinemann, 1977).

Phillips Sawyer, L., *American Fair Trade: Proprietary Capitalism, Corporatism, and the 'New Competition,' 1890–1940* (Cambridge: Cambridge University Press, 2018).

Phimister, I. R., *An Economic and Social History of Zimbabwe: Capital Accumulation and Class Struggle* (London: Longman, 1988).

——— *Wangi Kolia: Coal, Capital and Labour in Colonial Zimbabwe, 1894–1954* (Harare: Baobab Books, 1994).

Pilossof, R., *The Unbearable Whiteness of Being: Farmers' Voices from Zimbabwe* (Harare: Weaver Press, 2012).

Prebisch, R., *The Economic Development of Latin America and Its Principal Problems* (New York: United Nations, 1950).

Raftopoulos, B., and Mlambo, A. S. (eds), *Becoming Zimbabwe: A History from the Pre-colonial Period to 2008* (Harare: Weaver Press, 2009).
Raftopoulos, B., and Moyo, S., *The Politics of Indigenisation in Zimbabwe* (Harare: Institute of Development Studies, University of Zimbabwe, 1995).
Raftopoulos, B., and Yoshikuni, T. (eds), *Sites of Struggle: Essays in Zimbabwe's Urban History* (Harare: Weaver Press, 1999).
Ranger, T. O., *Bulawayo Burning: The Social History of a Southern African City, 1893–1960* (Woodbridge: James Currey, 2010).
Richardson, C., *The Collapse of Zimbabwe in the Wake of the 2000–2003 Land Reforms* (Lampeter: Edward Mellen, 2004).
Rowe, D. M., *Manipulating the Market: Understanding Economic Sanctions, Institutional Change and the Political Unity of White Rhodesia* (Chicago: Chicago University Press, 2001).
Sachikonye, L., Raftopoulos, B., and Kanyenze, G., *Building from the Rubble: The Labour Movement in Zimbabwe since 2000* (Harare: Weaver Press, 2018).
Skålnes, T., *The Politics of Economic Reform in Zimbabwe: Continuity and Change in Development* (London: Macmillan Press, 1995).
Stockwell, S., *The Business of Decolonization: British Business Strategies in the Gold Coast* (Oxford: Oxford University Press, 2000).
Strack, H. R., *Sanctions: The Case of Rhodesia* (New York: Syracuse University Press, 1978).
Thompson, C. H., and Woodruff, H. W., *Economic Development in Rhodesia and Nyasaland* (London: Dennis Dobson Ltd, 1953).
Watts, C. P., *Rhodesia's Unilateral Declaration of Independence: An International History* (New York: Palgrave Macmillan, 2012).
Welensky, R., *Welensky's 4000 Days: The Life and Death of the Federation of Rhodesia and Nyasaland* (London: Collins, 1964).
White, L., *Unpopular Sovereignty: Rhodesian Independence and African Decolonization* (Chicago: University of Chicago Press, 2015).
Wiseman, H., and Taylor, A. M., *From Rhodesia to Zimbabwe: The Politics of Transition* (New York: Pergamon Press, 1981).

Unpublished Theses

Chambwe, T., 'A history of African entrepreneurship in Southern Rhodesia, 1944–1979', (PhD, University of the Free State, 2020).
Chipembere, E., 'Colonial policy and Africans in urban areas, with special focus on housing, Salisbury, 1939–1964' (MPhil, University of Zimbabwe, 2006).
Clarke, D. G., 'The political economy of discrimination and underdevelopment in Rhodesia with special reference to African workers, 1940–1973' (PhD, University of St Andrews, 1975).
Daimon, A., "Mabhurandaya': the Malawian diaspora in Zimbabwe: 1895 to 2008' (PhD, University of the Free State, 2015).
Gwande, V. M., 'Foreign capital, state and the development of secondary industry in Southern Rhodesia, 1939–1956' (MA, University of the Free State, 2015).

Johnson, D., 'The impact of the Second World War on Southern Rhodesia, with special reference to African labour, 1939–1948' (PhD, School of African and Oriental Studies, 1989).
Machingaidze, V. E. M., 'The development of settler capitalist agriculture in Southern Rhodesia with particular reference to the role of the state, 1908–1939' (PhD, School of African and Oriental Studies, University of London, 1980), 182–98.
McKenzie, J. A., 'Commercial farmers in the governmental system of Zimbabwe, 1963–1980' (PhD, University of Zimbabwe, 1989).
Madimu, T., 'Farmers, miners and the state in colonial Zimbabwe (Southern Rhodesia), c.1895–1961' (PhD, Stellenbosch University, 2017).
Maphosa, L., 'Fuel policy in Rhodesia during economic sanctions, 1965–1979' (MA, University of Zimbabwe, 2015).
Mlambo, N., 'Arms production and war supply in Southern Africa, 1939–1945: limitations of the industrial war effort of South Africa and Zimbabwe during the Second World War' (PhD, University of Cape Town, 2000).
Mlombo, A., 'Southern Rhodesia's relationship with South Africa, 1923–1953' (PhD, University of the Free State, 2017).
Mseba, A., 'Money and finance in a closed economy: Rhodesia's monetary experience, 1965–1980' (MA, University of Zimbabwe, 2007).
Ncube, S., 'Colonial Zimbabwe's tobacco industry: global, regional and local relations, 1947–1979' (PhD, University of the Free State, 2018).
Ndakaripa, M., 'State, civil society and the politics of economic indigenisation in Zimbabwe, 1980 to 2016' (PhD, University of the Free State, 2017).
Nyamunda, T., 'Financing rebellion: the Rhodesian State, financial policy and exchange control, 1962–1979' (PhD, University of the Free State, 2015).
Pangeti, E. S., 'The state and manufacturing industry: a study of the state as regulator and entrepreneur in Zimbabwe' (PhD, University of Zimbabwe, 1996).
Selby, A., 'Commercial farmers and the state: interest group politics and land reform in Zimbabwe' (PhD, University of Oxford, 2006).
Tevera, D. S., 'Location of manufacturing industry in Zimbabwe: a geographical investigation' (PhD, University of Cincinatti, 1984).
Tow, L., 'The manufacturing economy of Southern Rhodesia: problems and prospects' (PhD, Columbia University, 1960).

Internet Sources

African Union, 'Flagship Projects of Agenda 2063', 6 February 2020, https://au.int/en/agenda2063/flagship-projects, Accessed 7 September 2020, 5:01pm.
Tralac Trade Law Centre, 'African Continental Free Trade Area (AfCFTA) FAQs', *Questions & Answers*, Issue No. 1 (update) 2018, https://www.tralac.org/documents/resources/faqs/2377-african-continental-free-trade-area-faqs-june-2018-update/file.html, Accessed 7 September 2020, 5:05pm.
Rhodesia Oil Conspiracy in 1976, Freight Services, http://schuitemaberend.blogspot.com/2012/01/howrhodesiagotitsoil.html, Accessed 14 May 2022, 1:04pm.
Reserve Bank Of Zimbabwe, 'Press Statement on the Introduction of Bond Notes', 26 November 2016, https://www.rbz.co.zw/documents/publications/press/

press-statement-on-the-introduction-of-bond-notes.pdf, Accessed 28 November 2021, 11:40pm.

Panapress, 'Zimbabwe adopts National Industrial Development Policy 2019–2023', 12 June 2019, https://www.panapress.com/Zimbabwe-adopts-National-industr-a_630592424-lang2-free_news.html, Accessed 28 November 2021, 10:48pm.

Index

Lightning Source UK Ltd.
Milton Keynes UK
UKHW021209210922
409162UK00001B/1

9 781847 013330